DIY Detroit

DIY Detroit

» Making Do in a City without Services

Kimberley Kinder

University of Minnesota Press
Minneapolis · London

The University of Minnesota Press gratefully acknowledges the generous assistance provided for the publication of this book by the Margaret S. Harding Memorial Endowment, honoring the first director of the University of Minnesota Press.

This project received financial support from the Taubman College of Architecture and Urban Planning at the University of Michigan.

Portions of chapter 3 were published as "Guerrilla-Style Defensive Architecture in Detroit: A Self-Provisioned Security Strategy in a Neoliberal Space of Disinvestment," *International Journal of Urban and Regional Research* 38, no. 5 (September 2014): 1767–84.

Published by the University of Minnesota Press
111 Third Avenue South, Suite 290
Minneapolis, MN 55401-2520
http://www.upress.umn.edu

Library of Congress Cataloging-in-Publication Data
Kinder, Kimberley.
DIY Detroit : making do in a city without services / Kimberley Kinder.
   Includes bibliographical references and index.
   ISBN 978-0-8166-9707-6 (hc)—ISBN 978-0-8166-9709-0 (pb)
1. Community development—Michigan—Detroit. 2. Urban renewal—
Michigan—Detroit—Citizen participation. 3. Municipal services—
Michigan—Detroit—Citizen participation. 4. Civic improvement—
Michigan—Detroit. 5. Urban policy—Michigan—Detroit—Citizen
participation. 6. Detroit (Mich.)—Economic conditions—21st century.
I. Title.
   HN80.D6K56   2016
   307.1'40977434—dc23   2015008728

Printed in the United States of America on acid-free paper

The University of Minnesota is an equal-opportunity educator and employer.

21 20 19 18 17 16   10 9 8 7 6 5 4 3 2 1

❰ For Charlotte and Cora ❱

Contents

Introduction

Self-Provisioning in Detroit

» JAMEL, THE CIVIC ACTIVIST

"We have a group of young neighbors that have a potluck club. So once a month, we all make dishes and get together. This month, I believe it's going to be an Earth Day theme, a vegetarian deal. Before that, we did a brunch. Before that, we did Italian. Before that, I think we did Mexican. And that has been a great opportunity to dialogue with newer neighbors [and] educate them on the way things are."

Jamel was an African American freelance consultant in his midthirties.[1] A lifelong Michigander, he grew up in Detroit, attended college in the state capital of Lansing, and then lived in the Detroit suburbs until 2012 when a slowly growing crisis of conscience brought him and his wife back inside the city limits. "The whole reason why we moved back into the city," Jamel explained, was "for us to help effect change. . . . If I was going to help—truly help—move the city along, I had to be a part of it. I couldn't just be a bystander. I needed to be in the mix, and that included paying taxes and all of that." Jamel initially fantasized about living hipster-style in a gigantic, decaying mansion with ballrooms and servants quarters. For financial reasons he bought a modest bungalow near his parents' house, instead.

After moving in, Jamel immediately joined his neighborhood civic association and became an active member of the volunteer board. For him civic activism and neighborhood vitality were synonymous. "That's what I remember growing up on my block," he told me. "We had a block club, and the neighbors were really engaged." They planted flowers and cleaned trash from public boulevards, and they raised money to plow city streets and build a neighbor-hood playground. The neighborhood was losing population when Jamel moved in, but it still outperformed citywide averages. Jamel described the tree-lined streets, manicured lawns, beautiful homes, and family-friendly parks as important selling points. "Well, it didn't *magically* get there," he insisted. The neighborhood was "a great place to live because of the people that were so active in it," the people who built community amenities and protected them from disinvestment.

Jamel's potlucks were about encouraging other young newcomers to be as active as he was because, without civic activism, he felt the neighborhood would not survive. "At some point, the leadership we have right now in the neighborhood is going to get to a point that they can't do it anymore. So someone's got to come behind them." He was optimistic. "It's what we all want," he said. "We realize, when you sign up to live in the city, everyone accepts a certain bit of re-sponsibility. There's certain things we just can't expect the city to provide. And [this] has been a neighborhood that never really relied on it anyway."

For Jamel, living amid disinvestment was about getting organized. It was about using democratic participation and civic activism to manage public works at the neighborhood scale. Residents like Jamel with college degrees, comfortable incomes, and professional work histories had a distinct advantage when it came to civic organizing. Those resources enabled participation, gave volunteers confidence in their abilities, and gave residents the professional skills and con-nections they needed to secure outside grants and hold governments accountable. Success from this perspective meant maintaining func-tioning property markets, reliable basic services, and an active citi-zenry supporting those processes. All that was needed, it seemed, was for residents to get active, get organized, and make it happen for themselves.

》 ELENA, THE URBAN HOMESTEADER

"Me, personally, it's really hard to do stuff, because I have a two-year-old." Elena gestured toward the toddler playing at our feet. "Before I had her, I would do a lot more things. . . . And my mom [who lives upstairs] does a lot of volunteer work in the community. While I was gone on vacation, my mother and some neighbors got together. They walked around door to door in our neighborhood . . . and they cleaned up all the garbage that has been dumped. . . . Because, literally, when I tell you there is garbage around here, it's not even pieces of paper. It's clothes. It's tires. It's boats. It's pieces of cars. And they walked all around, and they got some people together, and they cleaned it all up."

Elena, a Latina stay-at-home mom in her midtwenties, was a lifelong Detroiter. Her husband worked seasonally in landscaping and was laid off every winter. He used the off-season to read books about electrical wiring and drywall installation to save money on home repairs. In 2009, when Elena was seven months pregnant, the couple bought their first home, a bank-foreclosed duplex, for $8,500 cash. "We had to fix the walls," Elena recalled, "'cause they were cracked and leaking. And there was no sinks, 'cause [scrappers] stole the sinks out of the bathroom." With help from her husband's brothers, the family plastered, sanded, and painted the walls. They repaired the furnace, replaced the stolen water heater, and built a large backyard garden where Elena and her daughter could grow their family's food.

After repairing the house, Elena's husband developed a seasonal work routine to manage the neglected public spaces around their home. In the summer he mowed five vacant city-owned lots behind their house. Cutting those lots helped the family. "We park the cars in the back," Elena explained, "because they break into cars. They steal cars and all that stuff." In the winter he plowed the entire public alley behind their house. And several times a year, Elena's mother cleaned piles of illegally dumped trash from their street.

This family work routine improved the physical condition of the neglected public spaces around Elena's home. "You have to take matters into your own hands here," Elena explained. "'Cause if not, if you wait, then you wait, and wait, and wait. You're going to end up frustrated, and it's probably going to not get done." The family focused on tasks with immediate practical benefits. Elena could not eliminate crime or provide public works on a macroscale, but she could use her family's domestic resources to do a little extra housekeeping on the public spaces that most intimately affected their residential quality of life. It wasn't perfect. Cutting grass and shoveling snow did not make the vacant and vandalized house next door disappear, and the family built a privacy fence to screen it from view. Elena wanted to move to a nicer area, but until they could afford it, she relied on this combination of practical problem solving and selective tunnel vision to negotiate daily life in her underserved neighborhood.

For Elena, living amid disinvestment was about helping friends and family members solve small logistical problems. She used self-interest as a guide for intervention. Jamel's activism was also self-interested, but Elena's neighbors had fewer opportunities for formal collaboration. Some of her neighbors feared arrest or deportation, and many wanted to avoid fines for property code violations they could not afford to fix. These anxieties about public exposure discouraged official campaigns but not individual action. Success in this context meant reshaping nearby public spaces to create more manageable living environments and sheltered oases for family life. All that was needed was a broom, a shovel, and perhaps a long-term plan to relocate.

» MARA, THE SOCIAL REFORMER

"I happen to believe that our economy is going to collapse, basically. I don't think that what we're doing now is sustainable. And I think being able to make a living locally is very important." Mara was passionate and expressive as she imagined the possibilities. "This could be an ecotourism destination," she said, with "hospitality, homemade products, [and] little restaurants or cafes or workshops [or] crafts."

Mara, a white European woman with a mixed-race adopted family, was an avid urban gardener. She lived in Jamel's neighborhood from the 1980s until the mid-2000s, when she moved two miles west onto a heavily abandoned street to build the socially progressive community of her dreams. "Most Detroiters and, I think, most Americans are still very much stuck in what they think is American prosperity. You get yourself a good education and a nice house in the suburbs and a beautiful car. And that's the good life." Mara shook her head. "That might be sustainable for some people, but it's not sustainable for people in this neighborhood. They can't afford that. So what are your choices then? You're going to lead an undignified life? Or do you recognize that there's other ways to live that make life beautiful and dignified and fulfilling without having to have all of that?"

In her new neighborhood, Mara immediately got to work. She cleared several empty lots to make space for her vegetable garden, chicken coop, and goat shed. She started a youth market garden down the street and began going door to door delivering self-published newsletters encouraging her neighbors to plant gardens, as well. There were setbacks. "We've never done this stuff either," she said, "so we're just trying it out. Because we can afford to lose, you know what I mean? Most other people in this neighborhood cannot afford to lose anything. If something happens to us, well, we'll just replace it. And if we have too many chickens and somebody else wants chickens, we can teach them how to build a chicken coop and teach them how it gets done."

For Mara, living amid disinvestment was about social reform. Her outlook emphasized creativity, compassion, and self-direction as an alternative to the broken dreams and passive lifestyles of American consumer culture. This approach was especially prevalent among small groups of charismatic, grassroots activists living in scattered clusters across Detroit. Success did not mean reproducing the economic and government institutions of the past that, Mara felt, had not benefitted low-income communities of color. Instead, success meant empowerment, generosity, stewardship, and solidarity. All that was needed, it seemed, was for people to recognize their overlooked talents and put those talents to collective use.

» THE LOGIC OF SELF-PROVISIONING

Jamel, Elena, and Mara were all involved in urban self-provisioning. They approached the process with different expectations. Their resources varied, and they reconciled private needs with public interests in various ways. But they each self-provisioned alternatives to the abandonment that had already overtaken so much of their city. Their efforts included private homesteading and grassroots activism, but this book focuses primarily on the work they and their neighbors performed in "gray spaces,"[2] the spaces that private owners abandoned and public officials neglected. These in-between spaces were sites of conflict where residents competed for resources and social control.

Self-provisioning was creative and adaptive, and a few lucky residents treated it as an opportunity for countercultural experimentation.[3] But this book intentionally does not focus on those romantic variants, because, for most residents, self-provisioning was not romantic. It was simply something residents felt compelled to do out of necessity, since existing market practices and government policies did not meet their basic needs.

Urban disinvestment fueled self-provisioning. Disinvestment is a structural and ideological phenomenon with profound implications for everyday life. Political economists study these trends from the structural context down, and anthropologists investigate it from the social world up. These are complementary views. There are many intersections between structural theories of racialized capitalism and ethnographic accounts of everyday practice and affective agency. These overlapping and entangled dynamics coproduce the city. This book's exploration of that coproduction focuses on residents who respond to disinvestment by physically intervening in the devalued landscapes around their homes. Through these interventions, residents rework the physical, financial, and social logic of urban spaces.

Residents like Jamel, Elena, and Mara were optimistic, but they also recognized the precariousness of their self-provisioned accomplishments. It is unfair to expect fragmented self-provisioning to reverse Detroit's trenchant history of disinvestment, racism, and crisis. Some readers might therefore interpret self-provisioning as a limited coping mechanism, not a combative strategy for systemic reform. I share this concern. Self-provisioning was a weak weapon. Jamel's volunteerism, Elena's caretaking, and Mara's gardening were signs of strength, but that strength was pitched against national consumer-based delivery models that failed to meet their needs in a context where citizenship rights no longer protected them from vulnerability.

These are important caveats, but self-provisioning nonetheless produced real and significant local benefits. Residents insisted that it made them safer and more comfortable in their homes. It provided invaluable short-term solutions to otherwise intractable problems. And it reworked the logic of urban life by organizing people in space, mediating access to shared resources, and transforming the normative expectations residents had about their neighborhoods.

These productive outcomes meant that, for many residents, the challenge was not to discard self-provisioning because it was a weak weapon but rather to strengthen it by connecting it more meaningfully to other scales and modes of collective activism. Civic organizations were important allies in that endeavor. Large foundations and charities publicized self-provisioning, provided small grants to support it, and applauded residents for doing it. Small block clubs and local community groups helped, as well, by coordinating goals and working methods among neighbors. These local organizations also helped residents access the financial and legal expertise needed to scale up the work and accomplish more tasks collectively.

Some self-provisioners welcomed this organizational support, and these programs' influence cannot be overstated. However, many residents did not live in areas with well-developed civic organizations, and many people did not want to be involved with formal programs that came with messy internal politics, exposure to external scrutiny, and long-term demands on time and resources. These factors helped explain why some residents continued using provisional working methods even when institutional alternatives were nominally available.

Self-provisioning was a collective phenomenon. It appeared deceptively idiosyncratic, since residents often did not know each other, coordinate with each other, or share common goals. But disinvestment was a common citywide condition, and residents developed similar provisional responses to those shared circumstances. They mobilized the resources of friends, family members, and neighbors to accomplish the work. They borrowed tactics and vocabularies from social movement activists and civic agencies. And those social interactions reworked collective systems of mutuality, reciprocity, and belonging.

Self-provisioning transformed the social and spatial logic of the city. It created new clustering logics among families and friends. It reinforced some market practices while undermining others. It created informal mechanisms for civic participation among vulnerable social groups. It influenced the citywide distribution of scarce government and nonprofit resources. And it reworked normative moralistic expectations about governance, lifestyle, and entitlement.

These practices did not reverse Detroit's long history of racially mediated disinvestment, but they did rework the physical and social landscape that disinvestment produced.

» DISINVESTMENT IN DETROIT

Jamel, Elena, and Mara were similar to other residents in cities nationwide. They owned homes, had families, and developed friendships with neighbors. They represented a mix of racial identities, income levels, and family structures. They had hopes for the future and anxieties about the present. And they lived in a context of increasingly generalized economic instability, social inequality, and government incapacity nationwide. As Detroit residents in the early 2010s, however, Jamel, Elena, and Mara faced an especially acute moment of urban crisis. Their city's precariousness was not unique, but studying self-provisioning in that context revealed—in a heightened form, on a citywide scale, and across a range of issues—how contemporary logics of self-provisioning rework the logic of urban life.

Detroit grew rapidly during the early twentieth century. Industrial manufacturing fueled the city's growth, transforming it into the fourth-largest city nationwide by 1920. This period of industrial growth coincided with the creation of a strong public municipality with unprecedented economic, bureaucratic, and legal capacities to coordinate public interests and provide basic services. This dual market and government centralization created a growing city of middle-class residents enjoying household comforts and financial stability.

Since the 1950s, however, Detroit experienced several waves of disinvestment. Suburbanization reversed centralizing impulses and brought racial tensions to a heightened pitch. White flight across municipal boundary lines fragmented metropolitan-wide economic resources and political decision making. Global economic restructuring during the 1960s and 1970s accelerated this trend as investors pulled resources out of the central city and reinvested them in the more profitable suburbs and Sunbelt. Regional racism in hiring, housing, and transportation prevented African Americans from accessing jobs and services outside the city limits, further eroding the central city's economic and political clout. Precariousness intensified again in the 1980s and 1990s when concerned government officials cut social programs in an unsuccessful attempt to improve the city's credit rating. And the housing market crash of the late 2000s was especially pronounced in cities like Detroit, where predatory mortgage lenders had targeted low-income and minority homeowners.[4] Officials, investors, philanthropists, and community activists tried to reverse these trends. Charismatic Detroit mayors used federal money for downtown redevelopment projects, like the Renaissance Center, which unfortunately attracted few tenants and did not stop private disinvestment. Urban planners built new housing in areas like Victoria Park and Jefferson Village, but those projects consumed large subsidies, generated low sales prices, and did not stimulate similar reinvestment in the surrounding areas. Black inner-city churches embracing liberation theology constructed housing, established co-ops, and provided emergency relief for people living nearby, but limited funding, manpower, and expertise made it difficult to sustain that work.[5] In recent years some market analysts have optimistically trumpeted the renewed economic vibrancy of select downtown and midtown neighborhoods, but 94 percent of Detroit's fifty-four neighborhoods still lost population between 2000 and 2010.[6]

These waves of disinvestment transformed Detroit into a national symbol of crisis.[7] In 2012, as Jamel joined his civic association, Elena's family mowed public lots, and Mara planted vegetables, a public–private consortium released a report summarizing the conditions in Detroit. The city had lost jobs, people, and money for six consecutive decades. Nearly eighty thousand housing units stood empty. Over 60 percent of streetlights were broken. One-third of public roads were in poor condition. Public transportation served only 9 percent of the population. Detroit exceeded national averages in rates of asthma, obesity, and heart disease. It had the second-highest violent crime rate among large U.S. cities, and the household poverty rate was 36 percent and rising.[8] Then, in 2013, Detroit became infamous as the largest U.S. city ever to declare bankruptcy, at least so far.[9]

This image of decay contrasted sharply with the surrounding suburbs. While Detroit lost over one million residents between 1960 and 2010, the two suburban counties bordering Detroit to the north gained nearly one million residents. By 2010, inside the city limits, Detroit was 82 percent African American and only 10 percent white, whereas the northern two counties were 77 percent and 85 percent white and only 13 percent and 8 percent African American.[10] Residents in the suburbs were also significantly more affluent, with a median household income of $54,141, nearly double the $28,356 median income inside the city.[11]

Race in this context was inescapable. Racial discrimination and state-sanctioned laws preventing regional resource sharing fueled Detroit's crisis. The segregation emblazoned in the stark city–suburb dividing line also threaded, in more modest forms, throughout the urban core. Whites in Detroit were overrepresented among the city's civic leaders and business investors, and white community organizers and black religious leaders have historically viewed each other with mutual suspicion.[12] Alongside those long-standing black–white fault lines, new racial tensions were emerging during the 1990s and 2000s in places like southwest Detroit, where few African Americans lived in the city's growing Latino communities and vice versa.

Class differences added further complexity to this racialized landscape. The neighborhoods of Grandmont Rosedale and Brightmoor, which shared a boundary, provided an illustrative case in point. At 92 percent and 87 percent African American, respectively, the two neighborhoods were nearly identical in racial composition, but residents on both sides of the divide described crossing the humble, two-lane street separating the neighborhoods as a journey into another world. Crossing the street marked a shift from a median household income of around $69,000 to around $26,000, from a poverty rate of 12 percent to 44 percent, and from a homeownership rate of 83 percent to 45 percent. The street divided a neighborhood known for having one of the lowest vacancy rates citywide from one of the city's most notorious landscapes of abandonment.

These internal dividing lines, buried within the larger urban–suburban pattern of segregation, threaded through the entire city, and the four neighborhoods included in this study represented some of that diversity. Jamel's Grandmont Rosedale neighborhood was a stronghold of middle-class African American homeownership with architecturally distinct housing and strong neighborhood organizations. Elena's heavily Latino neighborhood of Springwells Village included primarily low-income homeowners and renters with little formal education, high rates of informal employment, and many clusters of extended families. In Brightmoor's vast landscape of impoverishment, vacancy, and rental housing, Mara was building a subneighborhood of slightly higher-income white and African American homeowners. I also spoke with residents in MorningSide, a predominantly African American neighborhood polarized by class with high-income blocks on its eastern edge that inversely mirrored the low-income streets to the west.[13]

The differences between these areas illustrated there was no such thing as a "typical" Detroit neighborhood, and yet, despite classed and raced differences, residents shared the problems of global restructuring, regional racism, and municipal insolvency. They also developed similar self-provisioning responses to those constraints. This book emphasizes those similarities. Instead of telling Detroit's story neighborhood by neighborhood and reinforcing perceptions of a disparate, fragmented metropolis, this book proceeds thematically, organized around shared self-provisioning strategies that crossed neighborhood boundaries and helped residents in a variety of circumstances to maintain and control the gray spaces around their homes.

» ETHNOGRAPHIC ENGAGEMENT

I initially went to Detroit to study home remodeling in a context where property values were so deeply depressed that investments often generated little resale value. I expected money-saving, do-it-yourself strategies to be especially prevalent in that context. The residents I met told me about their remodeled bathrooms, rebuilt porches, repainted living rooms, and relandscaped yards. But residents also moved seamlessly between descriptions of work they performed at home and discussions of work they completed on the neglected public and private spaces around them. Residents installed gutters on vacant homes, fertilized abandoned lots, and repaired playground equipment in public parks. These early conversations quickly demonstrated that do-it-yourself home improvement in Detroit was not just about investments in private homes. It was also about managing the larger municipal environment that threatened to undermine household safety and stability.

I started my research in southwest Detroit, where newcomers

from Latin America were remodeling Anglo-style homes and where informal activities carried little cultural stigma. I met residents like Elena at large public meetings, small block club events, and neighborhood holiday parties. Those residents introduced me to friends and family members who would not have trusted a white outsider without some community vetting. In exchange for interviews, I helped residents clean trash from their blocks, and I gave interviewees small gifts of cash for their time.

Professional colleagues helped me move beyond that close-knit, predominantly Latino community by arranging initial introductions in the predominantly African American neighborhood of Morning-Side on Detroit's East Side, where university researchers had been active for several years. Using similar snowball recruitment strategies, I interviewed residents until the birth of a child interrupted the work. I completed fewer interviews and observations in MorningSide than in Springwells Village, but those conversations confirmed my sense that race and ethnicity had little effect on self-provisioning in gray spaces. Unlike private home spaces where residents invested heavily in intimate expressions of race, class, and culture, residents across racial backgrounds rarely described long-term emotional or financial connections to the neglected gray spaces around them, and they generally secured those spaces with as little investment as possible.

Returning to work brought me to Jamel's neighborhood of Grandmont Rosedale, where civic organizations were comparatively strong and resident activism was reputedly high. Older residents with professional work histories and strong community ties were especially responsive to interview requests. Their life experiences illustrated the mutually reinforcing feedback loops that developed between individual interventions in gray spaces and collective responses to disinvestment. In appreciation for residents' time, I adapted the interview structure to include a series of oral history questions, and I gave the local community development organization a booklet containing some of the memories and anecdotes that residents shared.

My fieldwork ended in Brightmoor, where Mara and about fifty other neighbors were building a small but rapidly growing urban agricultural movement. The group was about half white and half black. Most of the whites had moved into the neighborhood to enjoy alternative lifestyles, and their experiences differed from the predomi-

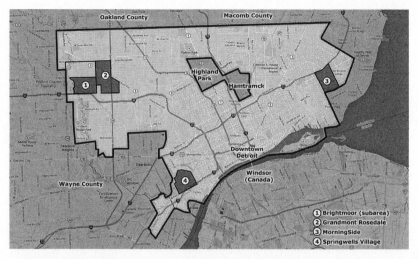

Map 1. Map of Detroit showing the locations of the four research sites.

nantly African American renters and squatters living nearby. I faced significant difficulty gaining access to their nongardening African American neighbors, many of whom worked long hours at low-wage jobs, expressed suspicion of white outsiders like me, or were in the middle of personal crises. Mara's subneighborhood was also considerably smaller than Springwells Village, MorningSide, or Grandmont Rosedale. These constraints meant that the interviews I conducted there were less diverse and fewer in number and that the residents with whom I spoke included committed community activists who also engaged in self-provisioning.

I intentionally chose neighborhoods that were different from each other, although I did not anticipate in advance how deeply fruitful this multisited approach would become. Even though self-provisioning residents had a lot in common, local subcultures developed around certain goals and methods. In Jamel's Grandmont Rosedale neighborhood, for instance, where people had strong vested interests in existing market processes and government connections, residents sharing Mara's vision of an alternative society were less publicly visible. Similarly, Elena's neighbors enjoyed strong social ties, but the fear of attracting unwanted government attention deterred official organizing and large-scale collaboration. Speaking

Map 2. Map of the boundaries for two research sites. Brightmoor appears on the left, including the southern subsection that was the focus of this study. Grandmont Rosedale appears on the right.

with people in many neighborhoods provided different windows for viewing self-provisioning practices that were evident everywhere but that assumed a weighted presence in certain contexts.

The qualitative data discussed throughout this book came primarily from qualitative interviews and participant observations. I conducted seventy-three formal, semistructured, tape-recorded interviews with residents across all four neighborhoods in 2012 and 2013. I recruited residents through community organizations, participant observations, kinship networks, and personal introductions. We spoke in living rooms, kitchens, cars, libraries, community centers, break rooms, and restaurants. Interviews lasted seventy-two minutes on average, with some conversations continuing informally for several hours or across many months. Residents described their homes, streets, and neighbors, as well as their experiences with private landowners and municipal authorities. Alongside the seventy-three resident interviews, I completed an additional nine interviews with nonprofit directors, administrative judges, public service providers, and other officials who shared valuable insights but who were not embedded in any one neighborhood.

Map 3. At the left are the boundaries of Springwells Village. The right shows the boundaries of MorningSide.

Participant observations were equally important. I attended eighty community meetings, brown-bag lunches, neighborhood celebrations, and local service projects. These activities led to scores of impromptu conversations with residents as we worked, ate, and rested together. These untaped conversations yielded fewer direct quotes, but they were invaluable as ways to make connections with new people and observe self-provisioning in action. These events also provided opportunities to hear residents discuss neighborhood conditions, government services, media reports, and crime incidents, as well as self-provisioned responses to those trends. These conversations among peers gave voice to details and prejudices that residents did not always share in formal interview settings.

In recruiting residents for interviews, I focused on people who used community-sanctioned practices to improve their living environments. Community-sanctioned practices were sometimes illegal, but residents distinguished between technical illegality and social harmfulness, and I followed suit. I also did not seek out residents with evident psychotic disorders, nor did I recruit professional scrappers, drug dealers, or arsonists for interviews. Those residents

Table 1: Neighborhood Demographics

	Brightmoor (subarea)	Grandmont Rosedale	Morning-Side	Springwells Village	Detroit (citywide)
Area (square miles)	2.3	2.2	1.6	1.3	138.7
Population					
Number of residents (2010)	8,182	14,406	13,411	16,859	713,777
Population change (2000–2010)	–36%	–15%	–26%	–14%	–25%
Population density (people per acre, 2010)	6	10	13	19.5	8
Number of households (2010)	3,034	5,356	4,419	5,106	269,445
Percent children (under 18, 2010)	31%	24%	32%	35%	27%
Percent elderly (over 65, 2010)	7%	11%	7%	6%	12%
Economics					
Median household income (2010)	$26,234	$69,623	$37,672	$15,761	$28,357
Household poverty rate (2010)	44%	12%	25%	36%	35%
High school attainment (age 25 and over, 2010)	80%	90%	81%	46%	77%
Bachelor's degree (age 25 and over, 2010)	9%	28%	13%	3%	12%
Housing					
Number of housing units (total, 2010)	4,341	5,984	5,887	6,429	349,170
Percent change in housing units (2000–2010)	–7%	0%	–5%	–4%	7%

Owner-occupancy rate (% of occupied units, 2010)	51%	47%	61%	83%	45%
Vacancy rate (2010)	23%	21%	25%	10%	30%
Number of vacant housing units (2010)	79,725	1,323	1,504	628	1,307
Number of vacant housing units (2000)	38,668	570	495	161	568
Race/ethnicity					
White alone (2010)	8%	21%	6%	5%	9%
Black alone (2010)	82%	5%	91%	92%	87%
Hispanic (2010)	7%	72%	1%	7%	2%
Property ownership					
Number of government-owned properties (2012)		253	544	52	680
Number of bank-owned properties (2012)		16	68	15	15
Number of properties owned by 3 biggest private landowners (2012)		113	83	35	470

Sources for census data:

Brightmoor: Estimates based on Social Explorer census data for census tracts 5441, 5436, and 5438 and for block group 3 of census tract 5434.

Springwells Village: Data Driven Detroit, "2012 Data profile: Springwells Village."

MorningSide: Estimates based on Social Explorer census data for census tracts 5013, 5019, and 5020 and for prorated areas of census tracts 5014 and 5018.

Grandmont Rosedale: Data Driven Detroit, "2012 Data Profile: Grandmont Rosedale."

Citywide: Data Driven Detroit.

Sources for property ownership: whydontweownthis.com.

Table 2: Research Data

Brightmoor		Recruit New Neighbors	Protect Vacant Housing	Repurpose Abandonment	Perform Public Works	Promote Public Safety	Produce Local Knowledge
	B01	■					■
	B02			■			
	B03	■	■	■	■	■	■
	B04	■	■				
	B05			■	■	■	
	B06	■			■	■	
	B07				■	■	
	B08				■	■	
	B09				■	■	■
	B10		■	■			
	B11	■		■			
	B12			■			■

Grandmont Rosedale		Recruit New Neighbors	Protect Vacant Housing	Repurpose Abandonment	Perform Public Works	Promote Public Safety	Produce Local Knowledge
	G01	■	■				■
	G02						■
	G03		■		■		■
	G04	■					■
	G05				■	■	
	G06	■					■
	G07					■	
	G08	■					
	G09	■					■
	G10				■		
	G11			■			
	G12	■			■		
	G13	■					■
	G14		■				■
	G15		■			■	
	G16	■					
	G17				■		
	G18	■	■				
	G19						■
	G20					■	■
	G21	■					
	G22					■	■
	G23	■	■				
	G24	■					■
	G25					■	
	G26		■			■	
	G27		■		■		■
	G28		■		■		■
	G29				■		

Table 2: Research Data, *continued*

Formal Resident Interviews	Recruit New Neighbors	Protect Vacant Housing	Repurpose Abandonment	Perform Public Works	Promote Public Safety	Produce Local Knowledge
MorningSide M01						
M02						
M03						
M04						
M05						
M06						
M07						
M08						
M09						
M10						
M11						
M12						
M13						

Formal Resident Interviews	Recruit New Neighbors	Protect Vacant Housing	Repurpose Abandonment	Perform Public Works	Promote Public Safety	Produce Local Knowledge
Springwells Village S01						
S02						
S03						
S04						
S05						
S06						
S07						
S08						
S09						
S10						
S11						
S12						
S13						
S14						
S15						
S16						
S17						
S18						
S19						
N=73	37	33	20	34	26	34

Table 2: Research Data, *continued*

Extended Resident Conversations							
		Recruit New Neighbors	Protect Vacant Housing	Repurpose Abandonment	Perform Public Works	Promote Public Safety	Produce Local Knowledge
Brightmoor	BU13		■				
	BU14		■				
	BU15	■	■	■	■		
	BU16		■	■	■		
	BU17		■	■			
Grandmont Rosedale	GU30		■				
	GU31				■	■	
	GU32	■					■
	GU33				■		
	GU34	■			■		
	GU35				■		■
	GU36						■
	GU37	■					
	GU38	■	■				■
	GU39	■					
MorningSide	MU14					■	
	MU15					■	■
	MU16				■		
	MU17				■		
	MU18					■	
	MU19				■		
	MU20					■	
	MU21		■			■	
	MU22				■		
	MU23	■					
	MU24	■	■				

Extended Resident Conversations							
		Recruit New Neighbors	Protect Vacant Housing	Repurpose Abandonment	Perform Public Works	Promote Public Safety	Produce Local Knowledge
Springwells Village	SU20			■			■
	SU21					■	■
	SU22	■	■	■			
	SU23			■	■		
	SU24				■		
	SU25		■				■
	SU26	■					■
	SU27		■		■		
	SU28		■				■
	SU29	■		■			■
	SU30		■				
	SU31	■		■			
	SU32	■					
	SU33	■	■				■
	SU34	■					
	SU35		■				
	SU36		■				
	SU37		■	■			
	SU38	■			■	■	■
	SU39		■			■	■
	SU40		■				
	SU41	■	■				
	SU42		■	■			
	SU43		■	■			■

made informal use of urban gray spaces, and I spoke with some of them informally when other residents were around. But to avoid incriminating them and to protect my own safety, I restricted myself to less aggressive forms of self-provisioning among residents interested in neighborhood improvement and community benefit.

Three other data sources influenced this work. At the project's outset in 2012, I led a team of students who completed semi-randomized door-to-door surveys with seventy-one residents in two of the four neighborhoods asking about the strategies they used to improve local living conditions. About half the residents surveyed said they performed basic maintenance on nearby property at least once a month, usually for free, and mostly on vacant homes and lots. Then, in 2013, I completed a visual survey of 245 randomly selected vacant residential lots across all four neighborhoods, looking for physical signs of care. That survey showed that people of all income levels adopted vacant lots. Areas with the highest stewardship rates were not necessarily areas with higher income levels or property values and instead seemed to be the places where community groups actively encouraged residents to do self-provisioning work. Throughout the research process, I reviewed past and present newsletters, social-media pages, and newspaper reports relevant to Springwells Village, MorningSide, Grandmont Rosedale, Brightmoor, and Detroit in general.

At the end of 2013, I read these transcripts and field notes, reread them, and read them again looking for recurring themes. I coded the seventy-three formal resident interviews several times to test (and debunk) working hypotheses. These methods were qualitative, not statistical, and the interview sample skewed toward residents with activist agendas and stronger-than-average community ties. Nevertheless, the coded transcripts provided a useful way to gauge the commonality of certain types of self-provisioning practices relative to each other.

I decided early in the process to focus on gray spaces that absentee owners and underfunded government officials neglected and that adjacent residents tried to control. I eventually settled on six self-provisioning themes: recruiting new residents, defending vacant homes, repurposing abandonment, performing public works, improving public safety, and producing local knowledge.[14] These themes were not all-inclusive, and their conceptual purity overlaid a messier on-the-ground reality. I cannot say whether these strategies made meaningful statistical differences in preventing neighborhood decline and improving life opportunities at an aggregate scale, but the residents with whom I spoke believed their work made critical differences in their home environments and their neighborhoods' likely future.

The chapters that follow explain the logic of collective self-provisioning in gray spaces and the implications of self-provisioning for urban life. Chapter 1 explores the history and theory of self-provisioning in nineteenth- and twentieth-century cities, and it explains the effect urban disinvestment and neoliberal policy agendas have on self-provisioning practices. Chapter 2 describes resident interventions in real estate markets that reorganize people in space and create intimate, personalized landscapes of occupancy and authority. Chapter 3 analyzes the guerilla-style architectural strategies that residents use to control vacant homes, and it highlights the ethical dilemmas that emerge through politics of trespass and vandalism. Chapter 4, on posturban visionaries, explains how residents adapt tactics from popular countercultural movements and use those borrowed strategies to create symbolic landscapes of hope and pride. Chapter 5 describes the provisional working methods residents use to improve public works and increase their neighborhoods' access to scarce municipal resources. Chapter 6 explains the spatial mechanics of resident surveillance and the negotiated norms of belonging that emerge. Chapter 7, on resident researchers, explores the role local knowledge plays in solving seemingly intractable problems and encouraging grassroots activism. The concluding chapter reflects on these self-provisioning trends, their transformative social effects, and their implications for collective responses against neoliberal governance in other cities nationwide.

Do-It-Yourself Cities

1

» THE POLITICS OF SELF-PROVISIONED URBANISM

The Great Recession that began in 2007 deepened an already well-entrenched and growing trend toward precarious life in the United States. Within two years unemployment increased 4.7 percent, a change that pushed around eight million people into economic hardships and degraded the working conditions of countless others. Home and business owners lost one-third of their equity; retirement accounts lost one-fifth of their value; and the wealth of American families fell 28 percent. Within five years concentrated poverty rates had risen 21 percent in urban centers and 105 percent in suburban areas, and several million housing units had gone empty.[1]

These changes triggered unprecedented budget crises at all scales of government, with especially troubling implications for urban municipalities. Cash-strapped cities like Sacramento, Colorado Springs, and Honolulu made deep cuts to their police departments, public school districts, and public lighting authorities. The situation was especially dire in Detroit where in 2013 and under the authority of a state-appointed emergency manager the municipal government declared bankruptcy. The recovery years following the crisis did not fully reverse the losses. Some services were restored; others were privatized; and some neighborhoods and amenities simply disappeared.[2]

These accounts of government contraction may give the misimpression that all residents were equally without help in navigating the economic crisis. As urban scholar Ananya Roy has shrewdly surmised, in the contemporary neoliberal climate "the rich have state help [and] the poor have self help."[3] Evidence of this situation was palpable in metropolitan Detroit. While suburban auto companies and young, white entrepreneurs received federal bailouts and small-business subsidies, the City of Detroit and its predominantly low-income, African American residents saw significant budget cuts in social spending, public works, and public safety.[4] In this context of inequitable aid, Detroit emerged as a quintessential do-it-yourself city, a place where residents swept public streets, adopted vacant lots, and organized neighborhood safety patrols.

Although extreme, Detroit was not alone. The rise of market-based governance has made basic services unavailable or unaffordable in urban areas nationwide. Countless residents now rely on household labor and neighborhood volunteerism to coordinate land use, maintain public spaces, and control social behavior. These practices provide meaningful, local, short-term "fixes," but Detroit's ongoing decline—despite ample evidence of widespread self-provisioning—challenges political ideologies that favor individual solutions to structural problems. Regrettably, more-lasting social reforms are slow in coming and may never arrive. In the meantime self-provisioning reflects a new social role vulnerable residents increasingly play in coordinating the logic and life of the neoliberal city.

Resident activism often looks like a sign of community strength. During the Great Recession, concerned citizens in Detroit and elsewhere organized petition drives to expand public bus routes. Neighborhood associations lobbied for improved street lighting. Resident volunteers collected litter from public parks and planted flowers alongside public streets. Residents adopted vacant homes, converted overgrown lots into community gardens, and checked on neighbors during moments of concern.

These practices looked like signs of strength, but as in all things, context was key. The urgency of self-provisioning reflected the precarious conditions of everyday life. Residents in Sacramento did not need to self-police the streets so vigilantly until the police department lost 30 percent of its operating budget between 2008 and 2012. Residents in the Atlanta suburb of Clay County did not need such extensive grassroots ridesharing networks before the cash-strapped government terminated its public transportation program in 2010. And residents in East Saint Louis did not need so many urban gardens until two-thirds of its residents had moved away.[5] Resident activism in those contexts signified vulnerability, as well as strength. It dramatized a series of political economic changes that have reduced the institutional capacity for one of the richest nations on earth to deliver basic services—like police protection, public transportation, and land management—to a growing group of increasingly vulnerable residents.

Basic services were unavailable or unaffordable in many rural areas, as well, but by 2010, 81 percent of the U.S. population lived in cities and suburbs.[6] In earlier eras urbanization meant improved access to jobs, education, health care, and utilities. Not everyone benefitted equally, and urban epidemics, pollution, drug cultures, and skid rows claimed more lives than boosters cared to admit, but cities were still places of relative opportunity. Unfortunately, the Great Recession was one in a series of economic crises that have fueled urban poverty and inequality since the 1950s. Government devolution, privatization, and austerity measures have exacerbated these trends, stripping residents of the physical and political infrastructure they once used to solve shared problems collectively. The situation was especially acute in "shrinking cities" where several consecutive decades of disinvestment, depopulation, and spiraling legacy costs eroded the municipal capacity to continue funding basic health and safety programs.[7] But even in shrinking cities, service cuts were not inevitable. Instead, they revealed the scarcity of politically viable alternative responses to economic instability and social inequality.

Self-provisioning is not new. Volunteer fire brigades were common in cities until the late nineteenth century. Urban homesteads and informal room rentals were widespread until the mid-twentieth century. Urban victory gardens proliferated during the crisis years of World War II, and an entire consumer-based industry of do-it-yourself suburban home remodeling emerged in the 1950s and 1960s.[8]

Despite this rich and varied history, the scope and urgency of self-provisioning diminished significantly throughout those decades. Municipal roads, waterlines, and fire trucks replaced amateur volunteers. Rising incomes, falling commodity prices, more stable employment patterns, and expanded social security programs made chicken coops and self-built homes redundant for the growing, urbanizing middle class. Zoning laws also made these practices illegal, which hurt minority groups, who received fewer benefits from the postwar social contract, but city-run welfare programs provided nominal alternatives to poverty in rural areas where self-provisioning remained more prevalent. Some city dwellers undoubtedly kept their tomato plants and informal remodels, but millions more happily traded the labor intensity of self-provisioning for the comfort of mass-built suburbs, chain grocery stores, rising property values, and municipal public works.[9]

Then, beginning in the 1970s, self-provisioning resurfaced with a vengeance. Deindustrialization undermined urban revenue streams. Employment instability increased; real wages fell; and welfare spending declined. Impoverished communities of color in segregated neighborhoods were among the first to revive older practices of self-provisioning in response to municipal breakdowns. In Boston's Villa Victoria and Roxbury neighborhoods, Long Island's Corona, Brooklyn's Greenpoint-Williamsburg, Harlem's El Barrio, and Chicago's the Flats, residents exchanged food, clothing, child care, and car rides to help friends and family members meet everyday needs. They organized community cleanups, neighborhood safety walks, and housing redevelopment campaigns to counter market disinvestment and municipal neglect.[10]

Self-provisioning became more widespread as household vulnerability expanded, a national trend especially visible in the growing informal economy. Day laboring and sidewalk vending became more common, especially among African Americans and recent immigrants, who occupied the most precarious positions in the national labor pool. Subcontracting and self-employment also expanded among middle-income whites. Those jobs came with fewer benefits and less job security than did salaried or unionized labor. The growing group of residents being squeezed out of the middle class began relying more heavily on informal garage sales and unofficial room sublets to make ends meet.[11]

Alongside these economic changes, the neoliberal turn to market-based governance fundamentally transformed the logic of municipal public works. In Chicago, for instance, in the words of sociologist Mary Patillo, "the model has changed from one in which cities 'deliver' public services like education, health care, and protection from crime, to one in which residents 'shop for' these goods in a service landscape that includes more nongovernmental, private subcontractors."[12] In the 1980s and 1990s, large cities nationwide privatized street maintenance, waste management, ambulance services, legal services, and drug treatment centers. In the mid-2000s, small cities like Sandy Springs, Georgia, and Maywood, California, made headlines for subcontracting every municipal service to private companies, including public safety.[13] In these places, people no longer looked like citizens entitled to basic services and instead were simply residents who could buy services, beg charities for help, self-provision alternatives, or go without.

Nonprofit organizations and community activists encouraged residents who could not afford to shop for services to collectively self-provision them. On the outskirts of El Paso, for example, nongovernmental agencies in the mid-2000s recruited low-income Latina women to work as volunteer community leaders and unpaid laborers bringing school busses and water systems to their communities. Similarly, police officers and block club activists in west Seattle encouraged impoverished African American residents to self-sacrifice their time, bodies, and emotional energy by cleaning trash and organizing safety patrols in their chronically underserved neighborhood. Community-supported self-provisioning was also crucial in hurricane-damaged New Orleans, where government-funded subcontractors rebuilt business centers and high-end condominiums but left low-income residents to self-organize their own disaster recovery.[14] These trends illustrate an evolving division of labor where more affluent residents and businesses continue to receive services through markets and market-based governing but vulnerable residents neglected by those market models have to self-provision their cities, instead.

Self-provisioning is not always an act of desperation. For some lucky residents, self-provisioning comes with countercultural cache. Taco trucks, pop-up beer gardens, artist enclaves, and guerrilla gardens in Los Angeles, Detroit, Philadelphia, and Boston resonate with social protests against capitalism, consumerism, environmental destruction, and white privilege. By the late 2000s, city planners were describing urban informality and provisional spatial development as a way to stimulate reinvestment by making neighborhoods feel trendy and public streets feel lively.[15]

These trends are important, but they are only one small part of the self-provisioning story. Urban gardening involves significant manual labor, and taco trucks come without retirement benefits or health insurance. Residents with overwhelming work and family obligations or physical disabilities have trouble sustaining the work. Also, the romanticized spatial cracks and fissures of capitalism look much more ominous to middle-income residents watching those cracks engulf them through falling property values, rising crime rates, and decaying infrastructure.[16]

For many residents in Detroit, self-provisioning was not about countercultural reform but about a way to buttress collapsing markets and avoid countercultural lifestyles. The residents I interviewed wanted to live in a functional city. Informal gardens and pop-up coffeehouses reversed disinvestment on a few blocks, but self-provisioning was much more expansive than that. Residents became informal realtors helping empty housing find new occupants. They adopted or destroyed vacant structures to prevent unsanctioned theft and vandalism. They cleaned trash, cut grass, and shoveled snow from vacant lots and public parks. They monitored street activity to keep each other safe, and they publicized positive images of strong and vibrant communities. Almost none of the residents I spoke with described these activities in countercultural terms. Instead, they tried to reinforce—not undermine—the capitalist status quo.

It remains unclear whether self-provisioning can stimulate the political activism needed to overcome racial inequalities or challenge market-based governing agendas. In Detroit, self-provisioning rarely came with an explicit political message. The work was usually fragmented, and the benefits were local. Self-provisioning was especially prevalent, however, in areas where other efforts at community capacity building and political mobilization were also under way. This coincidence underscored the mutually reinforcing connections between resident activism at the household scale and collective mobilization at the neighborhood and district levels.

It would be unreasonable to expect self-provisioning alone to solve the problems that daunt policy makers, community groups, faith-based organizations, and socially conscious investors. But self-provisioning practices created new urban logics by reorganizing people in space, changing the way people accessed collective resources, and influencing the normative expectations residents had about their neighborhoods. And when combined with other modes of activism, self-provisioned alternatives to disinvestment and decay had powerful effects on local quality of life.

Stories of residents sweeping streets and planting vegetables in public spaces are wonderfully inspiring, but the capacity for residents to adapt and "make do" hardly justifies the prolonged lack of amenities available in chronically underserved areas. These atomized responses to collective problems are difficult to sustain, and the continued deterioration of every neighborhood included in this study despite resident activism suggests that self-provisioning, whatever its benefits, is no panacea. Rather than romanticizing informality as a model of bootstrap urbanism to emulate elsewhere, it is perhaps best to interpret these narratives as cautionary tales. Self-provisioning involved the short-term actions people took when no other options seemed available, with the hope that comprehensive solutions to disinvestment, racism, and vulnerability would eventually emerge.

» SELF-PROVISIONED STEWARDSHIP IN URBAN GRAY SPACE

Self-provisioning has many meanings, and it includes both individual and collective actions. The most basic definitions of self-provisioning describe urban homesteads where people build their own homes and grow their own food to reduce household expenses. These practices have a long history in U.S. cities, and they generally involve using manual labor on private property to meet household needs without going through cash markets. Self-provisioning also includes things like community associations where people come together in groups to raise money for special services or enact local land-use regulations. These civic-oriented practices have a long history, and the goal is usually to enhance property values and improve living conditions within designated areas.[17]

Alongside these activities, another subset of self-provisioning involves claiming, maintaining, and reusing gray space. "Gray space" is an apt phrase describing areas that exist somewhere in between the social categories of legal and criminal, fixed and temporary, and safety and death.[18] In Detroit, gray space includes places like abandoned buildings and overgrown parks. The private owners and municipal governments legally responsible for those spaces no longer exercise authority over them or control what happens there. These spaces, released from their previous social functions, become contested sites where neighbors and other potential users compete for control. In these loose, conflicted landscapes, new social norms and community expectations emerge as people with competing agendas self-provision alternatives to government contraction and market withdrawal.

Residents use homesteading and civic-style self-provisioning to control gray space, but they also use stewardship models that do not easily fit within these older categories. For instance, some urban homesteading residents build garages on abandoned lots or refurbish vacant homes for resale. Their civic–activist neighbors establish community gardens in neglected spaces and start nonprofit organizations to restore decaying homes. Alongside these practices, another subset of residents recruit handpicked relatives to squat in vacant homes, independently cut grass and plant flowers in public parks, and arrange the public streetscape to enhance neighborhood safety. These residents intervene in landscapes they do not officially control, and they do work that benefits their neighbors, which pushes beyond urban homesteading, but their actions stop short of organized social movements or formalized volunteerism. These stewardship self-provisioning practices in the gray spaces near residents' homes are the subject of this book.

These practices come with high stakes and high costs. Vulnerable residents using household resources to address public needs easily become even more strained and burdened. This stress, as well as the indeterminacy of the spaces involved, encourages residents to be selective in the types of tasks they undertake and the working methods they use. Their intimate decisions create a fractured geography of contradictory agendas and ethical dilemmas. Self-provisioning also reveals disconnects between utopian descriptions of residents actively engaging in home rule and the limited capacity of residents to transform physical interventions at home into meaningful structural reforms at the regional and national levels. These practices do little to challenge the fundamental role reversal where residents are becoming de facto property managers and service providers while market and government actors merely pitch in as occasional volunteers.

Residents in Detroit were often fully aware of these dilemmas, but they self-provisioned anyway—and with good reason. Doing-it-yourself seemed like the most effective option at the exact moment when residents, looking out their kitchen and bedroom windows, saw another longtime neighbor moving away, another service being cut, another police station closing, another drug house emerging, or another home burning. Structural reforms would be better, but they were slow in coming and might never arrive. Self-provisioning was local and ephemeral, but it provided immediate solutions to problems that could not wait. An awareness of the inherent unjustness of the situation and makeshift character of the fix did not stop residents from celebrating the work they accomplished, even as they hoped for a future where institutionalized, professional, shared services could once again make the self-provisioned city unnecessary.

» MANAGING SLOW DEATH WITHOUT PROMISES OF NEW LIFE

The resurgence of self-provisioning represents a new urban logic. It is not a regression to a preindustrial lifestyle but a reflection of the profound political loss of a multigenerational effort to build democracy and public good into urban life.

During the nineteenth century, municipalities were small and private. They coordinated trade and business interests, but they were not public service institutions. If a group of property owners wanted to pave streets, build playgrounds, or install streetlights, they could. But they had to pay for it themselves, and renters and neighbors living outside the project's work area had no legal voice in those decisions. That nineteenth-century period was also a period of social instability. People were moving from farms and overseas homes to U.S. cities, where housing markets were exploitive and workers received low wages for unstable jobs.

Self-provisioning played an important social role in that precarious environment. Wealthy residents were exempt, since they could use personal wealth and political connections to have infrastructure and amenities provided for them. But working-class families with enough money to escape tenement living had to do the work themselves. They used secondhand material and sweat equity to build low-cost homes in areas with many empty lots and unimproved streets. Men formed all-volunteer fire brigades. Women and children tended vegetable gardens and chicken coops. Fee-based companies sold fuel for heating and water for drinking and cooking, and residents looked to religious parishes, ethnic clubs, and mob bosses for help during moments of crisis. Race limited people's employment and housing choices, making it difficult for minorities to escape exploitive markets through self-provisioning, but some minorities still managed to build their own homes and grow their own food, and all working-class families regardless of race relied heavily on domestic labor to meet their daily needs.[19]

Urban homesteading helped residents avoid volatile cash markets and the dependency that came with it. Landlords, grocers, and taxes required cash, and workers received cash wages. But minimizing cash outlays was essential to protect workers from hunger and homelessness should they suddenly become ill, lose their jobs, or go on strike. For lucky residents sweat equity was also a means of upward mobility. As property values rose, residents could use that equity to secure small business loans, pay for their children's education, or purchase homes in better-served neighborhoods. Self-provisioning did not always create wonderful living environments. Inadequate sanitation and dangerous construction methods were widespread. But self-provisioning shielded households from capitalist exploitation.[20]

The twentieth-century invention of public municipalities with widespread enfranchisement, citywide resource sharing, and an explicit public works agenda brought many improvements. Centralized municipalities collecting citywide taxes and providing universal services created economies of scale. These municipalities constructed citywide water, power, and waste management systems. They built roads, schools, parks, fire departments, and streetcar lines. Public municipalities also enacted building codes and zoning ordinances, and they passed licensing laws for architects, real estate agents, and skilled tradesmen.[21] In the decades that followed, leading into the mid-twentieth century, the role of the federal government changed, as well. Elected officials developed homeownership programs and labor protection laws, and they invested in public education and social security. These changes were crucial in building the American middle class.[22]

Public municipalities were not perfect. They enabled wealth redistribution upward as well as downward. They created greater structural opportunities for public corruption. They incorporated racial bias into development agendas. They subsidized suburban growth at the expense of central cities. And they codified the legal subordination of public municipalities to private corporations.[23] These were significant problems, but the goal of collective governing and universal services was nevertheless a powerful impetus for social reform.

These institutional solutions to economic vulnerability used wealth redistribution, market regulations, and economies of scale to lift millions of households out of high-risk environments. Large-scale investors enjoyed lower infrastructure costs, and fires and epidemics became less common and less disruptive. Public municipalities and federal social safety nets helped middle-income and working-class whites gain easier access to affordable, sanitary, high-value homes.[24] Residents no longer had to be as physically active in the day-to-day reproduction of their physical environment, and they gained greater political influence over regional decision making. Far from a paternalistic state taking care of hapless citizens, residents were active governing agents using their money, votes, civic associations, and mass movements to negotiate urban life.

This era of centralized municipal services was not permanent. Mid-twentieth-century suburbanization fragmented decision making and resource sharing. Since the city government's legal authority to advance public interests stopped at the municipal boundary line, the investors and middle-income whites who moved to the suburbs no longer had to share their wealth and influence with low-income and minority residents in the urban core.[25]

The national rise of neoliberal governance undermined municipalities, as well. By "neoliberal governance" I mean market-based policies that emphasize individual, profit-based solutions to collective needs and oppose wealth redistribution for social programs. The rollback of welfare institutions and the rollout of market-oriented governing benefitted elites at the expense of lower-income residents, especially inner-city minorities. City-run colleges and hospitals were privatized. Government funding for unemployment benefits, public housing, job training, and childhood development was cut. These funding decisions reflected new spending priorities where private companies received tax incentives and development subsidies even as social spending declined.[26]

These dual market and government reforms generated a "splintering" effect as municipalities sold public infrastructure and privatized municipal services.[27] These changes left residents with limited resources dependent on community organizations, churches, and charities that tried to coordinate economic development and provide social services in areas that profit-oriented investors neglected. These civic responses helped, but like municipal governments, nonprofit organizations faced increasing pressure to adopt revenue-neutral operating methods. These organizations also came with narrow mission statements, limited work areas, no electoral accountability, and limited professional expertise that despite good intentions left many basic needs unmet.[28]

Some neoliberalizing cities weathered these upheavals and re-emerged as icons of so-called lean, green, competitive reurbanism, but many did not, and recurring economic recessions have steadily pushed a large and growing subset of municipal governments toward bankruptcy. Nearly 130 cities, towns, and villages in the United States dissolved between 2000 and 2010 due to financial strain, a nearly unknown phenomenon in previous decades. Another thirty-five counties, municipalities, and municipal utility companies declared bankruptcy between 2010 and Detroit's notorious filing in 2013.[29] Detroit was the largest and most prominent city to become so fully engulfed in fiscal collapse, making it an especially apt place to see how government contraction and fragmentation restructured daily life, but Detroit was not unique. By the early 2010s, after many decades of suburbanization and privatization, the experience of living in neighborhoods with unavailable or unaffordable services had become routine, not only in shrinking cities like Detroit, St. Louis, and Camden[30] but also in subsections of prospering cities like Seattle and Boston.[31]

In some ways, the resurgence of self-provisioning in today's market-oriented environment is similar to urban homesteads of the past. Residents grow food, salvage waste, and reduce housing costs by doing work themselves or foregoing improvements. The erosion of municipal capacity and the growing precariousness of daily life marks a return to the situation where people are entitled only to the services they can personally afford. Wealthy residents with the resources to shop still receive market commodities and state assistance, whereas lower-income residents have to meet everyday needs and manage collective affairs alone. Block clubs, nonprofit foundations, and neighborhood gangs are the twenty-first-century counterparts to the nineteenth-century religious charities, ethnic clubs, and mob bosses. And new forms of self-provisioning are once again becoming an important part of urban life.

However, self-provisioning in today's postindustrial, neoliberal world is not simply a throwback to premunicipal lifestyles. It comes with a shifting—rather than a backsliding—pallet of chores, needs to be met, services to be filled, and spaces to be managed. Vacant homes, violent crimes, and unprecedented debt create a fundamentally different set of challenges that residents try to manage. Instead of deciding how or when to upgrade their homes and streets, residents have the responsibility for managing other people's decaying infrastructure foisted on them. Instead of opting out of exploitive markets, residents try to keep their families safe and their living conditions dignified in a context of market abandonment. Instead of translating into incremental upward mobility, stewardship-based self-provisioning rarely increases household resources, and the end result is often not the gradual building up of a neighborhood but simply a mediated decline that nonetheless keeps on coming.

» MORAL GEOGRAPHIES AND ETHICAL DILEMMAS

Self-provisioning produces moral geographies. A "moral geography" is a cultural landscape where certain people, practices, and objects appear to belong and others do not.[32] The twentieth-century era of rationalized technocratic urban planning created landscapes where commercial areas were separate from residential neighborhoods, affordable housing was underrepresented in suburban enclaves, and investors with storefronts had more rights than did vendors with pushcarts. These geographies reproduced classed, raced, and gendered hierarchies. African Americans looked suspicious in the lily-white suburbs. Homeless people on park benches and women athletes in public spaces looked like less legitimate users of public space than did their wealthier male counterparts.[33]

Moral geographies are not always harmful. They include mixed-race areas where white and Latino homeowners refuse to abandon African American or Asian American neighbors and landscapes of social capital encourage reciprocity and communal problem solving. But prominent discussions of moral geographies focusing on social injustice often emphasize how elites use normalized aesthetics to accumulate wealth and privilege at the expense of underprivileged residents. These black-and-white cases provide important political critiques, but most residents experience some form of vulnerability that decenters simplistic categories of dominants versus subordinates or big guys versus little guys.

The resurgence of informality is reworking the functional and moral valences of built environments. Latino immigrants facing employment discrimination use freeway ramps as impromptu peer-to-peer markets where they sell oranges and roses to traffic-jammed motorists. Retired Asian American women living far from their childhood homes meet at night to perform tai chi or other traditional dances in empty downtown parking garages after the daytime office workers have left. Mexican Americans put Guadalupe statues and old sofas on front curbs to celebrate their heritage and create quasi-public spaces where they can socialize with neighbors in otherwise alienating suburban environments. And stay-at-home housewives concerned about their families' falling incomes transform suburban living rooms into self-run clothing stores and day care centers.[34] These unintended uses of space create economic and cultural opportunities that markets and governments do not provide.

Provisional reuses of space are not ethically neutral. Business owners may suffer when sidewalk vendors sell goods without incurring rental fees or licensing costs, and neighbors may dislike the noise and foot traffic that home-based businesses generate. But owners and neighbors do not always take action against these technically illegal practices. Fast-food merchandizers may tolerate street vendors selling books and oranges but not hot dogs and French fries. Little old ladies performing meditative dances elicit greater public sympathy than do punk rock teenagers holding warehouse raves.

Neighbors may tolerate women running informal day care centers in their living rooms but complain about men repairing cars for cash on their lawns. These zones of tolerance illustrate inconsistencies between the moral and legal geographies governing everyday life.

Detroit's legacy of disinvestment complicates matters further. In cities like San Francisco, New York, and Los Angeles where land rents are high and vacancy rates are low, people often use public infrastructure or private home spaces to support provisional activities. But in areas with acutely weak property markets, gray space becomes a prime site for informality. In 2010, Detroit had 80,000 vacant housing units, 30,000 open and dangerous structures, and 114,000 vacant residential lots. At least half of those spaces were abandoned by absentee owners who had no intention of returning.[35] Unlike public sidewalks and freeway exit ramps, through which most people moved quickly, these domestic gray spaces were embedded within residential areas where neighbors lived full time, and the provisional activities occurring there easily spilled over to affect the neighbors' living conditions. Also, unlike residents who used their personal homes for commercial or civic purposes and who could be held accountable for those actions, many provisional users of Detroit's gray space used those spaces because it allowed them to be intentionally illusive.

These characteristics inflected the moral geographies that self-provisioning neighbors produced. Some neighbors enjoyed the idea of a pop-up beer garden outside their living room window, but most residents preferred to see new owner-occupants moving in. Similarly, the slim hope that an informal occupant might contribute to neighborhood vitality paled against the more statistically likely realities that the person seizing the space would sell cocaine and heroin instead of beer, the structure would be burned instead of painted, or the user would steal electricity but not cut the grass or trim the hedges.

Fears that someone might (mis)use the gray space next door prompted many residents—most of whom were low-income minorities living in precarious circumstances—to preemptively intervene in those spaces to create morally laden landscape aesthetics of exclusion and control. Concerned neighbors disguised vacant homes and recruited new occupants to keep domestic landscapes private, and they mowed public parks and cleaned trash from public streets to visually signify that the formal rules of public decorum still applied. These interventions created illusions of authority even though the private owners and government officials legally responsible for those spaces remained absent. When residents could not sustain those moralized landscapes, they sometimes chose to eliminate gray space by dismantling abandoned structures and repurposing vacant lots to push unwanted activities off their blocks. These practices inverted the usual countercultural logic of seized space and provisional reuse. Vulnerable residents intervened not to liberate space from private capitalist dictates but rather to rescript space as off-limits for provisional uses they felt were objectionable or dangerous.

The line between sympathetic and dangerous was blurry, and neighbors often disagreed over the types of self-provisioning practices they supported. Residents usually condemned scrappers who dismantled buildings and sold the material for personal gain, but those same residents also demolished decaying structures and re-used the wood floors and wall insulation in private home-remodeling projects. Residents concerned about trespass and vandalism technically trespassed and vandalized vacant homes themselves while disguising them, boarding them, and converting them into community spaces. And neighbors concerned about arsonists who endangered their lives sometimes set fire to buildings to displace other risks, especially the violent drug trade. All of these activities were technically illegal, but from a local perspective, one set of actors appeared socially legitimate. Informal norms varied by neighborhood, and residents used on-the-ground intuition negotiated among their peers and at arms length from state lawmakers to guide their interventions.

This extreme devolution of land management generated a landscape of care that sometimes diverged sharply from normative expectations of what so-called safe and clean cities were supposed to look like. Preemptive interventions in gray spaces were communicative acts. Neighbors adjusted building facades and ground surfaces to deter unwanted activities and welcome desirable newcomers, but the grammar of communication was not universal. A boarded window that indicated abandonment was also a sign neighbors cared about the building and were protecting it. A patch of clean, bare dirt that looked unmaintained compared with a manicured lawn was nonetheless an accomplishment in areas where residents spent several weekends each year clearing trash and debris from abandoned lots. Similarly, although everyone agreed a pile of trash was a sign of blight, strategically arranged debris blocking driveways and doorways was also an act of stewardship preventing people from using those spaces as drug houses and chop shops.

These communicative landscapes spoke locally, not from a god's-eye view. Residents engaged in thematically similar practices citywide, but they tweaked their methods and aesthetics in response to local conditions. These adaptations emerged partly from necessity. Neighbors with limited resources and no formal claims to the spaces they adopted valued frugality. Local stewardship innovations also generated feedback loops that reinforced neighborhood-specific sensibilities of what stewardship ought to look like. Validation came from neighbors who applauded residents' efforts and from potential users who respected their claims to space rather than from government authorities following binary legal strictures of right and wrong, clean and blighted, or occupied and abandoned.

State actors remained important in these subjective moral landscapes. Residents sometimes received grants and encouragement from public entities to maintain vacant spaces and repurpose public lots. Residents used public displays of caretaking to access scarce government aid and demand municipal accountability. Authorities could also fine residents for trespass and vandalism or arrest and deport people who attracted their attention, which limited the types of stewardship residents undertook—especially for residents with criminal records, undocumented family members, or limited incomes.

Despite this state influence, situated ethical judgments were paramount. Analyzing self-provisioning through the lens of citizenship would presume a person's relationship to the state was crucial. But when self-provisioners in Detroit assessed the morality of their work, relationships to government entities generally took a backseat to the contexts of risk and the logics of practice they shared with their neighbors.

This ethical fragmentation of the cityscape reflected the precariousness of everyday life. Residents lived with many risks, and self-provisioning in gray space involved trade-offs. Self-provisioning was a means to negotiate social norms and acceptable behaviors. It helped residents with no legal authority over neglected environments to create landscapes where certain people and practices seemed to belong and others did not. Markets and governments still mattered, and the lifestyle choices of residents could not reverse structural trends. But residents nonetheless intervened to create localized moral geographies as protective buffers around their homes.

» DEFINING SUCCESS, AWAITING SOLUTIONS

City planners and urban economists frequently cite growing populations, rising property values, and expanding corporate investments as measures of urban vitality. When measuring self-provisioning against this economic yardstick, the scale of disinvestment in Detroit dwarfed individual attempts at neighborhood improvement. Areas with high levels of resident activism have continued to deteriorate, and the mushrooming rates of unemployment and foreclosure during the Great Recession intensified disinvestment faster than self-provisioning (or other forms of community activism) could counteract it. More homes became abandoned and burned. Problems with trash, grass, and rodents intensified. And as more people moved away, fewer residents were left to carry the workload.

Emotional accounts of self-provisioning were often equally dispiriting. Most residents did not describe it as romantic and satisfying. Instead, they characterized it as incredibly unfair and relatively ineffective at solving citywide problems. The regional, national, and global dynamics producing disinvestment all too easily erased the atomized improvements neighbors made on their blocks. Defensive interventions rarely supplemented low incomes or improved public services. The labor was time consuming, physically taxing, and stressful, making it impractical for elderly, disabled, or overextended households. Residents also worried conservative state officials might notice their do-it-yourself efforts and mistakenly conclude expanded welfare and greater corporate accountability was unnecessary.

These concerns raise doubts about the potential for domestic microremedies to scale-up into something approximating urban revitalization. Uplifting stories about active residents do not necessarily mean communities are strong or improvements are permanent. Self-provisioning at the household scale cannot replicate the general social security programs or regional development policies federal governments and city halls once managed. These are not new concerns, nor are they limited to self-provisioning. Scholars raise similar questions about the limited capacity of civic groups and nonprofit organizations to manage collective needs in an era of neoliberal offloading. Civic organizing is better than inaction, but communities are often ill equipped to assume municipal functions in coordinated, sustained, and significant ways.[36]

These limits are important, but saving Detroit from a progrowth perspective is not the only measure of success. Self-provisioning in gray space has limited—but still real—benefits for quality of life. These practices help residents build stronger community bonds, solve practical problems, access scarce resources, control social behavior, and build posturban communities. Many self-provisioning residents also value their autonomy in a context where charitable funds come and go in unpredictable ways and the few government programs that do exist often feel paternalistic or cause more trouble than they are worth. These values come with their own measures of success that differ profoundly from market-based logics of growth. Reducing risk, displacing nuisance, or buying time helps, even if it does not permanently eliminate hardship or reverse structural inequality.

Organizations are crucial in helping residents self-provision and helping those activities add up to meaningful reforms. Community organizing and resident activism are mutually reinforcing, and self-provisioning is most effective as one in a series of integrated, multitiered responses to precarious life. Organizations raise public awareness about the benefits of self-provisioning, and they teach residents how to work more efficiently. Community groups also bring residents together to self-provision collectively and to demand greater government accountability, legal reforms, and foundation support to aid their work.

While giving self-provisioning its due, ongoing urban decline and municipal fragmentation underscore the need for greater reforms. Neighborhoods where vulnerable residents do not have access to basic services are not neighborhoods where residents have failed. Instead, those areas demonstrate the inadequacy of market-based governing policies that favor individual solutions to collective problems. Do-it-yourself urbanism cannot replicate institutionalized revenue sharing. It drains households of resources they could otherwise use to generate alternate life paths. It does not eliminate racism, make global capitalism more humane, or reverse structural disinvestment. Instead, it reflects the precariousness that emerges when neoliberal capitalism is unrolled over the top of long-standing racial inequities in a context of growing social precariousness. Self-provisioned neighborhoods are not abandoned and lifeless, but they are spaces of feeble lifelines and constant struggle. They are places where defying expectations is one measure of success and where the pressing need for new social policies is sorely visible.

I do not pretend that self-provisioning will "save" Detroit. Instead of reading self-provisioning through a utopian lens of salvation, this book emphasizes that self-provisioning in gray space has other implications for urban life. It reorganizes people in space, mediates access to collective resources, and reworks the moral geographies of the city. These practices do not save the city of the past. They bring a new type of city into being.

2

Seeking New Neighbors

» **RESIDENT REALTORS**

"Are you looking for someone?" A twentysomething, muscular Latino man stood, arms crossed, tattoos glimmering, watching me from a nearby porch. I was surveying vacant lots, and I had lingered to inspect a thin strip of bare dirt sandwiched between two tall houses, one occupied and the other boarded and vacant. "Are you looking for someone?" he repeated. It was a polite but firm question commonly used in the neighborhood to assess the purpose and legitimacy of strangers.

"No," I answered. We exchanged names. I gestured vaguely toward the patch of dirt and told Rey I was looking at some empty properties. Rey, assuming I meant the vacant house and not the empty lot, told me its story.

In 2012 Rey's neighbors walked away from the house over an outstanding debt of $2,400. Several months passed before the bank foreclosed and took formal possession of the building. By then, scrappers had already removed the copper pipes, hot-water heater, and plumbing fixtures. Bank subcontractors renovated the house three times over the following four months. Each time, the new appliances and equipment were stolen within a matter of days. Then, Rey's two young children began finding hypodermic needles on the sidewalk. Rey started to fear the "crackheads hanging out in the shadows" by the building's open doors and windows.

Fed up with the theft and drug activity festering from the bank's botched management, Rey took action. He became an informal advocate for the house. When bank contractors began a fourth round of renovations, Rey insisted they secure the doors and windows with fourteen-gauge reinforced steel plates every afternoon before leaving the job site, and he chained his personal guard dog to the porch every night. During the day Rey assisted free of charge with simple manual labor tasks, giving him an excuse to monitor the work—and workmen—on a daily basis. It also gave him an opportunity to memorize the building's specifications: its size and layout, the renovations completed, the materials used, and the quality of the craftsmanship. This knowledge was useful when, at Rey's insistence, bank officials agreed not to advertise the vacancy. Rey promised to find "a good buyer" for the house himself.

A month had passed since then. The renovations were still intact, and Rey's children had stopped finding needles while playing. "It's a good house," Rey told me. "Big, with a good layout." He asked if I wanted to see inside or if maybe I'd like to move in and become his new neighbor. I felt bad saying I couldn't buy the house, but it did not remain empty for long. A few weeks later, Rey convinced the cousin of another family on the block to move in, instead.

Rey had essentially become an impromptu "resident realtor," an apt phrase describing neighbors who work unofficially to help homes find new occupants. The economic recession and housing market crash of the late 2000s doubled residential vacancy rates citywide. Residents responded to this massive change in many ways. Some people absorbed vacancy by transforming duplexes into single-family homes or buying and demolishing vacant structures next door. Others bought homes to rent or sell at a loss just to get them back on the market. A smaller subset of residents organized promotional home tours, mural tours, potlucks, sock hops, garden tours, holiday celebrations, and award banquets to build a neighborhood "buzz."

For residents like Rey, buying and maintaining extra housing wasn't practical. He did not have the money, and he did not want to be a landlord. The real estate buzz from mural tours and taco trucks did not help him directly, either. With nearly 1,500 empty units in his neighborhood, it was unlikely one of the few newcomers inspired to move into the neighborhood would choose the unadvertised and repeatedly vandalized house next door. And so, like countless other residents, Rey became an informal realtor and matchmaker, searching for just the right person—a friend, family member, or kindred spirit—to move onto his block.

Matchmaking took many forms. Residents drew on personal connections of kinship and friendship to identify potential recruits.

Matchmaking arrangements generally involved quid pro quo, with residents offering financial or logistical assistance to ensure that newcomers moved into specified vacancies and not other units farther away. Among these recruits some became official owners or renters, and others lived informally as squatters. The criteria residents used to select potential occupants varied depending on block conditions and personal relationships, but subjective morality judgments were paramount. Matchmakers helped people gain access to housing they otherwise could not afford or may not have found. In exchange matchmakers expected the peace of mind that came from having a trusted—or at least known—person fill an otherwise troubling vacancy.

Half of the residents I interviewed (51 percent) described acting as informal resident realtors, and that number was consistent across all four neighborhoods, regardless of differences in income levels and vacancy rates. Community organizations developed formal programs to combat vacancy as well, and resident realtors often appealed to those groups for help in dealing with specific homes on their blocks. But since organizations had limited financial resources and preexisting programmatic commitments, organization leaders generally refused those requests. Even in areas with strong community groups, many resident realtors said they worked mostly alone.

Among homeowners, residents like Rey had vested financial interests in stabilizing local property values, but matchmaking was rarely mercenary. Residents recruited newcomers for emotional and practical reasons. They wanted to support family members, build alternative communities, deter vandalism, and eliminate uncertainty. Matchmakers helped young relatives and aging parents buy or rent the vacant units next door. They helped friends and family members facing financial difficulties become informal caretakers living unofficially in vacant homes. These squatters often paid utility bills and sometimes paid taxes, but they did not pay rent. Matchmakers also helped socially conscious friends and colleagues build communities whose alternative lifestyles and philosophies mirrored their own. Even when these arrangements did not create ideal living conditions, they still offered significant benefits for both the matchmaker and their recruits.

Matchmaking was a means of negotiating disinvestment. Property markets in Detroit created vacancy not occupancy. But disinvestment was not evenly distributed citywide, and resident realtors pulling people from other neighborhoods reinforced that lumpiness. Matchmaking created geographic clusters of people who shared common bloodlines or common interests. Markets still mattered, but disinvestment created a context where personal connections, social reciprocity, and subjective morality judgments became especially important mechanisms reorganizing people in space.

The general logic of matchmaking was exclusionary not egalitarian. Connecting friends with desirable homes and neighborhoods was as much about keeping "problem people" away as it was about bringing preapproved people in. With property markets collapsing, residents feared that vacancies left to the marketplace would attract low-income residents who would not maintain their property or who would bring "nuisance" behaviors from their old neighborhoods with them. An even greater fear was housing would remain vacant and become prime targets for the underground economies of scrapping and drug dealing. Despite the sympathy matchmakers felt for low-income families climbing the housing ladder, matchmaking was fundamentally about replacing faltering market mechanisms of class-based exclusion with personal judgments about the people residents felt would make good neighbors.

Resident realtors represent a category of self-provisioners who are easy to overlook. Matchmaking leaves no overt telltale signs in the street. Houses become occupied, but the history of how people came to be in those spaces fades from view. These market-buttressing practices also lack the guerilla romance of the urban gardeners, installation artists, street sweepers, trash collectors, watchdogs, spies, and blackmailers described in the chapters that follow. But scrutinizing this everyday form of self-provisioning underscores that instead of embracing Detroit's "free spaces" as sites of autonomy and liberation, most residents wanted to live in neighborhoods with functioning housing markets and conventional lifestyles. If recruiting new residents failed to stabilize markets, only then did residents adopt more explicitly insurgent strategies of spatial appropriation.

» LOCATING AGENCY IN PROPERTY MARKETS

Rethinking real estate through the lens of self-provisioning creates opportunities to reevaluate the role resident agency plays in shaping property markets. Political economic theories of investment cycles and rent gaps emphasize that markets are socially mediated (not naturally occurring) phenomena, since government policies, social hierarchies, and hegemonic ideologies guide the workings of capitalism. While acknowledging these superstructural influences, political economy theories also underscore the severely circumscribed role of place-based activism. Global social forces, not grassroots meanings or individual preferences, determine the form and fate of local environments.[1]

These structural analyses debunk consumer sovereignty explanations of urban inequality as the outcome of lifestyle choices, which is an important political step in struggles for racial integration, environmental justice, and rights to the city. I concede this point. But structural forces, while unavoidable, may not be as totalizing as they sometimes appear.

Important case studies illustrate residents can restructure local housing markets. The Dudley Street Neighborhood Initiative in Boston's Roxbury community is one well-documented success story. Roxbury in the mid-1980s was a predominantly low-income community of color with vacancy rates and social challenges similar to those in Detroit. Concerned residents took action. They formed a nonprofit organization to create and implement a resident-driven physical redevelopment plan involving the construction of several hundred affordable housing units on abandoned land. They used eminent domain to transfer blighted parcels from negligent owners to their organization. Then, when no professional developer would agree to oversee the construction, they designed and built the homes themselves. New people moved in, and the project's success galvanized neighborhood activism and social support networks.[2]

Case studies like these are exceptional. Many residents want to improve their neighborhoods, but efforts often fail to overcome the structural pressures of disinvestment, or equally troublingly, they lead to gentrification and displacement. Brooklyn, for instance, was once a disinvested landscape similar to Roxbury with low incomes, decaying housing, and marginalized residents. In the 1960s socially conscious middle-income professionals began moving to Brooklyn and renovating neighborhood brownstones. They used their professional skills and connections to pressure banks to stop redlining

Brooklyn and to provide new mortgage resources for remodeling. They also used home tours, literary references, and historical documents to promote the neighborhood to like-minded activists. Their interventions galvanized a back-to-the-city movement that by the 1980s had pushed real estate values so high working-class and middle-income residents alike could no longer afford to buy brownstones in Brooklyn.[3]

In Detroit in the early 2010s, some residents living near downtown and midtown redevelopment areas voiced gentrification concerns, but disinvestment and falling property values remained predominant citywide.[4] Within this structural context, many community groups and concerned residents tried to counteract decline by renovating homes, promoting neighborhoods, and working as informal realtors and matchmakers. It is unclear whether these grassroots campaigns had a meaningful market impact on real estate values, and preciously few areas saw the scale of change that occurred in Roxbury or Brooklyn. But markets are only one measure of success and only one element determining the arrangement of social groups in space. These practices may not have reversed structural disinvestment, but they modified its effects and created deeply personal, extramarket logics organizing people in space.

» DEPOPULATION AND THE INTERNAL HOUSING SHUFFLE

Resident realtors are not new to Detroit, but the pressure to intervene in property markets expanded significantly during the foreclosure crisis of the late 2000s. The Great Recession quickened an already existing trajectory of depopulation and disinvestment in Detroit. The city lost nearly 900,000 people between 1950 and 2000, and it lost another 237,500 residents—or 25 percent of its remaining population—between 2000 and 2010, with the biggest drops occurring after 2006. Throughout the years, residents left—and stopped moving to—Detroit for many reasons: fewer employment opportunities, racial anxieties, sensationalized crime reports, rising property taxes, rising insurance rates, declining school performance, and federally subsidized suburban alternatives, not to mention the moves and deaths associated with illness and age.[5] The late-2000s

foreclosure crisis compounded the problems. Over 63,000 properties went through mortgage foreclosure between 2005 and 2011, and
about 45,000 properties went through tax foreclosure in 2011 and
2012 alone. Most of those properties remained vacant for several
months or years thereafter.[6]

For many residents, moving was not an option. Some people
lived in housing they inherited mortgage free, purchased for cash, or
had already paid off. While siblings, parents, and children may have
moved on, residents with chronic health problems, unstable employment, or advanced ages often said they just didn't have the financial
resources to relocate. For owner-occupants and resident landlords,
falling property values meant lost personal wealth, further undercut-
ting their ability to move. Some residents were indifferent to these
market shifts, and some felt trapped despite their desire to leave.

Other residents fervently wanted to stay in Detroit. They cherished local friendships, family ties, and daily routines. Residents
working independently or in peer-to-peer economies were reluctant
to move away from their clients and business connections. Many residents enjoyed Detroit's nominally low home prices, which allowed
them to get more house for less cost.[7] For residents with options,
staying in Detroit was often a moral statement against market waste
and regional racism. Some people used Detroit's cheap housing to
escape unsatisfying wage labor or bureaucratic jobs in the suburbs,
but they were the privileged few. Not everyone wished to stay, but
resident realtors were most prevalent among people either resigned
or committed to living in Detroit for the near future.

However long people imagined they would stay, residents citywide were drawn into an extensive housing shuffle occurring both
within and across municipal boundary lines. The precipitous drop
in property values during the recession created opportunities for
people to relocate. Urban scholar Thomas Sugrue, an expert on race
and urban development, shrewdly summarized these trends in a 2011
New York Times editorial. Falling prices allowed minority homebuyers to cross the color line, moving from underprivileged Detroit
to better-served suburbs. "It was not until the economy of the entire
metropolitan area slumped," he wrote, "thanks to the faltering auto
industry and the foreclosure crisis, that black buyers finally found
whites willing—desperate, in fact—to sell their suburban houses,

especially in the working-class and lower-middle-class towns bordering the city."[8] Detroit's population decline partly reflected this increasing opportunity for African Americans to move to wealthier, whiter, better-served neighborhoods outside the city.[9]

The outflow of residents to the suburbs, including minorities seeking a better life, dramatically increased vacancy in the city they left behind. The neighborhoods where I interviewed residents all lost population between 2000 and 2010, ranging from a drop of 14 percent in Rey's Springwells Village to 37 percent in Brightmoor, the hardest-hit area I studied. Residents partially compensated for outmigration by spreading out—for instance, by converting duplexes into single-family homes. Housing demolition partially offset losses, as well. Municipal bulldozers leveled as much as 7 percent of the local housing stock. These expansions and demolitions did not keep pace with population loss. Vacancy climbed from 2 to 10 percent in comparatively stable Grandmont Rosedale, and it reached 30 percent in hard-hit Brightmoor.

Climbing vacancy rates and dropping property values generated a tumultuous internal housing shuffle that aggregate studies of citywide trends often overlook. Just as residents left the city for improved life chances in the suburbs, disinvestment inside Detroit created opportunities to shed debt and climb the housing ladder by relocating to other homes inside Detroit. For example, Derrick, an African American therapist, short saled his house in 2012. "I was underwater," he told me. "I bought the house for $125,000 in the late '90s. Once I went underwater, it was worth, maybe, $50,000. But I was still paying a mortgage. . . . I was able to get a short sale to get out of it." Selling the house meant losing his accrued equity. It was also devastating emotionally. Derrick left his home and his social support networks while carrying a sense of personal embarrassment and failure. With hindsight Derrick identified an unexpected boon. With housing values dropping, he was able to use his savings to purchase another house for cash, a fixer-upper in an architectural style he preferred in a neighborhood he felt was more stable than the area he left behind.

Lower-income homeowners relocated, as well, often without their banks' consent. Rosa, for instance, a Latina woman who moved from Mexico to Detroit for love, said she strongly wanted to "walk away"

Figure 1. A mix of occupied and vacant housing. Photograph courtesy of Irwin Danto.

from the house (and the spouse) she once affectionately cherished. After having paid $50,000 or $60,000 on her mortgage, the house appraised for only $9,000 in 2011. "And we're still paying." After hearing the new assessment value, Rosa stopped maintaining the building and made plans to relocate. Her former neighbor was her inspiration. The woman next door allegedly asked the bank to let her pay off her mortgage for $10,000 instead of the outstanding $50,000 due. When the bank refused, Rosa said, the neighbor found "a better and bigger" house a few blocks away for $10,000. She paid cash for the house and then forfeited her previous deed to the bank. After the foreclosure the bank resold the house to a new buyer for $10,000, the same amount the original homeowner initially offered. Rosa hoped to do the same. "I don't care about this house," she said. "I just want to save money and buy another one. Now that they are cheaper, you can find a cheaper house somewhere else."

The sudden loss of so many longtime neighbors left those who stayed behind feeling abandoned and bereft. One of Rosa's neighbors, for instance, explained how he felt when he lost his next-door neighbors in 2010. "It had nice neighbors living there," he said. "Real nice. But one day, I went to go take 'em some tamales, and there was nobody answering the door. So I looked through the window, and it was just vacant. Everything was gone out of there. The people across the street told me they had left the house. They walked away from it. So it was like, wow." He shook his head sadly. "They didn't say anything to me. They left the house. . . . As far as I know, they still own it. It's just a vacant, burnt house."

Many residents watching this internal housing shuffle were afraid falling home values would reduce neighborhood exclusivity and lead to increased turnover, lower maintenance standards, and increased nuisance. A conversation I observed between two African American men, both professionals, one retired, aptly illustrated this anxiety. The retiree said he had noticed foot traffic around the vacant house next door. His friend optimistically suggested the strangers might be potential homebuyers. The retiree responded, "I hope not." He had heard rumors that nearby homes appraising at $100,000 in 2005 were selling for as little as $10,000 in 2013. "With that low price point," he said apprehensively, "who knows who would be moving in next door?"

Residents in lower-income neighborhoods expressed similar concerns about maintaining exclusivity. Residents in Rey's neighborhood, for instance, knew the mayor and his city planners wanted to "right-size" the city by encouraging residents from sparsely settled areas to move into denser neighborhoods.[10] Instead of welcoming this densification proposal, many residents were afraid newcomers from high-poverty, high-crime areas would bring "social problems" with them. As one man explained, "The new tenants can be fine, and carefully screened. But then their boyfriends come, and the drugs come, and there's lots of problems." These residents wanted higher-income stabilizers—not bargain hunters—to move in. If that was not possible, then residents wanted to hand select the lower-income newcomers themselves to exclude people they did not want living next door.

›› THE LIMITS OF CIVIL SOCIETY

The scenes just described might suggest residents were without help or resources while weathering the massive changes affecting Detroit. But every resident I spoke with had at least one community-based or faith-based organization actively investing in housing stabilization in their area. Some of these were homegrown organizations, rooted in resident volunteerism. Others were professional branches of national foundations supporting development in several areas citywide. Residents often asked these civil society entities for help getting housing on their blocks reoccupied. Despite a few noteworthy exceptions, very few people had success. These organizations played an important role in general neighborhood development, but their preexisting workloads left them ill equipped to accommodate impromptu requests for help dealing with specific, newly arising vacancies.

Successful collaborations were generally those where, by happenstance, the property met very specific criteria and where residents assumed a significant portion of the workload. The most inspiring example from my field notes involved Constance, a loquacious, middle-aged African American woman who despite living in a highly stigmatized neighborhood, insisted hers was "the best block in the world." Her passion for community activism eventually brought her in contact with a neighborhood church that had just received its first federal grant for housing redevelopment and was searching for somewhere to spend it. As Constance explained publicly during a community meeting, "I saw the blight around me, and I prayed to God, 'Lord, I know about NSP [the Neighborhood Stabilization Program], but I need some help!' And within two weeks my prayers were answered by a man from [the nearby church]. He knocked on my door and said he had been sent to me because I know people in the community. I'm a community person. He said he wanted to renovate some houses, and would I help him."

Arising from this unexpected encounter and using money from the church's federal grant, Constance and the church official gutted and renovated six or eight long-vacant homes on her block.[11] She decided which structures to remodel, and she vetted the several-hundred people who applied for the units. She guided successful applicants through the federally mandated home-management training programs, and she helped them file paperwork for additional grants to cover their portion of the subsidized sales prices.

In this unusual example, the serendipitous confluence of organizational capacity, financial resources, and Constance's personal willingness to devote countless hours of unpaid labor created an opportunity to funnel resources onto her block. Constance also benefitted from geography. Only about a dozen subneighborhoods citywide were pre-authorized to receive Neighborhood Stabilization funding, so she was able to access federal resources that were unavailable to other equally eager residents living only a few blocks away.[12]

This fruitful collaboration was ultimately short lived. Once the one-time grant money was spent, church officials declined to pursue a second round of fund-raising and renovation. Inspired by the experience, Constance moved forward independently, writing new grant applications she hoped some foundation might someday approve.

In some Detroit neighborhoods, residents established community-based organizations to facilitate housing redevelopment more systematically. Residents in Grandmont Rosedale, for instance, built one of the strongest and most lauded community development corporations citywide. Within this solidly middle-class neighborhood of predominantly African American homeowners, their organization's small professional staff and large circle of regular volunteers were almost entirely composed of neighborhood residents. As the director explained to me, residents founded the organization in 1989 to combat a small uptick in neighborhood vacancy. The organization bought, renovated, and sold long-standing vacancies at a financial loss to new owner-occupants to stabilize the market and prevent disinvestment from growing. In the late 2000s the group was using donations from the Kresge Foundation, Ford Foundation, Michigan State Housing Development Authority, and federal Neighborhood Stabilization Program to cover the average $15,000 to $20,000 loss they incurred per house. The organization also offered down-payment assistance to mortgage-qualifying homebuyers. As the foreclosure crisis mounted, they developed an additional foreclosure-prevention program to purchase short-sale homes from underwater residents and resell them to the original owners, which prevented vacancy by allowing homeowners to shed debt without relocating.

As a model of community-based development, organizations like these deserve attention and encouragement. Despite their many accomplishments, however, the scale and structural nature of disinvestment in Detroit surpassed their capacity to reverse these trends. As the organization's director explained, the Grandmont Rosedale group partially stabilized property markets during "normal" decades

Figure 2. Resident volunteers encouraging neighbors to support vacant property upkeep. Photo courtesy of the Grandmont Rosedale Development Corporation.

of disinvestment, but the severity of the Great Recession quickly overwhelmed their efforts. The organization renovated twenty-five homes between 2010 and 2012, which reflected a significantly increased workload compared with previous years' but still left over six hundred neighborhood homes vacant.

Residents living next door to those vacancies said they frequently approached community organizations for help but to no avail. One African American woman who was also a high-ranking employee within the Grandmont Rosedale organization asked the board of directors to buy and renovate a long-standing and rapidly decaying vacant building next to her home. Even with her inside connections, the organization was unable to help. As she explained, "That house needs so much work. Nobody's done anything to it for a number of years. . . . I was trying to get GRDC [the organization] to buy it. The program that they had would buy these kind of homes, and they didn't have to worry about whether or not they made a big profit. They could put the money into the home and bring it back up to where it should be."

She sighed. "They don't have those funds anymore." The community group was renovating nine homes that year, but as an organization operating at a loss and dependent on fund-raising, they could not take responsibility for a tenth home on short notice.

These capacity limitations were common. In personal interviews and press statements, nonprofit directors with organizations like Bridging Communities, Habitat for Humanity, and Restoration America said they received many calls each week from residents hoping to donate homes or from neighbors asking them to buy vacant housing on their blocks. Administrators refused most requests. Some structures or streets were deemed "too deteriorated" to justify the investment. Others stood outside narrowly defined geographic work areas. Another challenge was that organizations focusing on new construction had preciously little money available to spend on renovations.[13]

Civil society organizations helped address vacancy concerns at the neighborhood level, but in the rapidly shifting housing market of Detroit, they were usually unable to help residents address spot-specific, spontaneously arising concerns. Even the most successful organizations were overwhelmed by the scale of the vacancy spike occurring in the late 2000s, and the existing momentum of programmatic commitments left them with little residual capacity. These limits encouraged residents to find other ways to get empty housing reoccupied—for instance, by becoming informal realtors and matchmakers for their blocks.

» PATRICE, THE OPPORTUNITY MATCHMAKER

Patrice grew up in a segregated public housing project outside Buffalo, New York. As a twentysomething African American in the 1970s, she uprooted her life and moved to Detroit. Despite deindustrialization, she found a place where, in her words, "there was so much opportunity for people of color." She got a job as a bus driver and used a now discontinued Housing and Urban Development program to buy a three-bedroom home in what turned out to be a comparatively stable neighborhood. Over the following decades, Patrice used that house as a springboard for her extended family. Her sisters and their children wanted to follow her to Detroit, and she let them stay with her—sometimes for many months—while they looked for jobs and apartments of their own. These relatives spread out across the city as they became financially independent. Patrice was the only homeowner in the mix.

During the Great Recession, Patrice became concerned about the number of homes going empty on her street. She also noticed her nieces and nephews—who were living in even harder-hit areas—were struggling with unresponsive landlords and deteriorating living conditions while sturdy, single-family homes on her block sat empty. She was especially close to one of her nephews, a self-employed barber, and she overheard him venting frustration one day over the lack of opportunities in his life. As he later told me, "It's hard for some people to get ahead because you need somebody to help you out, so to speak. Somebody has to have some money. You can have an idea, but you have to have somebody to back your idea." Patrice immediately thought of the solidly built homes sitting empty on her block. She offered to buy one of those houses for him and let him buy it back from her over time.

Patrice initially planned to work with a professional realtor, but when she learned about the annual Wayne County tax foreclosure auction, she changed tactics. When Detroit landowners default on their property taxes, the county covers the expense for two years. If owners remain in default, the county forecloses in the third year and auctions the property online. In 2012 the auction included 20,000 parcels citywide, making it, according to local media sources, the largest property auction in the world.[14] Of those homes, 178 were in Patrice's neighborhood. Patrice knew which house she wanted to buy, but she also looked around to see what else was available. "I started looking at prices," she said, and at "how cheap these homes were. . . . So we said, 'I'm going to bid on some of these properties.'"

Patrice entered the online auction with some trepidation. "I was never involved in this [kind of thing] before. I was kind of scared." Quickly, however, she felt swept up in the action. "That bidding was something else," she recalled. "I mean, I got the hang of it! You know? And you bid every $100. Every increment, $100, $100. . . . I went crazy. I went berserk. Because I was at home, and it was just me, and [there was] nobody there to stop me. . . . The more I looked around, I thought, 'Wow, this [house] is nice!' So I wound up getting seven houses. Seven! Outrageous! All in this neighborhood."

Patrice paid between \$13,100 and \$22,100 for each of the homes. She then began calling her nieces, nephews, and sisters to find people to live in them. She told them how wonderful her neighborhood was, and she offered them the same rent-to-own deal she had already made with one nephew. "The deal is: You rent. Pay me. And once I get back what I invested, I'll turn the home over to you. And you'll have a home."

For Patrice, helping relatives was clearly important. But she considered doing that by buying real estate only after she became concerned about the rising vacancy levels on her block. She also bought property only within a tight geographic radius around her own home. "I pretty much sold them on here, *this area*," she recalled. Although Detroit had several similarly strong neighborhoods, by recruiting relatives to her block she built a local kinship cluster that she, as a single woman living alone, found useful and comforting as she aged. Patrice also took steps to help her nieces and nephews become "responsible" long-term neighbors. She insisted they attend a nonprofit homeownership seminar, and as a verbal condition of sale, she told them, "You must keep the property up. OK? 'Cause I'm going to be watching you."

This matchmaking example was an especially vivid one among many more mundane accounts of residents connecting new occupants with vacant homes. Most stories, like Patrice's and Rey's, involved vacancies that arose as neighbors died, lost homes through foreclosure, or simply walked away. Among the subgroup of residents who approached matchmaking as an opportunity, most people recruited aging parents and growing children to live nearby. Matchmakers often purchased the properties on their recruit's behalf, usually paying between \$500 and \$4,000. Patrice was unusual in the number of homes she bought and the extent of financial assistance she offered, but her motives and working method mirrored her neighbors' citywide.

Matchmaking residents emphasized the importance of serendipity and mutuality in their decision-making process. Unlike other residents who acquired property for rental income, most matchmakers, like Patrice and Rey, said they never considered intervening in real estate markets until they confronted a particularly troubling vacancy on their block. Similarly, although residents wanted to help friends and family, concerns about neighborhood safety and stability were what prompted them to take action. These comments underscored that even though matchmaking was mutually beneficial, it remained entangled in defensive efforts to control access to housing on residents' own blocks.

» JANET, THE DEFENSIVE MATCHMAKER

Janet, a white woman in her early fifties, had lived within the same one-mile radius all her life. In 2013 she lived in one of three occupied homes on a block that once contained twenty-six houses. She worked odd jobs for a cleaning company, and her husband worked the janitorial night shift at a nearby hospital. Despite the disinvestment around them, the couple took pride in maintaining a clean and tidy home. "Everybody tells us we got the nicest lawn in the neighborhood and nicest house on the block." Despite this caring attention, Janet felt trapped. "I'm afraid," she said. "Especially with my husband working midnights, and I'm home alone. I'm afraid. I don't sleep at night. I sit here in my chair with a baseball bat." The couple avoided debt until a small house fire forced them to overspend on their Home Depot credit card. In Janet's eyes that debt, combined with their low incomes, advanced age, and home's negligible resale value, made it financially impossible for them to move.

Like Patrice, the opportunity matchmaker, Janet recruited a family member to live in the vacant house next door. Unlike Patrice, Janet's matchmaking was nearly entirely a defensive affair. She described watching, one by one, as 85 percent of the homes on her block went empty and disappeared. Drug dealers squatted in them; scrappers dismantled them; and arsonists set them on fire. Then, in 2012, Janet's immediate next-door neighbor moved away, and she became distraught over the building's likely future. "Them scrappers are going to get it," she told me. "Or have a drug dealer move in and set up shop. Have prostitutes running in and out of there. And what's to stop these drug-induced customers from coming in here? And then what? Rape me? Beat me to death? Rob me? I'll stick a match to that house myself before I let that happen. Make it to where it's not livable. I'd rather live next to a burned-out, gutted-out house than go through that."

In the first month the house stood empty, Janet said she "chased away" scrappers several times. Searching for a more lasting solution, she convinced her brother to squat in the house just to have it occupied and, by extension, off-limits. She described her brother as a homeless alcoholic who had been living in his girlfriend's car for several years. When we met, he had been squatting in the house for nine months, relying on his sister's garden hose for water and an extension cord running through her kitchen window for electricity. Even then, Janet said, "they [the scrappers] still keep coming around. People keep asking me, 'Well, what's going on with that house?' I'm like, 'My brother lives there. Leave it alone.'"

To prevent unwanted people from using the property, Janet recruited an occupant she trusted, and she offered him free utilities in exchange for living in the house. This trade worked partly because her brother's long-term struggles meant that squatting, even in a building without basic utilities, improved his living situation, and Janet felt safer having him there. Her brother's alcoholism made him an unreliable protector from neighborhood violence, but the void on the block was filled, which was all it took to keep other people away.

Defensive matchmaking had many similarities with opportunity-oriented recruitment. Both types of matchmakers pulled family members and friends from other neighborhoods to live in the properties that concerned them on their blocks. Residents also incentivized relocation by helping with acquisition costs and utility expenses or, in other cases, with yard work and promises of in-home care and social support.

Despite these similarities, the heightened anxiety surrounding defensive matchmaking created important differences. Defensive matchmakers were more willing to approach people who were, as they said, "living hard" or "down on their luck." They were more likely to describe their recruits as short-term placeholders filling a space until, as they hoped would happen, a more permanent solution appeared. For these reasons defensive matchmakers were more likely to consider squatting as a viable alternative to vacancy. Neighborhood discussions about squatting were politically charged, and most residents complained that unrecruited squatters stole electricity and were involved in criminalized economies. These concerns were important, but if a squatter was "your" squatter, prescreened and handpicked, other people on the block were more likely to accept the arrangement. As part of the exchange, matchmakers became sponsors arranging introductions with neighbors and vouching for their recruit's good character.

Unlike opportunity recruits, who usually became owners and renters with legal claims to property, handpicked squatters had to consistently demonstrate their merits and worthiness to stay. As one matchmaker put it, he expected his squatter to "be a good neighbor and not have the drug dealing coming in and out." Sponsoring matchmakers who felt their recruits violated their subjective moral codes could withdraw their support—for instance, by cutting off utilities or informing officials of the squatter's presence. Conversely, matchmakers said they felt constant pressure to continually reseduce so-called good squatters into staying, sometimes by offering more assistance over time. These relationships produced tangled webs of morality judgments and patronage organizing people in space.

» MARA, THE IDEALIST MATCHMAKER

Mara, an urban gardening social activist, frequently moved to follow her passions. She immigrated to the United States in 1980 to marry an American university student she had known only a few months. Thirty years later and still happily married, they left their comfortable home in a comparatively affluent section of Detroit to realize their passions for social activism and farming. Residents in their new neighborhood recruited them, as Mara explained, to "take over" the mortgage for a woman who had walked away. The couple built a large garden and began encouraging their neighbors to join them in building an off-the-grid sustainable community. Despite her outreach, Mara felt her new neighbors were hesitant converts to her cause. "They just want things to be safe, and they want to have a decent house, and they want their garbage to be picked up," she told me. "Well, they're not going to get that." To jump-start a larger social revolution, alongside her local outreach, Mara connected with people citywide who shared her ideals and who might be convinced to move into her neighborhood to build the gardening community of her dreams.

One white couple Mara recruited had been previously living in a comparatively affluent area with few empty lots. As the couple approached retirement, they became involved in the growing citywide food justice movement, and they discussed relocating to a higher-vacancy area to build a community garden. As the husband explained, "It wasn't too much after that, . . . we got an email from Mara. And it was an email to lots of people that Mara knows. And she was saying, 'We really are doing some creative things in terms of gardening [and] in terms of community building. And we have a house that a non-profit organization has sold us. And so this is an invitation. Anybody that wants to come and join what's happening in this neighborhood, here's an opportunity.'" The message came with links to media interviews and photographs describing Mara and her neighbors' fledgling gardens and farms. It circulated through food justice e-mail Listservs and online blog posts. Several Detroiters responded. As a direct result of this outreach, the retired couple moved into the nonprofit house, and Mara connected a young African American family with a second vacancy on the same block.

A few months later, a local pastor asked Mara to help him find a "deserving" occupant to take responsibility for a dying man's house located a short distance from her home. From her previous connections, Mara arranged an interview between the ailing man and a young researcher studying food justice. After the interview, "I got the nod," the researcher told me, and she said, when the man died, "they gave me the house." She received the deed at no monetary cost, with the verbal promise she would "do something good" with the property. Doing good in that context meant living in the house, respecting the neighbors, and planting a vegetable garden in front of another vacant house next door.

Idealist matchmakers like Mara intervened in real estate markets to advance broad social causes. These residents used social events and service activities to identify potential recruits. They arranged cycling tours of street murals and taco trucks, home tours of period architecture, and walking tours of prized flower patches and vegetable gardens to find kindred spirits. Residents relied heavily on friends, family, and colleagues with personal connections to other parts of Detroit to informally advertise these events to unknown but like-minded people. Idealist matchmakers adhered to the same basic principles of serendipity and mutual benefit other resident realtors followed. And their outreach created geographically clustered groups of people contributing to a shared ideal.

Unlike in opportunity or defensive matchmaking, idealist recruits were usually strangers. Social networks were important, since recruits tended to be friends of friends, but no preexisting personal ties or feelings of reciprocity connected matchmakers with newcomers. These matchmakers framed relocation as a decision about how to live rather than where to live, and matchmakers helped newcomers access specific homes. But recruits understood they were responsible for the full financial costs of relocation and occupancy.

Symbols of neighborhood identity were crucial to these matchmaking goals. Ideals rather than kinship mattered most, so presenting a compelling vision of place was crucial. Matchmakers used symbols and narratives to inspire people to move in despite disinvestment, blight, and negative stereotypes. They used organizations, like block clubs, churches, and community development groups, to help circulate their messages to broad audiences. Since recruits could be difficult to find, idealist matchmakers, like their defensive counterparts, were sometimes willing to make compromises by tolerating squatting if necessary. If recruits could assume formal occupancy, so much the better.

⟫ DERRICK, THE INVERTED MATCHMAKER

Derrick, the African American therapist who short saled his house during the Great Recession, was no stranger to discrimination. As a child, he said, he wanted to be a carpenter. "The goal was: you get in a program, you go to school, you become a carpenter, [and] you get a journeyman's card. Once you get a journeyman's card, then you can automatically command $100 an hour for your work. It's like, you're set for life." Life circumstances pushed Derrick in a different direction. "Racism was so rampant that it was very few African Americans that could get a journeyman card. In the South it was easier for African Americans to do," he explained, because "the whites kind of stuck to the whites, and the blacks to blacks. So if you knew a black carpenter, it was real easy to connect. But there wasn't that many journeyman black carpenters in Detroit. . . . So it's like, do I want to do this? Nah, I think I'll just go to college. Get a degree."

Derrick laughed heartily. He related this experience of racism that inadvertently pushed him into a white-collar career with an unmistakable sense of irony, but Derrick did not take discrimination lightly. Despite his concerns about snap judgments, within the tumultuous environment of Detroit, he said, he often had to make uncomfortably quick decisions about whether to challenge newcomers on his block.

Matchmakers usually took the lead when connecting housing with potential recruits, but shortly after moving into his new fixer-upper, Derrick faced a subtle inversion of the matchmaking process. Instead of encouraging a known person to move into a nearby vacancy, Derrick considered the merits of an unknown squatter to stay. The stranger moved into a bank-owned house across the street, and Derrick became concerned. "I'm like, 'Wow, a squatter moved into the house. I don't want to live with a squatter!'" Most residents were wary of uninvited squatters who moved into vacant property and fortressed themselves inside, but a small subgroup of these stranger squatters used public displays of conservative morality to ask the neighbors for tacit permission to stay. Derrick's squatter fit that pattern.

Derrick was initially suspicious, but he later changed his mind and hoped the newcomer would stay. At a block club meeting early on, Derrick discussed the situation with a neighbor. His immediate concern, Derrick said, was to find the most efficient way to force the newcomer to leave. "And I'm like, 'Man, how do you get rid of squatters?' . . . So [the neighbor] asked me, 'Well, what is he doing?' I says, 'Well, I noticed he cut the grass and he trimmed the bushes.' He said, 'Does he have parties?' I said, 'No.' 'Is he causing a lot of problems?' 'No.' He says, 'Leave him alone!' He says, 'Better to have a squatter in there that's taking care of the house than [for] the house to be vacant, because that's when [scrappers] come in and steal the pipes and the furnace and gut the house.'"

Derrick considered this advice. He still felt uncomfortable living with a squatter across the street, but he saw clear evidence the man intended to take care of the house and be a courteous neighbor. After hearing about scrappers dismantling other vacant homes nearby,

Derrick decided to give the newcomer a chance to prove his worthiness as a potential neighbor.

In the months that followed, Derrick carefully scrutinized the man across the street. His new neighbor rode a bicycle out of the neighborhood every morning and returned in the evening, "like he was going to a job," a positive quality in Derrick's predominantly professional neighborhood. He did not have guests over who might create unwanted noise or foot traffic. He cut the lawn at specific times of day when the neighbors were around to see him doing the work, and he borrowed hammers and other small tools from the neighbors to let them know he was making small repairs inside the house, as well. These public displays of maintenance and responsibility altered the neighbors' attitudes toward him. As Derrick explained, "That kind of taught me my lesson about squatters. All squatters are not bad squatters. Some of them are actually good neighbors. And this one actually turned out to be a very good neighbor."

This example of inverted matchmaking, where residents evaluated people's worthiness to stay rather than their merits to come, illustrated the morality judgments at work in all matchmaking schemes. Most of the residents I spoke with disapproved of squatting, interpreting it as a sign of moral failing or criminal impulses, but their discussions of so-called good squatters illustrated a range of tolerance for informal occupancy. Some residents were more sympathetic to women than to men. Some wanted to confirm squatters were not stealing electricity. Most wanted verbal promises newcomers would not make noise or use drugs. Residents were also more likely to criticize people who lied about having family connections with the house. Silence was preferable to deceit. Physical evidence was also important. Squatters who simply lived in a house remained suspect, and those who caused damage were automatically disqualified, but people who made repairs, washed porches, and raked leaves encouraged tolerance.

All recruits were subject to similar scrutiny, but for unrecruited squatters visual performances of unflagging morality were crucial. The perceived legitimacy of their claims to space relied heavily on stylized performances of deservingness. Not all residents were willing to give unrecruited squatters a chance to confirm or refute their fears, but as vacancy climbed, people like Derrick pushed their neighbors to embrace "good" squatters as a deterrent against explicitly destructive users who might otherwise come.

» RESIDENT REALTORS AND LOGICS OF OCCUPANCY

As long as there has been real estate, there have been boosters painting impossibly seductive images of better lives in faraway places. Magazines advertising the earliest New England suburbs showed Victorian homes nestled in winding streets and wooded brambles with no industry in sight. Picture postcards of sunshine, bungalows, and lemon trees lured white Americans westward to Los Angeles and San Diego. Gritty art galleries and edgy loft conversions sold gentrification in Brooklyn, SoHo, and Alphabet City. These wish images presented vacancy as an opportunity, encouraging consumers to buy commodified property that rarely lived up to their dreams.[15]

Patrice, Janet, Mara, Derrick, and Rey were boosters of another stripe. They wanted to help their families succeed. They wanted to feel safe at home. Some of them even wanted to change the world. And they recruited new people to live next door to realize these goals.

These interventions were deeply personal. Matchmakers recognized not everyone would appreciate the value of the homes next door, and they believed they could manage property more effectively than could the impersonal market actors who were undermining their communities. Matchmaking was an intimate affair involving courtships, dowries, and reciprocity. These intimate interventions created alternatives to vacancy, reorganized people in space, and created new geographies of belonging.

Political economic theories of property markets categorize cities as either growing or shrinking. The market is either up or down. Disinvestment in one location fuels new investment somewhere else. The crumbling physical remnants of Rust Belt cities present ample evidence of the wastefulness of boom-and-bust capitalism and the extreme difficulty of using local cultural activism to combat disinvestment.

All of this is true, but a structural reversal of global market forces is only one measure of the relationship between people and place. Disinvestment is lumpy and multidimensional. Some people move in, whereas others move out, and some blocks decay much faster than others. In Detroit, where formal property markets generated voids and vacancy instead of occupancy, residents used their personal resources to negotiate property transfers and settlement patterns. These socially generative acts created deeply personalized real estate. Markets did not disintegrate into randomness, but market withdrawal created ample opportunities for family connections, social ideals, and morality judgments to exert extraordinary influence on residents' decisions about where to live.

These intimate practices were fragmented but widespread. Matchmakers did not necessarily know each other, and their working methods varied from person to person and block to block. But matchmaking was nonetheless one of the most ubiquitous stewardship self-provisioning practices residents described, and the sheer number of people doing this work created new organizing logics of clustered occupancy and moralized habitation.

3

Protecting Vacant Homes

» **DEFENSIVE ARCHITECTS**

"The next house over is actually abandoned," Rachel said, "that one right there." She pointed through her living room window across a grassy side lot to a small brick bungalow with white shutters, white curtains, and a lush green lawn.

"Wow, it doesn't look empty," I replied.

"Between us and the other neighbors on the other side," she explained, "we try to keep the yard up."

Rachel, a Wayne State University employee, was recruited to the neighborhood in 2010 when family friends took her kids cross-country skiing. Referring to the large park behind her house, she said, "I felt like that was important, for the kids to be able to live near something kind of natural." Rachel was white, her husband was Asian American, and they had three young children.

The house they bought was one of three vacancies in a row. About a year after moving in, they bought and demolished the second burned-out house next door and began taking care of the third vacancy, the one Rachel was showing me through her window. "The back window had got broken in," she said, "and the front door was open. For a while, people were kind of squatting in there . . . [and] there were animals living in it. We cleaned it up a little bit. And then my husband and another neighbor down the street worked to get it all boarded up in the back." They and their neighbor, a retired African American man, installed plywood over the back windows, hung curtains across the front ones, mowed the lawn, weeded the garden, and removed the litter. "So it's pretty secure now," Rachel said. I agreed. From the street it looked occupied.

In demolishing one vacancy and disguising another, Rachel and her neighbor created a defensive architectural landscape between their homes. Residential vacancy spiked citywide during the late 2000s, so that by 2010 one in four housing units stood empty. Those homes were routinely vandalized. Some people were afraid of arson and drug dealing. Others felt demoralized watching scrappers dismantle the neighborhood around them. These activities made it harder for residents to stay in their homes and more difficult to get empty buildings reoccupied.

To prevent these activities, residents like Rachel relied on self-made architectural defenses. Some people used curtains, children's toys, and holiday decorations to make empty homes look occupied. Others planted flowers and trimmed hedges to show empty homes were not abandoned. Residents also boarded windows and barricaded walkways to keep people out. Most residents tried to preserve the buildings, hoping new neighbors would eventually move in. Less often, if a building was severely damaged or the nuisance felt unbearable, residents dismantled housing to permanently eliminate the risks associated with vacancy.

Residents who tried to control other people's access to vacant housing used similar strategies to control empty lots. Detroit had over 114,000 empty residential lots in 2014. The city owned about half the lots, and about 5 percent were blighted.[1] People trespassed on those lots, "spinning brodies" and illegally dumping trash. To reduce nuisance, neighbors adopted lots by cutting the grass, building fences, parking cars, building decks, and treating those side lots as extensions of their private homes.[2] Some neighbors bought the land or invested in large building projects, but many people preferred informal solutions that reduced expenses and minimized their legal liabilities.

It was easier to adopt empty lots than vacant homes. Trespass and dumping occurred on both sites, but vacant structures also attracted squatters, drug dealers, scrappers, and arsonists. Reusing buildings was also more expensive, requiring structural renovations that had to meet municipal health and safety standards. Taxes were higher, and demolition was costly.[3] These characteristics discouraged neighbors and small community organizations from buying vacant housing, and it made informal control more difficult to sustain.

Residents often tried to encourage new neighbors to move in, but if that failed, residents like Rachel used defensive architecture to discourage nuisance and assuage fears. *Defensive* is an apt adjective to describe the actions residents took to prevent damage to buildings or disruptions to street life. These defenses were architectural in that residents modified doors, windows, porches, gates, and yards to discourage access. Neighbors used social defenses, as well, confronting trespassers and calling the police, but they hoped their physical retrofits would reduce the frequency of those encounters.

These practices raise important questions about the difference between seized space and defensible space. Theories of seized space focus on marginalized groups who push against oppression by coopting public spaces for nonnormative uses. Taco trucks on New York City sidewalks and tai chi gatherings in Los Angeles parking garages are prime examples. These vendors and dancers use seized space to earn a living and build community ties.[4] Seizing space is especially important in cities where existing built environments do not accommodate the needs of vulnerable residents and activities associated with low-income or minority residents are criminalized.[5]

Protecting marginalized groups from oppression is important, but the often romanticized moral valence of informality shifts when those sidewalk vendors and tai chi dancers return home to find scrappers vandalizing the buildings next door or drug dealers fighting in the streets. Those residents were also seizing space for informal economic and social activities, and many Detroit residents recognized social hardships and oppression fueled those practices. But the physical dangers and heightened criminalized overtones changed the tenor of the debate and prompted residents to look for ways to defend themselves from those types of spatial seizures.

Theories of defensible space from the 1970s focus on activities that disrupt and endanger the lives of low-income, minority residents living in high-risk environments.[6] Defensible space theories have many problems, however. The emphasis on physical landscaping diverts attention from social and political reforms, and exclusionary designs can create the inhospitable landscapes marginalized residents push against. This baggage means using terms like *defensive architecture* requires caution. Using this language responsibly requires making judgments about whether interventions are oppressive or empowering, a challenge, since life is rarely black-and-white. Social and political solutions that interrupt the renewed production of racialized poverty would be better, but those solutions have not materialized in Detroit, so vulnerable residents try to improve their lives by creating homegrown versions of defensible space.

Community organizations support this work. For example, Michigan Community Resources, a nonprofit organization that builds community capacity citywide, provided $5,000 grants from 2011 until 2013 to support resident-led defensive architecture.[7] Block clubs and neighborhood associations spent the money on buying the plywood residents needed to board homes and reimbursing neighbors for gas used to mow neglected yards. Many small organizations distributed leaflets encouraging residents to disguise and board vacant homes. This support helped, but for actual implementation, residents often worked alone.

Defensive architecture was one of the most widespread self-provisioning practices I encountered. Nearly half of interviewees (45 percent) described performing this work, and that frequency was nearly constant citywide. These residents disguised vacancy when possible, cared for homes that could not be disguised, barricaded access to vacant structures, and occasionally demolished empty buildings. These interventions gave residents a greater sense of control over their living environments. It is unclear whether these practices reduced crime rates, but residents said it helped them control social behavior, slow the spread of blight, and protect their families from harm, at least for a while.

Defensive architecture was a strategy of control. Residents used disguises, caretaking, booby traps, and sabotage to self-provision a public order the underfunded police department could not provide. Defensive architecture helped, but it was only a stopgap measure in a context where genuine solutions to disinvestment were not forthcoming. Defensive architecture required constant maintenance. It had a limited geographic reach, and it did not lead to larger social reforms. The residents doing the work had no legal authority over the spaces they tried to control, and scrappers and drug dealers challenged their claims of authority. These problems encouraged residents to recruit new occupants to fill vacant spaces instead or, if that failed, to consider embracing posturban alternatives.

» SPECTERS OF DEFENSIBLE SPACE

Terms like *defensive architecture* raise the specter of Oscar Newman, a prominent city planner who built his career around the concept of defensible space. Newman's foundational book *Defensible Space* appeared in 1973, and he published a follow-up article with the same title in 1995. Those publications spanning his influential career made a lasting mark on the field of urban design. In the early 1970s, public concerns about urban disinvestment, concentrated poverty, and racial segregation were growing while political support for federal programs addressing those issues was waning. Instead of looking to social policies, Newman searched for physical solutions. His work on social housing, for instance, extolled architectural and landscape designs that, he believed, could create safer living environments for marginalized residents without requiring social reforms to curb the reproduction of racialized poverty. He focused on spaces like large, grassy lawns and long interior corridors that dozens of households shared, spaces that existed between the public realm of the street and the private sphere of the home. For affluent residents these architectural spaces came with doormen and superintendents who acted as de facto guards, but those authority figures were absent in public housing.

Newman asserted that the indeterminacy of those spaces as neither fully public nor fully private meant many people passed through them but no one felt a natural sense of authority over what happened there.[8] His solution was to privatize shared space. For large lawns he recommended using fences and shrubs to subdivide the grass into private yards assigned to individual residents. For internal corridors he recommended adding stairwells and barriers to reduce the number of people passing through. Newman believed these changes would replace zones of ambiguity with spaces that looked like extensions of private homes where residents could exert greater social control.[9]

Newman's focus on physical designs and social exclusion was problematic. His work undertheorized criminality and inequality. He explicitly discouraged city planners and policy makers from using social, economic, and welfare planning to revitalize cities, create jobs, or redistribute income.[10] And by the 1990s private real estate developers were using the language of defensible space to justify the gated communities and privatized public spaces that cast outsiders as suspects and conflated homogeneity with safety.[11]

These criticisms are important, but Newman's underlying assumption that physical conditions influence people's perceptions of who legitimately controls space remains significant. All shared space involves exclusion. Whether those controls are oppressive or empowering depends heavily on the context.[12]

Most Detroiters have probably not heard of Oscar Newman, but many residents nonetheless created their own versions of defensive architecture in the gray spaces around their homes. Like the public housing residents in Newman's original studies, informal defensive architects lived in contexts of extreme disinvestment with real safety risks and few politically viable solutions. Also like Newman, these residents focused on indeterminate spaces that were neither fully public nor effectively private, and they used physical retrofits to push those spaces toward the private realm. These spatial interventions were territorial acts, claiming space as a means of social control.

Despite these similarities, residents' homegrown efforts to protect vacant housing diverged from Newman's theories in important ways. Newman's professional clientele of public housing authorities and neighborhood development groups had financial resources to spend, but residents in Detroit had to make do with whatever limited material they had on hand. Similarly, Newman's followers and Detroit residents both created landscape aesthetics of private control, but in Detroit those aesthetics were usually illusions that did not come with legal authority. Sympathetic neighbors might respect their claims to space, but police officers, absentee owners, and other potential (mis)users often did not. Newman's work also had little to say about booby traps, sabotage, or residents' tendencies to demolish unruly structures, nor did he discuss the ongoing social practices needed to reproduce defensible landscapes. Homegrown defensive architecture shaped moral geographies and offered many benefits, but it was also precarious, requiring constant work to replace aesthetics of abandonment with wish images of occupancy and control.

» PERCEPTIONS OF VACANCY, NUISANCE, AND DANGER

Between 2000 and 2010, almost every Detroit neighborhood lost population, but the unevenness of the process created different risks in different areas.[13] For example, neighborhoods like Grandmont

Rosedale with little vacancy, many homeowners, and comparatively high property values before the Great Recession experienced especially high rates of change. In that decade the number of vacant units increased by nearly 300 percent from 161 units (a 2 percent vacancy rate) to 628 units (a 10 percent vacancy rate). Residents observing that shift worried about steep drops in property values and the rise of unwanted squatting. Residents in Springwells Village voiced different concerns. That neighborhood experienced a lower rate of change, but the absolute number of vacancies was much higher, and residents had lived with those vacancies for longer. Vacancy in Springwells Village rose by 132 percent between 2000 and 2010, from 570 vacant units (a 9 percent vacancy rate) to 1,323 units (a 21 percent vacancy rate). Property values and squatters were still concerning, but anxieties about drug activity and arson dwarfed those debates.

Despite local variations, residents in every neighborhood described vacancy as one of the most significant problems they faced. The actual links between vacancy, property values, and crime were indirect, but emotions ran high, and the potential problems associated with vacancy were well known.[14] Residents in every neighborhood firmly believed vacancy put them in danger and put the long-term stability of their streets at risk.

Drug activity was an especially visceral concern that only the most affluent blocks escaped. Most residents made unprompted references to active or recently closed drug houses on their blocks. Some dealers worked in legally occupied spaces, but most residents said dealers used vacant homes to store drugs, evade police, and expand their trade. Late-night parties, celebratory gunfire, and public urination caused disturbances, but residents worried most about the foot traffic drug houses generated. As one African American man explained, "At one point, one of the houses was like a drive-through. That's how many people would line up to get the drugs." Other people made similar comments. "Every six or eight or ten minutes, all day long, you have a parade of people coming to the house. The worst sort of people. And then the entire block and the people on the street are nervous." The most provocative fear was that people buying drugs would break into other empty homes to get high, which neighbors felt put them at risk. Parents with young children were especially concerned and often refused to let their kids play outside for months at a time when they saw needles, pipes, and "crackheads" on the streets.

Scrapping was an even more ubiquitous concern, and it crossed neighborhood lines. Every resident I spoke with, no matter their address, had direct experience with people dismantling the buildings around them. Occupied homes were vulnerable when residents were away, but vacant structures were nearly defenseless and hotly targeted. A retired Latina woman shared an especially poignant memory of an elderly couple who purchased the house next door and renovated it until the husband suffered a heart attack and died. When his widow returned home two days later, "no cabinets were left on the walls, no fences left on the property, [and] no windows [were] left in their frames." Other residents described similar experiences watching people steal copper pipes, electrical wires, security bars, porch posts, rain gutters, window counterweights, aluminum siding, driveway bricks, air conditioners, roof shingles, furnace equipment, front doors, and bathtubs. Alongside the lost value of the stolen material, scrappers also damaged the buildings, making it harder for resident realtors to recruit new occupants. As an African American woman told her state representative during a public meeting, "You can't get a community back if the house for sale costs $25,000 and it costs $40,000 just to get the heat on."

A third concern was arson, a rare occurrence in comparatively affluent areas but an everyday event in neighborhoods with longstanding vacancy and blight. Local firemen in one neighborhood told me they responded to between thirty and forty house fires each month in their eight-by-ten-square-block area. They estimated 90 percent of the fires originated in vacant buildings, and about half the time, they spread to at least one occupied structure. They believed arsonists set between 90 and 99 percent of the fires, but investigators had the resources to prosecute only about 2 percent of the cases. Residents were especially worried about fire because many people in high-risk neighborhoods lacked homeowners insurance. Some people couldn't afford it. Others were disqualified for installing window bars (a fire hazard that nonetheless prevented break-ins) or because they could not afford to keep their homes code compliant. These residents lacked the financial safety nets they needed to rebuild after a fire. Since vacant structures often burned many times before burning to the ground, the threat to neighbors was long-standing.

Residents in higher-income areas with fewer drug houses and arsons were more vocal in their complaints about squatters and property values. Most residents had direct experience with people squatting on their blocks, but only residents on higher-income streets were concerned enough about squatting—regardless of whether squatters were also involved in other illicit behaviors—to create architectural defenses against it. Similarly, although property values were decreasing citywide, only comparatively affluent residents said property values alone were enough to motivate them to protect the vacant spaces next door. Informal defensive architects all wanted to feel safer at home, and cost was always a factor, but most residents were protecting daily routines and avoiding relocation expenses rather than shoring up formal markets and sunk equity.

Residents concerned about vacant housing often began with "legit" steps, like calling management companies, code enforcement officers, and police departments to report vandalism, nuisance, or suspicious activity. Those phone calls sometimes solved problems, but residents more often felt ignored or rebuffed. These disappointments encouraged residents to find their own ways to control social behavior, including using self-provisioned versions of defensible space.

» GENE, THE ILLUSIONIST

"Go and take a look," Gene instructed. "Can you identify what's so unique about them?" It was January 2013, and Gene wanted to see whether I would notice the glass balls on his Christmas tree had been painted from the inside. Later in the conversation, Gene recounted his childhood fascination with crepe paper. "I would feel like I wanted to create some kind of fantasy," he said. Money was tight, but for ten cents he could buy a roll of crepe paper and spend days decorating the basement for make-believe parties that never happened. Eventually, Gene showed me the house across the street. "Does that look like that's lived in?" he asked. By this time I knew the game. Gene had created an illusion, and he wanted me to confirm its effect.

The 1950s brick home looked warm and inviting. Pots of artificial bright-red poinsettias and an all-season carpet runner framed the front door. An illuminated porch light cast a soft glow over a small plastic wreath. Despite the cold weather, the grass was neatly trimmed and edged, and the shrubs were freshly pruned. A mini-van parked in the driveway faced the street, as though the occupant inside might emerge any moment for some postholiday shopping.

It was an illusion. There was no one inside, and there hadn't been since 2008. Five or six homes on Gene's block lost their occupants around the same time. Investors purchased a few of them, and Gene recruited an acquaintance who was down on his luck to squat in one, but the house immediately across the street remained empty. Gene had watched scrappers dismantling other homes nearby, and he knew from personal experience the understaffed police department could not respond to most complaints about scrapping and vandalism. So for five years Gene had been cutting the grass, hanging holiday decorations, and parking his car in the driveway to make the home look lived in.

Gene's disguise was an exercise in control. This kind of stage dressing reinforced normative expectations that housing was for living in only, not for scrapping, drug dealing, vandalism, or anything else. Gene had no more legal authority over the building than anyone else did, but he created a landscape aesthetic where certain people and practices looked like they belonged and others did not.

Disguising vacancy to look like occupancy was a common citywide practice. Gene had an unusual flair for detail, but his methods were otherwise ordinary. The simplest disguises involved decorating windows and porches. A group of Latino neighbors, for instance, used this approach to secure a bank-foreclosed building on their block. "Banks take everything out of the house, leaving it looking obviously empty," the subsequent owner explained. "The neighbors put window shades back on the house so it wouldn't look so obviously abandoned." These curtains provided a homey touch, and they prevented people passing by from seeing the bare walls and empty rooms inside.

The more props used, the more convincing the disguise became. As Gene explained, "You'll do tricks. Such as put wreaths on the door. Flowerpots. . . . If you've got an extra vehicle, park the extra vehicle up in the yard. Make it look like somebody's there." Some residents put plastic patio furniture on front lawns, using either old sets they no

Figure 3. A vacant home disguised to look occupied. Photograph by author.

longer wanted or salvaged pieces they collected from neighborhood curbs on garbage day. Other people placed rugs on porches and artificial flowers on steps and walkways. Some residents ran extension cords to power exterior porch lights and interior lamps, using the illusion of utility connections to imply occupancy. This stage dressing helped vacant structures blend in with occupied ones, making it less likely someone would single them out for (mis)use.

Especially elaborate disguises mimicked the dynamic liveliness of everyday activities as an antidote to the stillness and stasis of abandonment. Some residents rotated decorations seasonally by displaying holiday wreaths in the winter and plastic Easter Bunnies and pinwheels in the spring. Other people used the same props year-round but moved lawn furniture and children's toys to different spots in the yard every week. Neighbors left kids' toys looking intentionally disheveled, as though the toddlers playing with them had rushed inside but might return and resume their play at any moment. Residents hung drapes with books, toys, and artificial plants poking through the curtains to add a sense of authenticity to the scene. Neighbors also drove their cars up and down driveways and walked up and down stoops "to put some tracks" in the snow, so "it looks like someone is coming and going."

Residents disguising vacancy also erased evidence of absence, which mostly meant doing yard work. Neglected grass and shrubs undermined the illusion. In Gene's words, "Limbs on trees are a real problem. Dealing with the leaves that come down is a real problem. Overgrown brush, you've got to keep the brush clipped up." Maintaining other people's yards was hard work, which was why lawn care seemed so compelling as a sign someone must be living there. Residents also removed the fliers, coupons, handbills, phone books, and catalogs advertisers left on front porches. Those papers signaled new vacancies that delivery people had not yet learned to skip, which meant the most valuable building materials for scrapping were probably still inside. Collecting this detritus on a near-daily basis was a dominant theme in every neighborhood, something so ubiquitous and habitual residents often mentioned it as an afterthought.

In these disguises some spaces and elements mattered more than others. Residents like Rachel and Gene gave special attention to the view from the street by hanging curtains, cutting grass, and removing trash from the fronts of empty homes while leaving the less visible backyards wholly untended. These practices conformed to the glance test. As Gene explained, "If you can get it to look like somebody lives in it, then that's important. So whatever it takes to look at the property and just glance at it and say, 'Oh, somebody cares about that,' that's probably your best way to deter vandalism on it." For residents who had scrappers living on their blocks, no disguise, no matter how elaborately set, would keep the vacancy a secret, but most residents felt the biggest threat came from people living farther away who prowled the streets looking for new targets. That was the social group defensive architects hoped to fool.

Neighbors who disguised more than one home or who kept their illusions going for many years adapted the work to suit their personalities. Gene's interest in holiday decorations, for instance, was evident both inside his house and on the home he disguised. Another resident who enjoyed seeing well-groomed shrubbery through her windows pruned the bushes next door into elaborate, sculptural shapes. One of her neighbors who enjoyed manicured lawns hired a landscaping company to maintain his personal yard, and as a hobby he experimented with different types of fertilizers and lawn feed around the vacant house next door. Combining disguises with hobbies did not reduce the workload, but it made disguises more elaborate and helped people stay motivated.

Civic organizations encouraged residents to disguise vacant homes. Community groups distributed leaflets and newsletters asking people to "take immediate action" whenever they noticed someone moving out "to prevent further deterioration of vacant homes, prevent a breeding ground for criminal activity, and keep property values up." These fliers urged neighbors to remove litter, pull weeds, install solar-powered lights, put potted plants and holiday decorations on porches, and move city-issued trash cans back and forth from the curb every week to make those spaces look occupied.

Disguises helped, but they could not last forever. Residents hung curtains and trimmed hedges, but they did not replace broken windows, repaint exterior trim, or make structural repairs. Sometimes, new occupants moved in, making the ruse unnecessary. More often, property decay or vandalism eventually exposed the disguise for what it was: a self-made illusion of occupancy that ultimately lacked physical truth or legal authority.

» ELLEN, THE FOSTER OWNER

"We've always had a house that we adopted," Ellen explained. Ellen was a white research nurse who moved onto an all-white street in 1984. By 2012 that street was almost entirely African American, and she guessed that a quarter of the homes were empty. With vacancy rising, Ellen and her neighbors started a block club to clean some of the blight along a one-mile stretch of their street, starting with the block immediately to her north. "That was a block that was so depressing that I wouldn't even drive down it," she said. "And that's a strategy people use a lot, I think, to keep from getting too demoralized. People choose their route to avoid some of the worst places that are going to depress them. . . . When we started the block club, I said, 'My personal goal is, I want to be able to drive the length of [the street] without getting depressed [and] without wanting to close my eyes.' And everyone said, 'Yeah, yeah!' That resonated."

"So trash was a problem?" I asked.

Ellen shook her head, no. "What really got me started doing something in the community was when the house on the corner on this side, two doors down, got broken into."

"Was it occupied?"

"No," she said, "it was empty. And I kind of freaked out because [scrapping] had now invaded my space. . . . And I just realized, this is not acceptable. I'm not going to let this happen to our block." Ellen replaced the stolen front door with plywood and asked a neighbor to decorate it. "And within an hour, he had this great [mural]," she recalled. "He painted it so it looked like panels in a door." They also boarded the front window and painted an interior view with curtains, a table, and a vase of flowers. The boards made the house look unmistakably vacant, and Ellen compensated by planting new flowers in the garden and maintaining the lawn.

When the house sold for $8,000 several months later, she adopted a second vacant home and, then, a third. Her goal, she said, was to keep the homes intact until new neighbors moved in, which also helped keep existing neighbors from moving away. "When the first house got broken into . . . I mean, to call it a rape is extreme. I don't want to overstate it. But it felt like a violation." She paused and sighed. "It's a slap in the face that tells people nobody cares. The neighborhood's going to pot. And that alone can prompt people to decide to move. . . . People just see houses—or a whole block—that just get wasted. Then they say, 'Let me get out of here. I can't take it anymore.'"

Some telltale signs of vacancy were hard to disguise, like missing doors, missing electrical meters, boarded windows, and burned roofs. Residents like Ellen tried to mark those properties anyway, using signs and landscaping to create evidence of care. Stewardship could not disguise vacancy, but residents said it was still the most important thing—and oftentimes the only thing—they could do to indicate empty homes were not free for the taking.

Like their illusionist neighbors, resident caretakers used plants to discourage unwanted activity. One woman, for instance, saw the house next door go vacant, then become a drug house, and then go vacant again. After the drug dealers left, even though the broken windows and damaged porch made the building look obviously empty, she began cutting the grass, putting out potted plants, and planting rose bushes she "got cheap at an end-of-season sale [for] two dollars a bush." No one had entered the home since. Another resident down the street, a Latino man with several young children, woke early once a week to mow the front lawns of several vacant homes before leaving for work, a practice he believed kept drug users away and helped his wife feel comfortable letting their children play outside.

Paint was another medium of care. The mural Ellen's neighbor painted had such a transformative visual effect that she and her neighbors decided to paint murals on fourteen other boarded homes, as well. Similarly, in Gene's neighborhood a white woman spent several weekends and evenings painting the plywood on boarded homes so that they would blend in with the rest of the house. "That drives me crazy," she told me. "I hate seeing boarded-up houses. . . . So if it's a brick house, I'll paint [the boards] burgundy. If it's a white house, I'll paint 'em white." Other residents did similar work using leftover paint from home improvement projects. As Gene explained, "When the paint gets all mixed up together in five-gallon buckets, it makes a brownish-mauve color that suits the task fairly well."

Residents also used literal signs with words and pictures to discourage unwanted activity. Signs reading "Keep out," "No Dumping," or "This House Is Being Watched" were common. Neighbors made these signs using whatever material they had on hand. Janet, the defensive matchmaker, made a "No Dumping" sign for a vacant home on her block using a closet door salvaged from the living room and a paint bucket she found in the basement. Another resident in her neighborhood painted the words "If you can reading, we can see you dumping" on a broken sheet of plywood and mounted the sign on a salvaged fifty-five-gallon drum. A third resident used red spray paint to write the word "looking" in three-foot-tall letters across the front of a vacant house with the two o's in "looking" decorated to resemble eyes. Other signs warned of video surveillance. These warnings were not always true, but residents like Elena believed the ruse was an effective deterrent against illegal dumping. "Even though we know there's no cameras there or nothing like that," she explained, "just by putting that sign up saying you're on camera, they'll think twice before they dump it."

Unlike illusionists, who usually worked alone, foster owners often worked in small groups. Block clubs organized weekly or monthly cleanups at which a handful of foster owners who adopted property on their own blocks came together to clean other neglected properties spread across the neighborhood. These groups sometimes received small grants to hire professional lawn care companies or reimburse volunteers for gas money, but those groups were the lucky ones. Most volunteers brought trash bags, rakes, mowers, and fuel from home.

These stewardship practices helped, but they were also easy to ignore. Janet and Elena found new piles of trash dumped only two feet away from their "No Dumping" signs. Other residents said they had to clean vacant properties several times a year because despite their stewardship, people kept "going in and throwing things around again." The flowers foster owners planted needed weeding and watering, and the vegetation they cleared always grew back. The work was hard, but residents firmly believed it preserved buildings. "The only difference," Ellen said, "between those [adopted] houses and some . . . that have been completely stripped . . . the only difference I can see is that those were taken care of. And the other ones, people let the grass grow up and let mail and circulars pile up on the porch. And it's like an invitation: 'Hey, this house is empty, and nobody cares about it.' I have no concrete proof, just anecdotal evidence and my own feelings, that that's probably the single most important factor."

» CONNIE, THE BARRICADING BOOBY-TRAPPER

Connie was a self-described jack-of-all-trades. When her neighbors wanted a new sign for the neighborhood park, she poured them a concrete footing. When renters caused problems on her block, she blackmailed the landlord into evicting them. When the nuns down the street needed food, she gave them tomatoes and peppers from her garden. And when gang members moved their drug house from a few blocks away to the end of her street, Connie decided to solve that problem, too.

On a weekday morning after the drug dealers left, Connie knocked on her neighbors' doors asking for help. "The men on the block were shamed," she said. "Like, 'Hey, other people have already dealt with the original crack house. You guys all have children. What's up? By the way, we'll be picking up a couple cases of beer and starting a barbeque for anybody that wants to do some community service today.'" Connie's neighbors responded. They met at the home, removed the porch steps and the interior closet doors, and used the wood to barricade the doors and windows. "Everything was boarded from the interior," she explained. "I think there's probably three-hundred-and-some three-inch wood screws at every orifice there is."

In boarding the home, Connie and her neighbors joined other defensive architects who built blockades and booby traps around vacant homes. These residents nailed plywood over doors and windows. They built makeshift wheel stops across driveways, and they stacked debris in front of porches, walkways, and yards. These barriers prevented easy access in and out of empty spaces. They also challenged normative expectations about what an aesthetic of care was supposed to look like. In high-vacancy areas, debris, when strategically arranged, was a sign of attentiveness not neglect. What looked messy had a purpose. Those purposes challenged expectations that only tidiness—or the lack of broken windows—could signify care.

Boarding, the most conventional form of fortressing, involved nailing plywood across doors and windows. Residents often boarded single-family homes on their own or in small groups after foreclosures or after neighbors walked away. Most resident boarders, like Connie, Ellen, and Rachel, started doing this work after unnerving incidents of theft and vandalism or after fires left buildings damaged but not fully destroyed. A retired woman in Gene's neighborhood, for instance, helped board a vacant house after the utility-paying squatter moved out. "Next thing you know, air conditioner gone, furnace gone, pipes gone. Overnight. We, the neighbors, secured it," she told me proudly. "And we watched it. We boarded up the front door. We tried to lock up the back, which was very difficult. . . . We figured anybody that wants to come in, they can just work for it. So it kept people out."

In areas with comparatively low vacancy rates, residents preferred to disguise vacancy and described boarding as a last resort. Boards were telltale signs a building was empty, and they could attract unwanted attention. "It's the signal," one resident explained. "'Come and get whatever you want.'" Scrappers used crowbars to pry boards loose, and they used concrete blocks to break down boards. As vacancy levels rose, residents were more willing to switch from soft

Figure 4. Volunteers boarding a vacant home. Photograph courtesy of Neighbors Building Brightmoor.

defenses like disguises and stewardship to hard defenses like boarding. "We used to feel that [disguising vacancy] was the best way to protect the house," the woman continued, "but it's a safety concern today. . . . Now, there are just too many vacant properties." Boards were not inviolable, but they still helped keep buildings "from going to wreck and ruin."

Most residents supported boarding, but it was expensive and risky. Residents estimated boarding small single-family homes cost between sixty and one hundred dollars in plywood, bolts, and nails. This expense was significant in neighborhoods like Connie's where one-third of families lived below the poverty line and residents had to reboard properties several times a year. Boarding was dangerous because residents had to climb extension ladders or fire-damaged stairs to install plywood across upper-story windows. Some people hired contractors to do the work for them, but that added cost. Residents avoided large or complicated projects, like apartment buildings and corner stores, which required specialized equipment, more than one person, a full day of unpaid labor, and up to one thousand dollars in out-of-pocket expenses.

Small grants from foundations and charities helped residents overcome those barriers. One African American mother who wanted her kids to be able to play outside recruited neighbors to help her board eight homes on her street using plywood she bought with a $500 AmeriCorps grant. Another block club in the same neighborhood received a $5,000 SAFE grant from Michigan Community Resources, a Detroit-based nonprofit organization. As Mara, the urban gardening social reformer, explained, they used the money to buy a few communal lawn mowers and enough plywood for resident volunteers to board eighty-eight homes in one summer. Local business owners also contributed. A storeowner in Connie's neighborhood boarded over sixty structures in 2011 and 2012. When his delivery crew had downtime, he paid them to board the apartment buildings, storefronts, and upper-story windows residents had trouble managing on their own.

Charitable resources were crucial but unreliable. Mara, for instance, was incredulous that after having accomplished so much work with so little cash in one summer, she was unable to get the same grant again the following year. "We thought, well, OK. We'll get the SAFE grant again. Never heard anything from it. How can you plan? Or how much time do I have to spend trying to get a lousy $5,000 to board up eighty houses, free of labor?" Her frustration was palpable. The home-boarding businessman in Connie's neighborhood also pulled back after the second year, saying he could still donate his employees' time but the cost of plywood was simply too much. Resident volunteers often asked each other at community meetings whether those resources would come back. "Who knows?" their neighbors would respond. "The money is gone, so its up to us."

Residents like Connie and her neighbors salvaged wood and created guerilla-style barricades to reduce expenses. When moving vans drove away, neighbors rushed outside to nail the front doors shut, padlock the gates, and replace the locks with ones they salvaged from junkyards and demolition sites. Ellen's neighbor knew a welder, and on three occasions when homes on her block lost their owners, he came and welded the security doors shut. "Security doors [are] only as good as the screws you put into them," Ellen explained. Welding gates and nailing doors reduced out-of-pocket expenses by removing the weakest links in the buildings' preexisting security architecture.

Residents constructed makeshift wheel stops. Janet, the defensive matchmaker, was concerned people were using an empty garage behind a nearby vacant house as a chop shop to strip stolen cars, so she collected broken concrete blocks from a pile of illegal dumping and stacked them in the middle of the building's driveway. She then cut branches from the overgrown backyard and stacked them four feet high in front of the garage door. People still stole and scrapped cars in her neighborhood, but the barricades pushed those activities away from her home.

Residents like Connie also created guerrilla-style booby traps around empty buildings. A narrow walkway was all that separated Connie's home from the vacant house next door. After the neighbors moved out, she placed bricks on either side of the gate. They scraped across the ground, making noise whenever someone entered. Next, she laid a wood rail across the walkway to trip intruders in the dark. Then, at a pinch point she placed a metal garbage can filled with salvaged bricks an intruder would have to drag aside to continue down the path. The dragged can made a distinctive sound she could easily hear from her bedroom window. "So you can still get in," she said, "but we're going to know about it." Connie used similar techniques to barricade a second house where scrapping had become especially intense. "We wound up just felling all the weed trees from the alley in the lot," she said, laughing, "just to slow the traffic down. It's like, 'You will have to go out the front of the property in front of all the neighbors with what you steal. You're not cutting in and out of an alley at night. And if you do, you're going to have to trip over all these trees, and good luck!'"

These self-made barricades and booby traps went well beyond the tidy, privatized, defensible space designs professional planners like Oscar Newman envisioned, and they worked best when combined with disguises and stewardship. Rachel, for instance, used all three tactics to protect the empty home she showed me through her window. "If you look at the house [from the street]," she said, "you can see the curtains, but the boards are on the inside [nailed behind the drapes], so it doesn't look like a boarded-up house." Those boards created a physical barrier in case someone tried to break in despite her disguise. Residents boarding homes also removed litter and cut grass, making those structures both fortresses and objects of care. Those defenses helped, but they were not impervious, and residents sometimes decided it was better to eliminate the buildings altogether.

» MEG, THE DECONSTRUCTIONIST

Meg, a recently laid-off restaurant director, had lived in Detroit for twenty-six years. In that time, she purchased six single-family homes at auction. She lived in one, rented one, disguised one, gave one to her daughter and another to her ex-husband, and had the sixth home demolished. That sixth home was the house next door. "Different people had owned [it] and never done anything," she said. "I mean, they never even painted the kitchen for forty years. Anyway, the last people took a loan, bought a house, took the money, and walked away from this house. And this house was a mess. And I thought, I can't live with another person buying that house, maybe throwing a renter in it. So I bought the house in an online auction for $5,500. And then I spent $8,000 tearing that house down. And I had the same people do it who work for the city. It's gone."

Demolishing the house caused a rift on Meg's block. The neighbors on the opposite side were upset over her decision. "They are the only neighbors on the block who won't talk to me, and it's because I tore the house down," she explained. "They thought it should have been rehabbed." Meg disagreed. She had renovated homes before, and she thought the house was unsalvageable. Once the building was gone, she described feeling an overwhelming sense of euphoria. "It seemed like, all of a sudden, all this sunshine was coming in." Her comment referred both to the light entering her windows and to the emotional calm she felt when the house and its troubled past disappeared forever.

Meg was one of many residents who disguised, maintained, and barricaded some buildings but also demolished or sabotaged others to make problem structures disappear. Most people tried preservation first, with the hope a new neighbor might someday arrive. But when scrapping, arson, and drug dealing felt overwhelming, residents sometimes took more drastic steps, legal or otherwise, to make those buildings go away as quickly as possible. People like Meg said the city would eventually demolish those homes anyway, and accelerating the process saved residents from years of anxiety otherwise spent waiting for municipal bulldozers.

City officials and local philanthropists demolished thousands of structures in Detroit every year. Mayor Dave Bing, like many of his predecessors, campaigned on promises to demolish 10,000 housing units during his four-year term. By mid-2012 his bulldozers had razed 6,000 units, and he had eighteen months left to go.[15] That same year, Governor Rick Snyder contributed $10 million from a federal foreclosure-prevention fund to demolish abandoned housing in targeted neighborhoods, including 230 buildings near public schools in MorningSide.[16] Philanthropists like those with the Detroit Blight Authority organized demolition drives, as well—for instance, by demolishing sixty-seven units in Brightmoor in January 2014.[17] Community organizations lobbied these groups for help. In an especially creative campaign, residents in Grandmont Rosedale made a prioritized list of twenty-five homes they wanted demolished, and then they convinced the Southeast Michigan Council of Governments to use water department funds to pay for the demolitions, since it reduced impervious surfaces causing storm-water runoff.

Official demolition drives helped, but the process was slow, the scale was limited, and vacancy continued to rise. Contractors razed 26,000 housing units—nearly 7 percent of Detroit's total housing stock—between 2000 and 2010, but citywide vacancy rates still doubled that decade. Municipal project coordinators told me it took eight months or more to demolish high-priority structures—the open and dangerous ones that came with fanfares and media coverage. The wait time for lower-priority projects was much longer. Residents also complained they had too little control over which buildings came down first. These frustrations encouraged residents to take matters into their own hands.

Some neighbors sabotaged buildings to push them up the city's prioritized demolition list. One woman, for instance, followed the advice of a city planner and stopped taking care of the dilapidated home next door. "The man from the city said, 'Do not maintain it,'" she told me. "'The worse it looks, the more tickets [the owner] will get, and the sooner it will get chopped down.'" She stopped mowing the lawn and began piling her yard debris around the home to increase its blight. Connie used similar methods. She was one of several residents who used sledgehammers to damage the walls and stairs of empty homes, hoping to make them so uninviting squatters and drug dealers would not want to spend time there.

Other residents demolished buildings. Meg, for instance, hired municipal contractors to bulldoze the house next door, and she and her granddaughter dismantled the garage by hand. "We hired one of those big dumpsters," she recalled. "Forty yards. And in two days, we put that entire garage into that dumpster. . . . A dumpster's $400, so there's time elements. But my granddaughter comes from my family. That's how we work. We do it to completion."

Rachel could not afford contractors and dumpsters, so she asked a nonprofit organization to deconstruct the vacant building next door as part of their job training program. "It was a pretty rocky road for us," she said. The trainees were good at demolition, but no one knew which permits they needed or how to get utilities disconnected, so Rachel's husband had to do most of the paperwork. Once the home was finally gone, it took several more months for the organization to remove the foundation walls and backfill the basement.

The headaches and expenses of by-the-book demolition encouraged residents to find informal alternatives. An extreme case that made this trade-off especially clear involved a white activist who had demolished 113 crack houses around his home over the preceding twenty-five years. He said those demolitions followed one of two paths: "the legal way, and the easy way." Demolishing a house the legal way was complicated and costly:

> First, you have to find out who owns the house, which is challenging. Then you have to ask them to sell it to you, which makes owners think the house is worth all this money, because someone wants it, which it isn't. Then you have to get the deed, another hurdle, and then get everything ready for demolition. The water company charges $1,500 to come out and turn off the water. The electric or gas [company], one will turn off for free, but the other one, they charge $750 to disconnect. Then you take all those papers you've accumulated every step of the way, and you

> go down and get a permit to demolish the house. Then you
> have to take it down, which can cost $5,000 or more. Then
> you have to remove the basement walls and haul it away. Then
> someone from the city has to come out and do an open-pit
> inspection, looking in the hole to make sure you've poured
> concrete over the sewer connection in the basement so the dirt
> used to fill the hole doesn't get into the sewer system. Then you
> fill in the hole and do whatever you're going to do on top.

He clearly preferred demolishing housing the easy way. He said he followed the same steps, like disconnecting utilities and capping sewer lines, but he saved time and money by doing the work himself without formal ownership or official permission. In a quarter century of demolishing houses the easy way, he said no one had ever complained about his work.

In rare but extreme cases, residents in high-vacancy areas considered setting homes on fire to keep drug dealers away. A conversation I observed while eating lunch with a group of Latina neighbors was especially illustrative. One woman told her friends she had just purchased the vacant house next door just so she could control it. "If I hadn't got it," she said, "I would have wanted to see it burn rather than see it become a crack house."

Her friend nodded and shared the story of an adjacent home that had become a drug house, "and then mysteriously," she said with a wink, "a few months later, the house burnt down." She added she would rather have set fire to the house herself than live with drug dealers next door.

A third neighbor agreed. She said that sometimes when she called the police department to complain about a drug house, "the hotline operator has said, 'Are you sure you've got the right number? Are you sure you don't want the number for the Fire Department, instead?' Hint, hint."

Arson was a sensitive topic, and I felt comfortable pressing only one resident for details. She was a woman I had come to know well, and she once had a drug house on her block she believed corrupt city officials were protecting. The police raided the home many times, but the drug dealers always returned within a few hours, along with an undercover officer who she thought kept watch for them. One day, when the house was empty, she and two neighbors decided to challenge the officer. "You can leave," they reportedly told him. "Go back and tell your boss that the neighbors are going to take care of this." The residents then placed a military-grade plastic explosive in the center of the house on the ground floor and set it on fire. That way, she reasoned, the fire department could extinguish the fire before the flames spread to their homes but not before the vacant structure would be "fully destroyed and cave in on itself."

When discussing her involvement, the woman praised her skills as superior to those of neighbors who had set similar fires but worked more recklessly. She had taken a police-run arson investigation training course several years earlier, and she had used those skills at least once to preserve evidence a local businessman had set his storefront on fire for the insurance money. She was clearly sensitive to the physical and ethical hazards of arson, but when the alternative was living next to a drug house, she was willing to trade fire for the peace she believed would follow the flames.

These defensive fires were probably extremely rare, and they were qualitatively different from those set by the professional arsonists firefighters tracked who worked a neighborhood for kicks. For residents self-organized demolition was a natural extension of official efforts to remove "excess" and "dangerous" property from residential areas. Municipal bulldozers were preferable, and scrapping and arson were troubling, but precarious living conditions inflected the moral tenor of local debates. If a home was going to go, residents said it was better to have it go quickly and on the residents' terms so that maybe it would not take the rest of the block down with it.

» SELF-PROVISIONED TERRITORIES OF SOCIAL CONTROL

Bruno was Latino. He owned a small property management company, and he arrived at a community meeting with a bruise on his face. A neighbor near one of his rental properties called him the previous week to say the house was being stripped. Bruno rushed over and found his doors, window bars, and copper wires stacked in the back of a pickup truck. With the neighbor's help he tackled the scrapper and held him for forty-five minutes until the police arrived. "I'm the owner," Bruno said, "and I'm complaining." He chose his words carefully because police officers responded to scrapping only if there was an owner complaint. As the police sergeant for the neighborhood told me later, "Without the owner, there's no crime."

Bruno's voice became emotional and exasperated as he continued the story. He said the police refused to arrest the scrapper, because the building being vandalizing was vacant. "But I'm the owner," Bruno had insisted. The police disagreed. They told him he owned the company that owned the house, and the property was empty anyway, so his ownership claims were suspect. They also said they wanted to save jail space for "real" crimes. The officers let the scrapper go with a verbal warning, and Bruno stood on the grass, surrounded by the broken pieces of his house, as he watched the man drive away.

A few months after hearing Bruno's story about the feebleness of official ownership rights, another resident shared a hopeful story about the power of informal property claims. Meg the deconstructionist had adopted the vacant house across the street. She cleaned the trash, cut the grass, and paid her son to prune the hedges. I initially thought Meg would measure her success by how few incidents of vandalism occurred on the property, but she reminded me that it's impossible to know how often someone looked at the tidy yard and decided to dump or scrap somewhere else. Instead, her proudest moment came when a neighbor's son approached her and asked her permission to board the garage. "Why on earth are you asking me?" she wondered. "I don't own this house." Without her knowing, Meg's neighbors had watched her work, and they decided the property was hers in everything but name. "You've done so much work," the son reportedly replied. He would never dream of trespassing on "her" property without asking first. He offered her the gift of his help in return for her volunteer caretaking. With her approval he boarded the home and painted the boards.

Territoriality is a term describing nested claims to space and tools of communication that visualize social authority. It embodies the notion of a right to govern.[18] In U.S. cities private ownership laws and municipal zoning codes usually govern space, but disinvestment and depopulation loosen the hold of these formal systems. Laws still matter. But legal ownership does not automatically translate into authority, as Bruno's experience showed.

For Bruno, Meg, and other defensive architects, validation of spatial authority came informally from neighbors not officially from lawmakers. These residents used illusions, stewardship, barricades, and sabotage to create spatial landscapes of social control. Their interventions reinforced normative expectations that a house was for living in not for scrapping or drug dealing. They hoped the people who saw their self-made landscapes would react as though their illusions and assertions were true and, in doing so, make their social vision a reality.

These tactics worked, but they were weak weapons. Illusions were difficult to sustain, and neighbors had no legal recourse against people who violated informal territorial claims. Living in precarious circumstances also involved making trade-offs between various types of risk, which encouraged some residents to use ethically questionable but contextually rational methods to solve problems. If these efforts failed and empty homes could not be reoccupied, disguised, or controlled, then residents considered accepting abandonment and pushing toward an alternative, posturban future.

4

Repurposing Abandonment

In 1975 Camille followed her mother from rural Alabama to Detroit, and they became one of the first African American families to buy a house in a traditionally all-white neighborhood. Within a decade the neighborhood transitioned from mostly white to mostly black. Vacancies and rentals increased, and drug dealers took advantage. "We had the drugs," Camille recalled. "The meth. We had crack. We had heroin. We had that all over. . . . When the drugs came, that was it. People just started running, because people were getting killed. . . . If the house wasn't rented, [drug dealers] would literally bust in and take over your home. And the landlords that were in here were too afraid to put 'em out. So they literally had taken over the community."

By 2013 Camille's neighborhood was still notorious for crime and blight, but Camille said things were improving.[1] The few blocks around her home felt serene and hopeful. "People are actually taking an interest and wanting to move back in," she said. "People are building gardens like crazy. We're really living off the land over here tremendously. You'll find goats. You'll find chickens. You'll find rabbits. You'll find . . . ," she paused, laughing. "What else up in here? . . . Ducks! Oh, wow!" Many of the gardens Camille described were started by the "import," a term she and others used to describe white people who moved to the neighborhood and started urban farms and other "demonstration projects" in "postapocalyptic" living.[2]

Camille felt inspired by these changes and began planning a garden of her own. She wanted to turn two lots down the street into an edible playscape garden for the neighborhood kids. The city owned one lot; the other belonged to an absentee owner; and both were severely overgrown. She applied for a grant to cover her expenses, but funders denied her request, so she and a friend decided to "hustle." They organized two fish fries to raise the cash Camille needed for plants, and a local block club connected her with a group of faith-based volunteers from the suburbs who would do the initial digging and planting. Under Camille's guidance, the volunteers planted strawberries, gooseberries, raspberries, blackberries, plum trees, pear trees, and apple trees. They planted a tea patch in the shape of a turtle and a cluster of chai that looked like a volcano. They built a hay jumper, sandbox, splashing pool, and picnic area. "And the kids love to eat the broccoli [and] the eggplants."

In building the edible playscape, Camille became one of many residents repurposing abandonment and blight. Their motives varied. Some people wanted to increase household earnings. Others wanted to build alternative communities. Some, like Camille, wanted to improve living conditions and create spaces of hope. These residents turned vacant homes into community theaters, storage sheds, and art pieces. They turned overgrown lots into informal parks. They used salvaged wood, trees, and trash for raised beds, compost piles, and children's art classes.

These informal gardeners, artists, and recyclers used Detroit's urban prairie to build an alternative future. "Urban prairie" is an apt phrase that describes the plants and wildlife that grow up around the decaying rubble of abandoned steel, wood, and concrete infrastructure.[3] Not all vacant spaces disintegrate to urban prairie levels, but in 2012 Detroit's potential urban prairie included 36 percent of the city's commercial parcels, 22 percent of its industrial land area, and five square miles of empty residential lots.[4] These spaces no longer generated jobs, land rents, commercial activity, or tax revenue. Instead, their posturban decay cost the municipality money in maintenance costs, code enforcement, fire suppression, and depressed property values.

By the early 2010s, instead of trying to hold the urban prairie at bay, Detroit's mayor announced plans to accelerate its growth, at least in certain sections of the city. The municipality had been bulldozing properties for decades with the expectation reurbanization would follow, but decline routinely exceeded reinvestment. City planners eventually gave up the dream of a citywide revival and began discussing plans to "rightsize" the city. Rightsizing rhetoric began with the premise that a city like Detroit with 700,000 residents could not support an inherited infrastructure designed to serve the nearly two million people who lived there at its peak. Geographically consolidating residents and funneling resources into those designated subareas could theoretically help some neighborhoods achieve the growing populations, rising land values, and new business ventures they needed to be counted as an economic success.[5] These planning approaches offered many potential benefits, but they also privileged progrowth agendas, and they indicated some neighborhoods, like Camille's, would most likely return to seed.[6]

As the municipality stepped back from some neighborhoods, investors and nonprofits stepped forward with ideas about how to turn the incipient urban prairie to posturban ends. Some artists hoped the city would preserve decay and create a "national ruins park" or an "American Acropolis."[7] Agricultural companies like Hantz Farms imagined planting 15,000 hardwood trees on 1,500 residential lots where they could grow, undisturbed, for half a century until harvest.[8] Nonprofit organizations like EcoWorks (formerly the WARM Training Center) envisioned new blue-collar industries of workers dismantling housing by hand to salvage recycling for resale.[9] None of these interventions would stop the city's deurbanization. Planned art, forest, and salvage would only modify—not counteract—the posturban ecosystem that emerged and the methods used to get it there.

Residents had their own ideas about what do with the urban prairie. They drew inspiration from artists, farmers, and recyclers, but the process involved significant adaptation. Repurposing gained the most traction in areas where local activists used external resources to complete a few high-profile demonstration projects. Those experiments adapted countercultural working methods to fit domestic scales and household needs. The resulting projects were often small in scale and easy to overlook, but the intimacy of the interventions is what made them meaningful. At their best these practices transformed waste into opportunities and inspired neighbors to revalorize the vacant land around them.

Posturban experimentation is easy to romanticize, but repurposing blight was challenging work. Some imports brought money and skills with them from the suburbs. Some longtime residents "lucked up" and "hustled" for start-up funds and volunteers to get their projects started. Those resources helped, but the work was still hard. As Camille recalled, "I'm telling you, that garden was a project! It took many, many hours of volunteers to get it where it is now. Many hours of volunteers. When you['re] talking about building a garden, that's labor!"

Camille laughed good-naturedly, remembering the struggle. Two years after the initial planting, she was bursting with pride as we watched a few youngsters jumping along the path she had laid and snacking on the strawberries she had planted. The garden was her regenerative oasis. "It was an empty lot, and it looked horrible," she recalled. "And to see it now to be such beauty, it's wonderful! It's a nice place to sit and wind down and relax in the evening. And before, you couldn't even walk through it."

Camille's edible playscape was an important self-provisioning success story, but resident-led posturban transformations, while powerful, were rare. Only a quarter of the residents I spoke with (27 percent) said they participated in these activities. Residents were twice as likely to recruit new neighbors for vacant homes and twice as likely to create defensive architecture around empty spaces. Repurposing blight also had the most uneven geographic spread. In some neighborhoods, like Camille's, it seemed like everyone was doing it, but in other areas it was almost unheard of. This imbalance partially reflected different neighborhood levels of blight, but other provisioning practices were not so heavily stratified. Class-based aesthetics limited local support for informal posturban futures in some areas. Variable participation rates also revealed the importance of charismatic activists who popularized repurposing by adapting it to domestic contexts.

Residents repurposing the urban prairie imagined posturban possibilities. They wanted new homes, residents, and businesses to come to Detroit, and some would, but many more were lost forever. Parks, art, and salvage did not reverse shrinkage, but it did change the lived experience of shrinkage and its locally felt ripple effects. Markets and governments had walked away, but Camille stayed and reinvested her sweat and courage in the spaces other people left behind. Urban or not, her neighborhood would have a future, and she wanted it to be an imaginative, hopeful one.

To build that future, residents borrowed strategies from citywide cultural movements. This borrowing showed self-provisioning was not insular and it did not emerge solely from the ground up. Instead, residents like Camille reached up into the superstructure of collective activism and adapted the tactics they found there to fit their domestic agendas. These practices diffused countercultural innovations, and grassroots self-provisioners used them to informally reshape their neighborhoods.

» RACE, CLASS, AND THE COUNTERCULTURE

One spring evening, I joined Camille and about fifty of her neighbors in a soup kitchen for their monthly community meeting. About half of the residents were white. They wore flannel shirts and paisley prints and looked like the tanned granola farmers I would expect to find in places like Northern California. The rest of the group was African American and looked decidedly less country in their dress. I noted these stylistic differences and then quickly forgot about them as I watched the residents intermingle with ease, chatting and laughing cheerfully in each other's company.

About halfway through the meeting, a humorous exchange brought questions of black/white and urban/rural back into the spotlight. A middle-aged white man had volunteered to build a community "pole barn," and he invited the group to a "barn raising" he would host the following Sunday. "We'll do this Amish-style," he said. "My fire pit is almost finished, so I'll get some food cooking and make it a community event." A young, lanky black man sitting nearby raised his hand and asked, "What is a pole barn? Someone needs to explain that, because," as he said in overly affected Ebonics, *"we some urban folk!"*[10] The group laughed heartily at his joke and at the jarring juxtaposition of an Amish-style barn raising in the industrialized inner city. Their laughter suggested the residents recognized their differences but felt comfortable they were all on the same side.

Some of the whites present that evening had lived in the area for decades, but most were newcomers who moved to the neighborhood to join a small but growing group of urban farmers. These residents followed their countercultural inclinations to disinvested spaces where real estate markets were weak and property values were low.

From an academic perspective, this market disinvestment freed land from exchange-value constraints. As land without formal monetary worth, people disenchanted with modern, capitalist life could use these forgotten spaces to create alternative societies based on the principles of social justice and human creativity.[11]

From a practical perspective, this economic assessment overlooked the social trauma neighborhood disinvestment caused, and the arrival of so many whites with pioneering mentalities sometimes smacked of colonialism. Camille and her neighbors wanted new people to move in, but white newcomers came with very different life experiences, and it was not obvious the mostly white imports would automatically find solidarity with the mostly black neighbors already living there. The joke about the pole barn, which got its punch from its intentionally racialized delivery, highlighted the racial tensions that existed in the neighborhood outside that particularly convivial subgroup. White activists wanted to be there because they saw opportunities for alternative futures, but many African American residents said they simply had too few opportunities to escape to the "normal" neighborhoods where they wished they lived. Some longtime residents also resented the expectation they had to farm the city, join big volunteer groups, and live next to whites for their living conditions to improve.

These tensions infused self-provisioning with racial identity politics. White newcomers and black old-timers tried to use countercultural working methods to repurpose blight, but they approached this process differently. A pattern emerged where mostly white funders and activists advanced posturban visions and mostly black residents and youth rejected, supported, or adapted those messages.[12] These groups were not monolithic. Motives varied as widely within racial groups as across them, and residents with different racial backgrounds collaborated often. In Camille's neighborhood, where repurposing efforts were growing rapidly, a mixed-race group of residents found ample common ground.

Class differences were sometimes more difficult to resolve than racial ones. Painting, planting, and recycling were three key strategies residents used to repurpose the urban prairie. Comparatively affluent areas often boasted of an organized community garden and an official public mural or two, but middle-income residents whose property values and professional identities were deeply embedded in formal market systems often wanted to stabilize those formal institutions not replace them with informal posturban alternatives. These concerns meant that while residents built many cross-racial bridges within neighborhoods, the domesticated countercultural strategies emerging in lower-income areas rarely traveled well across spatialized class dividing lines.

Despite these race- and class-based tensions, Camille's pole barn–building neighbors forged ahead. Neighbors turned broken-down homes into self-made art. They transformed overgrown lots into pocket parks, and they used trash and debris as ingredients for community capacity building. Professional installation art, organized community gardens, and market-based salvage provided inspiration, but residents adapted the work to fit their needs and circumstances. Many residents still hoped their neighborhoods would come back someday, but Camille knew that city officials no longer planned to rebuild her block. The urban prairie had come; it would not be pushed back; and residents had to decide what to do with it.

» BECCA, THE RESIDENT ART DIRECTOR

Becca moved to an alternative community in Scotland after high school to escape what she described as the dull tedium of Detroit suburbia, and she did not plan to return. Then in the early 2010s, after seeing films and newspaper clips describing "all the cool stuff going on" in Detroit, she moved back—this time living inside the city limits—and wrote a senior thesis on site-based performance art. She and Mara, an urban gardening social reformer, became fast friends. Becca was thirty years younger than Mara, but they bonded over a shared philosophical commitment to the importance of beauty and color, which they felt was missing in Detroit's urban prairie. "These children grow up so quickly," Becca told me with a sense of urgency in her voice. "There's no time for these children to not be exposed to things that are beautiful and things that stimulate, visually. If you grow up looking at trash, and looking at things that are burned out and gray and black and ugly, that affects your mental state. . . . As a human being, I know that that is a deprivation for the mind, and for the heart, and soul, and all that good stuff."

Becca and Mara took action. They wrote a successful AmeriCorps grant for Becca to start an informal afterschool art program. Every Tuesday afternoon for the following year, Becca rode her bicycle around the neighborhood, inviting the kids to follow her to a nearby park where she set up easels, paper, and paint. When it was too rainy to paint outside, they met in vacant housing and painted on the walls just to have something creative to do and somewhere free to do it.

While Becca was painting in the park, Mara received a second charitable donation to pay local teenagers to board vacant buildings. The friends quickly combined their work. An African American teenager with several younger siblings inspired their first joint project. He wanted to board the dilapidated building next to his home, and his siblings were some of the most eager participants in Becca's afterschool art program. "His siblings were always asking me to do stuff," Becca recalled. "Always wanting to borrow chalk, and do this, and do that, and [asking,] 'When can we paint again?'" Becca, Mara, and the young teen came up with a plan to transform the boarded house into a canvas for the kids. "We designed it so they could draw on the house." The older brother and his friends built wood frames in geometric shapes. They mounted the frames on plywood, filled them with chalkboard paint, and nailed them to the side of the house. This secured the doors and windows while creating a reusable canvas close enough to home the youngsters could draw anytime they wanted without special supervision.

In the months that followed, the growing group of young boarders and painters experimented with different techniques. For damaged homes on the city's demolition list, elementary school kids painted plywood on easels, and the older teens used those paintings to board doors and windows. They later began wrapping entire buildings in wood, which reduced the amount of cutting involved and created murals the size of buildings. For homes in better condition that might be reoccupied someday, the teens carefully trimmed plywood to fit inside door frames and window trim, and they decorated the boards with custom murals. The process was iterative. "We have painted over a lot of stuff that was done before," Becca said, "because people were just not happy with it." As their artistic skills improved and as neighbors told them which paintings they liked, the kids revised their work.

Figure 5. Residents painting murals on a boarded home. Photograph courtesy of Neighbors Building Brightmoor.

Adding color and beauty to the decaying urban prairie was challenging. For people without artistic training, painting and drawing could feel frustrating rather than cathartic. Becca said the neighborhood teenagers felt "incredibly insecure" when she asked them to draw from their imaginations for the first time. Unlike boarding and weeding, the kids associated art with talent and inner selves. Painting made them feel anxious, "like, 'I'm not going to be good enough.'" The teens resisted, using debasing humor to deflect attention from their insecurities, until Becca took them on a field trip to see graffiti and street art in other parts of Detroit. That art looked accessible and homegrown. The kids first copied it, then embellished it, and eventually left it behind as their own ideas emerged.

By the year's end, Becca estimated around 150 African American kids from the neighborhood had helped paint murals on over eighty vacant homes across twenty-two blocks. Many images had pastoral themes, like starry skies, sunflower meadows, sunrises, fields, wildflowers, trees, leaves, waterfalls, vegetables, and turtles. Some murals were more geometric, and a few included biblical passages or other inspiring prose. Becca said the next-door neighbors usually worked with the kids, asking them to paint specific objects or psalms that reflected their tastes and values.

Some longtime residents watching the kids felt inspired to create similar art of their own. One woman painted a large sunset on her garage door that mirrored the mural of a rising sun the kids had painted across the street. Another resident borrowed Becca's brushes and paint, and she drew a row of flowers, a sun, and a bright-blue sky on a vacant home. A third neighbor, who enjoyed poetry, painted a boarded structure white with a simple blue border, and she used the house as a parchment where she wrote and revised lines of verse.

For residents without artistic inclinations, Becca created a system to help outside volunteer groups paint locally inspired murals on their behalf. "I had a lot of material from the kids, from their sketchbooks," she explained, and she assembled those images in a binder. Mara recruited large groups of volunteers from suburban churches, universities, and auto companies to clean trash and board homes. At the end of long, sweaty workdays, Becca would open a few gallons of paint and ask them to join her in "a little bit of fun . . . as kind of a dessert for the volunteers." The outside volunteers transferred the local kids' drawings onto the boarded buildings. This process reinforced the younger kids' confidence in their artistic potential. "We'd look at a house and say, 'Oh, that's S—'s drawing, which is now this massive mural!' So that's [a] really cool experience for them to see someone else take their idea and make it real and put it on a house." These practices also discouraged volunteer groups from tagging the neighborhood with outside symbols like religious crosses or university logos, and it replaced those tags with homegrown images and self-selected icons.

These locally created mural houses resonated, in some ways, with the work of professional installation artists. The art scene in Detroit received a lot of media attention during the Great Recession. In 2009 a newspaper reporter announced, "With many Detroit houses selling for less than a month's rent in the suburbs, artists seeking studio space and a blank urban canvas are buying property and starting art enclaves. . . . If Detroit has anything, it's cheap real estate."[13] Artists moving to Detroit had lower living costs than did their colleagues in Chicago or New York. Many artists used the wood and trash of the urban prairie as raw material in their work, and their creations voiced political opposition to capitalist systems of waste and disinvestment.

The Heidelberg Project was one of the most famous examples of professional artists turning blight into art in Detroit. I met the project's interim curator informally while working in another neighborhood, and she gave me a personal tour of the site. Toys, shoes, pieces of cars, and other found detritus collected from the surrounding blocks covered several large homes and vacant lots. The landscape, she said, was an expression of mourning for all the city had lost.[14]

Other installation artists did similar work. In 2006, for example, student artists from the suburbs painted dozens of crumbling buildings bright orange to attract public attention to the scale of abandonment in Detroit. Similarly, in 2010 artists from New York City sprayed a vacant Detroit house with water and encased it in ice as a symbolic protest against the national foreclosure crisis. These artists used the urban prairie to denounce global markets that destroyed homes, lives, and dreams.[15]

Becca and her neighbors knew about these professional projects, but they approached their art with very different goals. Professional artists worked with large audiences in mind, but Becca's kids and the residents who joined them painted murals and poems only a handful of people living on their blocks would ever see. Unlike professional artists, who focused attention on blight, Becca and her young partners used art to inscribe hope—not mourning—onto domestic landscapes. The residents' work also emphasized youth empowerment not political commentary.

Residents in other neighborhoods painted hopeful images, as well, but most of them worked at a smaller scale than that of Becca's art crew. Most residents began a mural project only if an activist directly encouraged them and a foundation provided some financial support. Unless residents wrote grant applications and asked neighbors to help them spend that money, homegrown art projects were rare. Another challenge in other neighborhoods was adults did most of the painting, not kids. These adults tried to paint alongside their work and family obligations, but even people who loved the experience and believed it helped their blocks still had trouble finding the time.

Organizations and charismatic leaders were crucial in overcoming these hurdles. Without the national AmeriCorps grant, Becca said she would not have spent a year bringing art to neighborhood kids. Mara's grant helped expand the work, and both women relied on a local community group to administer the funds. With organizational help these charismatic volunteers reached out to neighbors, many of whom lacked the time, motivation, or self-confidence to apply for grants and design art projects alone. Resident activists also helped their neighbors reconsider the value of street art. Reframing art as a vehicle for homegrown beauty instead of professional political critique expanded the range of people who participated and the goals they hoped to accomplish.

Painting was not a perfect solution. Residents wanted new neighbors to move in, and they wanted crumbling structures to disappear. But those changes came slowly. In the meantime, residents like Camille said the murals were "just so beautiful to see. Because it's brightened up the neighborhood tremendously. . . . It's really beautified the neighborhood, and [it's] giving hope to a community that a lot of people thought was gone."

» JACK AND DANI, THE COMMUNITY LANDSCAPERS

Jack and Dani were white activists who used urban gardening to combat racial injustice. Before retiring, Dani helped build a small community garden behind her church in one of Detroit's most upscale neighborhoods. After retiring, the couple moved to a new neighborhood onto a street that was mostly vacant. "We just wanted to live more simply," Jack explained. "We wanted to downsize." Living simply for them meant living in a smaller house, volunteering at a neighborhood soup kitchen, building a community garden, and informally mentoring underprivileged youth.

Jack and Dani's first big intervention into the urban prairie involved building a community garden on the vacant lots next door. "It was three overgrown lots," Jack explained. "Not much trash but a lot of downed trees and limbs and things like that." It took several months of intense manual labor to clear the land and build the garden. "It was all hand digging," Jack recalled. "We started digging three- or four-foot beds. They're about fifty feet long. And so we just dig away. And when we got a number of them dug, then we would begin planting." They uncovered broken bricks and fragments of cement as they worked, the remnants of three houses that once stood on the site. They also added several truckloads of new topsoil to improve the poor-quality fill dirt municipal contractors had used to backfill the basements after demolition. They did not officially purchase the land.

As they dug, planted, watered, and weeded, Jack and Dani stopped their work to chat with neighbors passing by. They wanted the garden to be a community space, and they invited their neighbors to participate. A few adults helped occasionally, but as with the mural projects, the kids on the block were the most enthusiastic. Within a few months a core group of African American kids aged five through eleven began spending afternoons and weekends digging, pruning, and snacking in the garden. For Jack and Dani the process was intentionally educational. "When the kids first came to work on the garden, they were scared by every worm they saw," Jack said. "Or every bug they saw, they wanted to kill, whether it was a good bug or not. And they weren't too sure what it was that we were growing." Dani's volunteer ethos and personal charisma transformed the afternoons of manual labor into fun afterschool activities. At harvest time the kids who worked in the garden got their pick of vegetables to take home. Dani helped the kids learn to cook the food, something she started doing after one of the youngsters asked for help reproducing a traditional breaded eggplant recipe his grandfather brought from the South.

Jack and Dani's community garden was part of a growing citywide urban agriculture movement. Detroit was a national leader in urban farming. The Catherine Ferguson Academy began using gardens to teach English, math, nutrition, and life skills to students in the mid-1980s. The Capuchin Soup Kitchen built its famous Earthworks Farm in the late 1990s to feed poor, hungry people while healing "a wounded Earth." Since the mid-2000s, the Detroit Black Community Food Security Network has used foundation grants to farm neighborhoods lots, like the locally renowned D-Town Farm, to address food insecurity in African American communities. Other nonprofit organizations, like the Garden Resource Program and the Greening of Detroit, made gardening classes, vegetable seeds, and logistical help widely available to residents, schools, and community groups. Farming was technically illegal in Detroit, but city officials overlooked these gardens as much as possible, and they worked with activists to pass new ordinances to allow and encourage farming at the household and community scales.[16]

Race was important in this agricultural movement. Gardeners, like artists, included a mix of whites and African Americans who built gardens and farms on vacant land to earn cash and reduce expenses. In other U.S. cities, white interest in urban gardening was rooted in nature preservation and back-to-the-land movements. For African Americans in Detroit, community gardening was often a symbol of protest and empowerment, as well. Popular academic studies and documentary films from Detroit—such as Monica White's "Sisters of the Soil," Leila Conners's *Urban Roots*, and Mark Dworkin and Jessica Moore's *We Are Not Ghosts*—popularized the persona of the local black activist using urban agriculture to resist white oppression, build solidarity, and enhance self-determination. These farmers earned little money for their labor, but weeding and watering brought fresh vegetables to food deserts, job training to unemployed youth, and personal dignity to marginalized residents.[17]

Empowerment is always a relation of power, and Jack and Dani walked a delicate line as white activists advancing food justice in a predominantly African American neighborhood.[18] They used their personal savings and unpaid labor to start a garden they hoped their neighbors would embrace. This was not the model of black nationalism, but it worked. The adults on their block told me they enjoyed watching the garden grow, and the local kids quickly made the space their own.

Jack and Dani's vegetable garden was wonderful but unusual. Other residents tried to start similar gardens, but many people lacked the knowledge, health, money, time, charisma, or even just the good luck Jack and Dani possessed. Another resident down the street tried to build a community garden, but she lived on a corner, and the closest vacant lot was across the street, where she lacked easy access to water. She planted anyway, but she could not afford new topsoil, and she was unable to convince any neighbors to join her. Then, in the autumn municipal contractors absentmindedly bulldozed the garden while demolishing the vacant house next to it. Demoralized and frustrated, she did not rebuild.

When discussing community gardening with residents, I heard more stories of failure than of success. Neighbors who initiated joint projects eventually argued, moved, and died. Disabilities intensified, crops failed, and motivation waned. These factors made food-based community gardens difficult to sustain. Many residents had backyard gardens where they grew herbs, tomatoes, peas, and okra, but these homesteading projects did not repurpose blight.

Instead of giving up, residents adjusted their expectations and began thinking about plants and landscapes in other ways. Once Jack and Dani's garden was well established, they looked for a new project that would give the neighborhood kids something extra to do when the normal working day was done. Dani had received a small grant from a local foundation promoting childhood development. She and the kids used the money to landscape the front section of an overgrown lot across the street. They cleared the weeds, built small benches, and planted perennials and shrubs that bees liked to pollinate. They arranged their honeybee garden along the sidewalk, and they mowed a patch of grass to separate their wildflowers from the urban prairie beyond.

The honeybee landscape adapted community gardening ideals to a domestic scale. The project still involved unpaid resident labor and outside charitable donations, but it was smaller than the vegetable garden, and it required much less maintenance. The perennials and benches did not become a community hub for job training and neighborhood solidarity like Earthworks Farm and D-Town Farm, but it replaced blight with a visual sign of hope and care.

Compared with vegetable gardens, non-food-based parks like the honeybee landscape were easier for residents to integrate into their everyday domestic routines, and many of Jack and Dani's neighbors built similar projects. For example, local high school students helped a woman living a few blocks north clear several overgrown lots next to her house, and an artist helped build a spiraling plank bench around a central cottonwood tree. The resident nailed a wooden sign by the sidewalk to give her homemade park a name. She also chained a hand-painted plastic garbage can to the tree and emptied it every other week. These furnishings mimicked the amenities of public parks and invited public use. Her neighbors enjoyed the space, but they also recognized her informal authority over it and asked her permission before using it. Jack and Dani, for example, asked to host a movie night in the park. They propped a makeshift screen against the cottonwood tree, made popcorn for the kids, and showed them a movie about bees.

Another neighbor two blocks away built a bird and butterfly trail on a government-owned lot. She selected plants birds and butterflies liked to eat, and she asked an outside group of volunteers to clear the lot and built a meandering wood chip path around her plants. Like the spiral bench park and the honeybee landscape, she used a wooden sign to name her park, and she did all the mowing, pruning, and decorating herself. Also like her neighbors, this woman did not own the lot or have legal authority over the space, but her landscaping created an informal public space with implied limits of use. The butterfly path connected to the sidewalk, inviting pedestrians to enter, but the narrow, undulating path contained no benches and it ended midlot. This arrangement encouraged brief, passive, visual enjoyment, and it discouraged rowdy games and "spinning brodies."

These wildflower paths and informal parks were humble and low maintenance, but that simplicity gave them their strength. Informal parks did not require long-term group commitments. Outside organizations helped create them, but residents could mow the grass and clean the trash by themselves in an hour or two each month. Residents changed the plants, expanded the beds, and decorated the gardens with pinwheels and statues as they pleased. Compared with the Catherine Ferguson Academy gardens or Earthworks Farm, the lack of explicit programming reduced the political importance of informal parks as spaces of explicit community activism, but the ability of residents to maintain these landscapes on their own made it easier for those spaces to survive despite unreliable external funding and neighborhood infighting. These informal parks domesticated the urban gardening movement and created tranquil environments residents could enjoy and maintain within the constraints of their everyday lives.

» BETH, THE RESIDENT RECYCLER

Beth, a lifelong Detroiter, was in her midforties. She had been a theater technician, golf caddy, delivery driver, community organizer, and house sitter. When she was between gigs or wanted extra cash, Beth worked as a "legal scrapper," scavenging suburban trash piles for appliances she could disassemble for the metal inside. Beth condemned "house strippers" who destroyed her neighborhood. Unlike them, she said, she always followed the rules, and she refused to collect metal from inside Detroit.

Beth was also an avid gardener. When she was a child, her fam-

Figure 6. Resident-maintained informal neighborhood park. Photograph by author.

ily "bought a postage-stamp house on a big-ass plot" to avoid being dependent on other people for food. As an adult renting a house on a much smaller lot, she covered every inch of her yard with pots of peppers, tomatoes, jalapeños, and greens. She was white, but she prided herself on her southern growing style. "I happened to be lucky enough to get trained by an old Georgian African American man on how to grow collards and things like that," she explained. Beth ate some of the food, sold some to local restaurants, and traded the rest with neighbors for gifts of cash, meat, and personal favors.

When Beth and I met in 2012, she was combining her skills to build a market garden "through salvage recycling, really guerrilla style." She made her own soil using grass and leaves collected from the neighborhood. "I cut several neighbors' lawns," she said, "which gives me lots of grass for compost." She also "politely gathered leaves" from several nearby empty lots and added them to the mix. She composted this material on the empty lot behind her house and enriched the compost with suburban scrap. "When all those rich people in the suburbs throw out their potted plants at the end of every summer," she explained, "I collect that, and I put that in my soil mix to get a nice, rich soil." She collected shelves, shovels, pots, and watering cans the same way. "Eventually I realized I was capitalizing a business, just without the cash outlay. I have several thousand dollars' worth of gardening material. Just through recycling and repurposing."

Beth's involvement in suburban salvage was unusual, but her reuse of local debris was not. Residents in several neighborhoods cut trees from vacant lots to sell for cash or to use as fuel to heat their homes. Mara used tree trunks from overgrown lots to build a personal storage shed. Jack, Dani, and a few of their neighbors collected sap from abandoned maple trees and used salvaged wood to cook the sap into syrup on their wood-burning stoves. People salvaged trash, as well. Janet, the defensive matchmaker, spent several months trying to catch a landscape company that illegally dumped debris on her block. When that failed, she loaded the dirt into a wheelbarrow and used it to build a small private garden on a vacant lot. Rachel, the defensive architect, had also seen lawn companies dumping leaves and grass in the park behind her house. She gathered the debris and added it to her personal compost pile. "I think they've been doing that for a long time," she said, "so that's a nice source of getting some good loamy dirt that has a lot of organic material in it." Janet and Rachel, like Beth, built their compost piles on vacant lots, which kept the smell away from their homes.

Beth also scavenged for water. The house next door was vacant, and she diverted the downspouts so the rain falling on its roof would run into her homemade rain barrel system. Beth's low-income neighbors often reused domestic water in similar ways, using rinse water from their sinks and washing machines to flush toilets and water backyard vegetable gardens. Beth was part of a smaller group of people who used rain barrels and other homemade devices to collect water from the urban prairie, and she was protective of that water source. After a scrapper stole one of the metal gutters off the front of the house, Beth replaced it with a plastic one. As she told me, laughing, "Who ever thought I'd be fixing an abandoned house to get water?"

While Beth was collecting water from the roof, her neighbor used the same house as a potting shed. The home was boarded, but he installed an industrial lock on the back door to keep it secure while giving him private access. He used the kitchen, stripped as it was of appliances and cabinetry, to store fertilizer, containers, rakes, and other gardening supplies. Residents in other neighborhoods stored tools and paint in vacant homes, as well, and Beth supported those activities. But she also knew vandals or bulldozers could appear at any moment. She needed her equipment for food and cash, so she preferred to keep her supplies at home.

Beth used the urban prairie to build a garden, but she used an approach different from Jack and Dani's. Beth salvaged objects from abandoned spaces, but she did not make long-term territorial claims to those spaces. Beth's work was also explicitly homegrown, rooted in childhood experiences and peer-to-peer economies instead of civic grants and activist newcomers. She looked to citywide resources for support—for instance, by submitting soil samples to a nonprofit organization for chemical testing and by selling vegetables through a citywide growers' collective. The urban agriculture movement also gave her a vocabulary to distinguish salvage and stewardship from scrapping and trespass. Like other community gardeners, Beth wanted to tame the prairie and save the world. But she did that work on the side by volunteering at neighborhood cleanup events and community task forces not by seizing abandoned land.

Beth's distinction between polite salvage and unconscionable house stripping raised important moral questions about the methods used to dismantle and reuse residential infrastructure. Bulldozers were the city's official solution to blight. The municipality hired private contractors to raze homes and haul the debris to landfills. But the city's prolific industry of underground scrapping demonstrated condemned structures had resale value. Beth and other "professional" scrappers told me bricks in good condition went for a dollar each, copper sold for around four dollars a pound, and appliances usually sold for between fifteen and forty dollars each. Other material like wood studs and hardwood floors had little scrapyard value, but small contractors could easily reuse those materials in custom renovation projects.

Nonprofit organizations like the EcoWorks sustainability group pressured municipal officials to use this untapped revenue stream to reduce waste and create local jobs. The EcoWorks training center ran a foundation-supported program employing young men and former prison inmates to disassemble homes by hand and sell the material to recycling centers and salvage shops.[19] This deconstruction model was not yet revenue neutral, but the training center was making progress. At residents' requests the city allowed EcoWorks to use foundation money to deconstruct ten homes in Beth's neighborhood as part of a pilot study in 2014.

One of the homes was on Beth's block. She had been lobbying her local community development corporation for two years to get the house removed and to do it in a way that promoted salvage. If bulldozers were coming, she asked for a heads-up so she and her neighbors could soft strip the hardwood floors and wood beams a day or two before demolition. If the EcoWorks crew was coming, she wanted them to save the foundation so that she could build a make-shift greenhouse on top. Beth refused to strip the home prematurely as a matter of principle, but she hoped to make as much use of it as possible before it went to the landfill.

Residents living near Becca, Jack, and Dani made similar distinctions between positive salvage and negative scrapping. Camille's pole barn–building neighbor, for instance, used the analogy of eating left-over food to distinguish "stealing" from "having the good sense to use what you can before you can't use it anymore. A lot of the insulation in our house comes from abandoned houses," he added, "and I want the opportunity to use material as salvage for building the community." Voicing proscrapping sentiments in a public setting was risky, and one of his neighbors responded with a swift, unequivocal rebuttal. "The scrappers are, in my opinion, the biggest source of destruction in our neighborhood," she said. "I've seen perfectly livable houses that, in two hours, are turned into a dysfunctional wreck." The pole barn builder agreed but said vacant homes put the community at risk, and their material could instead help the community rebuild. His critic eventually agreed. "Once a house is destroyed," she conceded, "we might as well go in and use what's left."

Most people described underground house strippers as a problem, but these conversations also illustrated that instead of shunning all forms of recycling, residents wanted to develop community standards about how material could be harvested and what people could do with it. The debate was not about insiders and outsiders, since local residents were sometimes the most prolific scrappers working the neighborhood. The timing, purpose, and method of extraction mattered more than the scrapper's address. For Beth if the building could not be reoccupied, if local residents did the work, if they left the building clean and secure until its eventual demolition, and if they reused the material for neighborhood improvement, then she was willing to support salvage-based community development. But even though she wanted to make productive reuse of the urban prairie, until her neighbors agreed on a community standard, she salvaged only grass, water, and leaves and left pieces of buildings for another time.

» DOMESTICATING THE COUNTERCULTURE AND THE POSTURBAN PRAIRIE

On a warm summer day, Neecy, an older African American woman, sat on her front steps watching her five young grandchildren play on an empty lot next to a vacant house. The house was wrapped in plywood from the basement to the rafters, and it was covered in colorful polka dots and hand-painted butterflies. A mutual friend introduced us, and I asked about the house. Neecy pointed a finger at the murals and said with emphatic pride, "Hey girl! My grand-baby put them painting up!" Her grandchildren rushed over, took my hand, and showed me their butterflies, the ones they had drawn and volunteers from General Motors had hung on the house facing their bedroom windows. The mural house was beautiful, Neecy said, and the kids were proud of their work.

Not everyone agreed. A few days after the home was boarded, a neighbor from the nearby cross-street knocked angrily on Neecy's door, demanding an explanation. She said he criticized the childish images, told her the paintings were ugly, and said the house was an eyesore. Without her knowing it, he had been working for months to get the house torn down. He looked the other way when scrappers vandalized it, and he called the city repeatedly to complain. Slowly, he was pushing the house up the prioritized municipal demolition list. Those efforts were now wasted, he said, because volunteers secured the house and made it into an art piece. He was furious, and he told Neecy he wanted to sue whoever was responsible.

Neecy was proud of her grandchildren's art, but it was a conflicted pride. Like many residents, she wanted to live in a "normal" neighborhood where avant-garde acts like making blight into art were unnecessary. Her neighbors, she said, did not see themselves as farmers, artists, or activists. They were glad for other people's volunteerism, but she was not ready to rebuild her life around the pipe dream of social reform. Neecy was also sympathetic with her angry neighbor who had been trying to combat blight in his own way. The dispute was about methods not goals. For Neecy practicality was paramount. If no one would move into the home and if the city would not demolish it, it was better to repurpose it as much as possible and move on with the business of life.

Landscapes like these were hybrid spaces of overlapping ambitions and nested scales of action. The grassy lot where Neecy's grandchildren played reflected the labor of Neecy's neighbor who mowed the lot on her behalf in exchange for free water she used to nourish a small vegetable garden planted in the back. The mural house was also a plural space, organized by local block club activists who encouraged the neighborhood kids to self-paint the boards and who recruited suburban corporate volunteers to install them. The resulting coproduced landscape was a disputed environment. Residents worried about blight and wanted to eliminate it, but Neecy and her angry neighbor worked at cross-purposes toward this shared goal. This overlapping mix of people and tactics unfolded with no official owners in sight to mediate the conflicts.

These juxtapositions underscored the generative interconnectedness of self-provisioning in Detroit. Self-provisioning was not an insular process emerging only from the ground up. Instead, it was part of a broad public negotiation over the future of the city. Residents, community organizations, and charitable foundations all played a role, and these groups borrowed ideas from each other and adapted them to suit new purposes. Tensions emerged; community gardens failed; artistic visions clashed; and anxieties about salvage abounded. Those tensions became generative moments, pushing residents to develop informal, constantly evolving standards for repurposing blight. These juxtapositions inspired new forms of self-provisioning. They connected those domestic practices to larger movements for social reform. And they reworked the moral geographies of the city.

5

Domesticating Public Works

PROVISIONAL SERVICE PROVIDERS

An elderly white woman hunching over a snow shovel came into view as I rounded the corner. It was warm, nearly eighty degrees, and she was panting. She wore a leg brace that helped her walk despite partial paralysis on one side. I heard her before I saw her. The shovel made a scraping sound as it slid rhythmically across the pavement. I recognized the woman. Her name was Jean, and she was seventy years old. We had met briefly at a community meeting earlier that year, and I was glad to run into her again on the street. We chatted a few minutes. Then I pointed to the snow shovel and the warm summer sun. I asked curiously, "What's this?"

Jean lived across the street from a large public elementary school that had closed eight years earlier. The school district hired maintenance contractors to mow the grass, but they came only a few times each year. When the workmen finished, they left two-foot-long grass clippings piled high in the gutters. Those clippings clogged the street drains, causing the neighborhood basements to flood when it rained. Jean lived at the other end of the block. Her asthma and mobility impairments made outdoor manual labor difficult. But she disliked the flooding. So three or four times a year, she followed along after the contractors and shoveled heavy mounds of dry, matted grass off the road.

A red pickup truck parked alongside us as we spoke. Jean's brother climbed out, grabbed a gardening spade from the back, and began shoveling alongside his sister. They talked quietly as they worked, exchanging news and gossip, and I learned they often met this way to keep their spirits up while doing the manual labor of the city. I was almost late for another appointment by then, so I left them in each other's company, the sound of chatter and shovels fading in the distance.

In clearing debris from the road and sewers around a public school, Jean had essentially become an unpaid, invisible, municipal public worker. Detroit's Department of Public Works was nearly 140 years old. Its employees collected trash, plowed snow, and maintained the streets. Their colleagues with the much newer General Services Department, founded in 2006, maintained the city's public parks, street islands, and vacant lots. For private property, code enforcement officers with the Buildings and Safety Engineering Department surveyed property, issued citations, and referred violations to these other municipal entities for maintenance at the owners' expense.

These departments had more work than their budgets allowed. Decades of disinvestment and depopulation had drained the city of financial resources. While tax revenue fell, the public workload increased. Tax foreclosures transferred thousands of private properties onto the public books. Scrapping, arson, and illegal dumping increased expenses, as well. The Great Recession of the late 2000s and the city's long slide into bankruptcy compounded the problems. Officials responded by cutting some services and privatizing others, which for many low-income residents looked like the same thing.

Service cutbacks and privatizations left a lot of work undone, and residents compensated with a range of strategies that helped fill a few of the most basic shortfalls around their homes. Some neighbors organized volunteer groups to cut grass, clean trash, and repair broken play equipment. A few residents hired private contractors to do the work, but cost was a limiting factor. Alongside these civic- and market-based responses, nearly half of the residents I interviewed (47 percent) domesticated public works by using personal labor and household resources to complete basic maintenance tasks. Like Jean with her snow shovel, these residents incorporated grass, snow, trash, and other infrastructure work into their seasonal domestic routines.

These residents worked provisionally in two senses of the word. By using household tools and sweat equity to maintain neglected public and private spaces, they self-provisioned alternatives to municipal contraction. But the working methods residents used were deeply provisional, as well. Cutting other people's grass, shoveling their snow, and cleaning their litter was difficult and tedious, and residents used psychological tricks and temporal working rhythms to make the labor feel more manageable. Some people worked incrementally, expanding the maintenance they already performed at home to cover neglected spaces nearby. Other residents pooled resources to accomplish larger tasks but kept those collaborations informal. These incremental mentalities and informal collaborations were provisional fixes not permanent solutions. For many residents, deciding to join in and do a little extra work once, even if they made that choice many times, was easier than deciding to become a permanent, unpaid, unacknowledged volunteer. These provisional strategies diffused emotional strain. They were also especially important in low-income neighborhoods because they allowed people in precarious circumstances to opt in and out at will.

Informal public works was about more than just local maintenance. Public displays of self-provisioning and volunteerism were also important tools residents used to increase their access to scarce resources. As city governments and their nonprofit partners replaced universal services with discretionary spending models, those entities encouraged resource allocation based on judgments about who deserved those resources and where they would do the most good. In this context residents who could show city officials and foundation leaders physical evidence of self-provisioned accomplishments presented themselves as deserving subjects who ought to receive discretionary aid. In exchange for cleaning other people's litter, adopting other people's vacant lots, and repurposing other people's blight, residents expected city officials to waive fines, provide occasional special assistance, and ignore the not-quite-legal tactics of many self-provisioners' work.

Provisional public workers could make small improvements to the living conditions on their streets, but they had limited resources and worked without the benefit of economies of scale. Residents could cut grass, but they could not repair collapsing sewer systems. They could clean trash but not resurface roads. They could provide alternative street lighting, but they could not improve erratic cell phone service or provide affordable municipal water. Resident self-provisioners recognized those limits, and they used their volunteerism on smaller projects to pressure the municipality to continue providing larger public works they could not complete on their own.

This evolving division of labor reflected the loss of universal services and the rising importance of market consumerism and discretionary patronage in allocating collective goods. My research focused on streetscape services like grass, snow, trash, and lighting, but self-provisioning was evident in other areas, as well. When public schools performed poorly, parents looked to homeschooling alternatives. When public libraries closed, residents set up mobile book shares. When ambulances were unreliable, neighbors organized dial-a-ride phone trees to get people to hospitals. These practices illustrated informal public workers were only one subset within a broad spectrum of residents searching for provisional alternatives to government and market systems that did not meet basic collective needs.

» THE RISE AND FALL OF MUNICIPAL PUBLIC WORKS

A strong municipal government with the capacity to manage public works was a historical anomaly in the United States, an anomaly that coincided with Detroit's rapid growth into one of the largest U.S. cities by 1920. As cities like Detroit expanded, investors began to recognize epidemics and fires on one block spread easily to other areas, which affected the health and economic productivity of the entire city. Those investors began supporting public works, like municipal water and sanitation departments, that protected their investments from those disruptions.[1]

Detroit was an early mover in these campaigns. The city council bought its first water company in 1835, and eight decades later, the water department had become the third-largest public water supplier in the nation. City officials also established a formal public works department in 1874 to collect trash and build roads. The state legislature established a similar municipal public lighting authority in the mid-1890s that replaced private gas and electric companies with a unified municipal street lighting system.[2] These investments and legal reforms incorporated formerly private services into the public domain, which reduced infrastructure costs for investors and reduced self-provisioning on those fronts.[3]

As manufacturing cities grew, their municipal boundaries expanded outward to encompass the developing landscape. Detroit annexed neighborhoods like Brightmoor, Grandmont Rosedale, MorningSide, and Springwells Village in the 1910s and 1920s. In the emerging era of universal services, annexation entitled landowners to municipal public works like road construction, water delivery, sewage treatment, and streetlights. The rhetoric of universal access that emerged during that period disguised a deeply inequitable landscape. Racial segregation increased significantly during the early twentieth century, leading to ghettoized African American neighborhoods like Detroit's Black Bottom and Paradise Valley where minority communities were routinely underserved.[4] But on the urban periphery, annexation encouraged development, and municipal services pushed outward.

The utopian promise of universal public works proved a double-edged sword. Annexation came with services, but it also came with new laws, taxes, and collective identities. Real estate developers and affluent residents who did not want to subsidize services for lower-income residents challenged municipal annexation rights in court. By the mid-twentieth century, investments in land and infrastructure continued radiating outward into the suburbs, but the municipal boundary line no longer expanded with it. The landlocked central city saw a decreasing share of metropolitan-wide investment, and urban residents had no legal claim to the rents and profits generated on their edges.[5]

The political boundary line dividing cities from suburbs gained renewed importance during the civil rights era. White voters leaving Detroit for the suburbs refused to pay for region-wide public transportation systems that would help minorities access higher-paying jobs outside the city limits. These voters used their physical distance from predominantly black neighborhoods to thwart truly integrated public education, and they used intimidation and mob violence to prevent middle- and upper-income African Americans from buying homes in the suburbs. These practices reinforced white middle-class privilege. Suburban residents had no legal obligation to support region-wide collective services, and they used the municipal boundary line to justify their isolationist stance. That boundary quickly became a color line reproducing long-standing neighborhood racial inequalities at the municipal scale. It also perpetuated the myth local public corruption and so-called cultures of poverty caused Detroit's troubles, as though structural patterns of disinvestment and segregation were irrelevant.[6]

The onset of the Great Recession worsened the city's economic vulnerability. State officials used fiscal shortfalls to justify canceling revenue-sharing agreements, which meant a loss of $732 million for Detroit between 2003 and 2013.[7] Depopulation and the housing market collapse also eroded municipal revenue. Although estimates vary widely, market analysts say median citywide housing values climbed to a peak of somewhere between $83,400 and $97,800 around 2005 and 2007, and they then fell to somewhere between $11,500 and $16,400 by around 2009 through 2011.[8] Lower sales prices meant lower property taxes, and rising unemployment and poverty rates made it harder for people to pay tax bills on time. In 2013 investigative journalists reported 47 percent of the city's taxable parcels were delinquent on their 2011 bills, which added up to $246.5 million in uncollected revenue.[9]

This shrinking fiscal capacity occurred alongside a growing public sector workload. Abandonment increased code enforcement and fire suppression expenses, and ballooning tax foreclosures transferred tens of thousands of private parcels into public hands.[10] These ownership transfers decreased the city's taxable land base and imposed new maintenance burdens on the already struggling municipality.

These trends undermined the city's financial ability to continue providing public works. Archives of community newsletters indicate in 1998 over 98 percent of the city's streetlights worked, but that number fell to 40 percent by 2012.[11] The General Services Department could afford to mow public parks and city-owned lots only twice that year. The Department of Public Works continued plowing snow from streets, but sidewalks in front of public parks and city-owned lots remained unshoveled. Government officials relied heavily on charitable donations, without which the municipality would have had twenty-three fewer ambulances, one hundred fewer police cars, and fifty-one fewer public parks operating in 2013.[12] Officials acknowledged these service shortfalls, but solutions were elusive. The conservative white suburban voting bloc made regional resource sharing politically unviable, and the state imposition of an unelected emergency manager in 2013 severely constrained residents' voices in democratic decision making.

The escalating crisis marked a clear turning point away from the goal of universal services. Universal public works was always a utopian ambition, but the abandonment of the ideal had profound repercussions. As the city slid toward bankruptcy, the mayor and emergency manager privatized services. These changes continued a national austerity trend that began in the 1970s with the privatization of city-owned hospitals, museums, and colleges.[13] Those trends resurfaced in Detroit in the late 2000s when officials privatized portions of the city's lighting, water, transportation, and waste management authorities.[14] Advocates promised improved services at lower prices, but for many residents private street lighting simply meant fewer lights, and private utilities meant higher costs and aggressive termination policies.[15]

Several civic groups and volunteer activists tried to counteract the dramatic decline in public services available during the recession and its aftermath. Merchants in Springwells Village, for instance, used Business Improvement District funds from foundation grants and business taxes to pay for extra streetlights, graffiti removal, and private security officers.[16] Residents in Grandmont Rosedale lobbied state and local officials to enact a Neighborhood Benefit District law that would allow residential property owners to levy special assessment taxes to fund similar work. Volunteer groups helped, as well. In the early 2010s, the informal Mower Gang of about twenty socially conscious suburbanites cut the grass on eight or nine city parks in northwest Detroit, and the Detroit-based Motor City Blight Busters organization used foundation grants and sweat equity to cut grass, demolish homes, and renovate abandoned buildings in the same neighborhoods.[17]

These efforts helped in small pockets of Detroit, but residents still faced significant service deficits citywide. Their mounting concerns prompted residents to find workaround solutions for their blocks by using provisional methods to perform public works and by using public displays of self-provisioning to increase their access to scarce resources.

» DALE'S INCREMENTAL LAWN CARE

"We have ... one ... two ... three ... four ...," Dale paused, counting aloud, "four abandoned houses and three empty houses. I distinguish between the two by saying the ones that I said were abandoned have been broken into and stripped. And ones that are empty are people [who] have just recently moved out or, like my neighbor, passed away."

Dale was a middle-aged African American renter. He worked for an auto company, and he had lived on the same street for over twenty years. That street, he said, never had empty homes until around 2008.

"With seven houses empty," I asked, "how has that changed the block?"

"Well, see, last summer," Dale replied, "me and my girlfriend were taking it on ourselves to go to the other empty lots to cut the grass and stuff. Pick up the trash and stuff."

"How did it start?"

"Just for wanting to keep the block up," Dale replied, shaking his head nonchalantly. "That was it. There was no big plan or meeting about it. We just said, that house is empty, the house looks horrible, let's just start doing it. . . . The neighbor . . . that died, . . . we were already taking care of his grass and stuff, too. So it was like, well, what's one more grass to cut."

The city's zoning ordinance required people to keep their grass cut below eight inches in height. The municipality was legally responsible for mowing the 66,000 publicly owned residential lots and for ensuring private owners complied with the ordinance. But the municipal agency could afford to mow public areas only twice in 2012 and once in 2013, which guaranteed city-owned property would be overgrown most of the year. Code enforcement officers could not write citations for government-owned property, which meant residents had little legal recourse against fields of grass standing five or six feet tall on public land. For private property officials could issue citations or cut the grass and send the owners a bill, but the process was impractical because elusive owners rarely paid fines.

Grass was a constant, ubiquitous element in Detroit's urban prairie. After neighbors walked away and bulldozers leveled their homes, the grass kept growing. Tall grass symbolized market and government failure. It attracted rats and possums, introduced allergens, concealed rotting trash, and created hiding places that made neighbors nervous. Elena, for instance, worried about the five city-owned lots behind her house. "The city doesn't come and cut the grass," she told me. "There's been times that the grass is [chest] high. And that's not good. What if there's somebody hiding in there, and I don't see them, and I'm coming with my daughter? I have my CCW [concealed carry weapons permit], but I don't want to shoot nobody."

To allay practical and psychic fears, residents like Elena and Dale began cutting grass themselves. Dale and his girlfriend approached the work incrementally. At the beginning of the summer, they mowed their own lawn, as usual. When their neighbor became ill, they cut his grass as a favor, and they kept cutting it after he died. Then one day, when the mower was out and the sun was shining, Dale decided to go a little farther. He mowed around a third house and, then, a fourth. By the end of the summer, without planning it, he and his girlfriend had incrementally expanded their mowing routine to include the front sections of every vacant property on their side of the street.

This incremental approach made it easier for Dale to domesticate public works. Dale was active in the community. He made a point of getting to know his neighbors, and he attended community meetings. But like many residents, he disliked the idea of becoming a regular, unpaid volunteer doing the city's dirty work. Instead of joining community cleanups or neighborhood associations, he simply expanded the domestic chores he was already doing at home to temporarily solve small problems on his block. This approach minimized his emotional commitment and psychologically downplayed his volunteerism by framing the work as a small, self-directed, nonpolitical act. For Dale, instead of attempting a grassroots revolution, his incremental approach gave him the strength to begin making personally meaningful improvements on his street with no long-term commitments and minimal disruptions to his seasonal maintenance routine.

Other residents did similar incremental work. Earl, an older African American man, had recently started mowing around a nearby vacant storefront. "I didn't mind cutting it by myself," he said. "I felt like I want to make that corner look as well as possible. It don't have to be the neatest cut, but at least you keep the grass maintained and pick up the trash." Like Dale, Earl framed the work as simple extensions of the maintenance he already did at home. "All you have to do is run your lawn mower," Earl explained. "I had the lawn mower and gas, so it just took a little time. Whatever time was convenient." This add-on approach subdivided the vast urban prairie into small, manageable chunks connected to people's homes, which made it physically and psychologically easier to provisionally incorporate public works into domestic routines.

Figure 7. Resident volunteer collecting trash and leaves from a neighborhood street. Photograph courtesy of the Grandmont Rosedale Development Corporation.

Snow was another troubling element in the urban prairie the municipality left unresolved. The city and county plowed the streets when it snowed six inches or more, and most residents said that was workable, but the sidewalks remained problematic. As with grass, absentee owners and municipal officials were supposed to shovel the sidewalks on their property, but neighbors said that rarely happened. Many residents cleared some of this snow themselves using the same incremental approach they used for grass. Dale, for instance, shoveled in front of his own home and continued for two houses to the left and three houses to the right to cover the nearest vacant homes on his street. Another of Dale's neighbors did similar work. "I blow the neighborhood snow with the snowblower," he said. "I just take two strips down. I go from here to the corner and then [come back] on the other side." He explained that blowing snow made it easier for him to walk to the corner without slipping on packed, lumpy ice. Then he added, "It gives me something to do," a statement that verbally minimized his civic contribution by reframing the work as a casual extension of his daily round.

Fewer people cleared snow from streets and alleys, but Elena's husband was an exception. Since the family owned a plow, Elena explained, "he'll plow the alley. The whole thing. . . . And it's nice, 'cause the neighbors are really happy when he does that. 'Cause its good for them. . . . Because the city doesn't even come out to do the streets. It takes them forever. So, good thing we have a plow." Most residents did not have the special equipment needed to do work at this scale, but Elena's husband did, and he treated the work as additive. The hardest part, Elena said, was finding the energy to hitch the plow to the truck to clear the family's private parking space. After that, whether he plowed twenty feet or two hundred yards made little difference.

Trash was another piece of the urban prairie residents addressed using domestic routines. Retirees with unhurried schedules incorporated trash collection into daily coffee breaks and walking schedules. "I'm up at 6:30 in the morning," one woman explained. "I go outside. And if there's paper trash around, [I'll pick it up]." Other older residents had similar habits. "We'll walk all the way down the street," one couple told me, "maybe a good half-an-hour [or] forty-five minutes' walk. We carry a couple of plastic bags with us." The couple collected paper trash and litter from the road and sidewalk, cleaning the public street as they went.

Younger residents with more chaotic schedules also cleaned litter, but they usually worked less systematically. Several residents, like Jamel the civic activist, had compulsive trash collection mannerisms that almost resembled nervous ticks. "I always pick up trash everywhere," Jamel explained. "It doesn't matter where. I hate litter. So I'm always picking it up." These residents filled their pockets and bags with garbage to throw away later. I observed some residents bending down, arching their backs and straining their knees, as many as two-dozen times in a single block while going about their day. Community groups encouraged these habits by chaining makeshift trash cans to street trees and mailboxes. These cans gave resident trash collectors somewhere to unload their pockets, and the nearby neighbors emptied them into their private city-issued bins for municipal collection.

Residents described this provisional trash collection work as a simple extension of their daily round and as distinct from organized volunteer campaigns. Several times each year, during Motor City Makeovers and Detroit Partnership Days, thousands of volunteers from suburban corporations, universities, and churches rode buses into Detroit to clean trash, mow overgrown yards, and board vacant homes in residential neighborhoods. Community organizations and resident activists helped shape those events. They contacted potential volunteer groups in advance and asked them to send people to specific locations. They provided rakes, boards, and food to the volunteers, and they asked county officials to provide dumpsters or special trash collection services to remove the debris volunteers consolidated on the curbs.

Residents expressed mixed emotions about these civic events, and their anxieties reinforced the emotional importance of self-provisioned alternatives. Earl, for instance, felt disheartened at the sight of "outside" volunteers picking up trash. "It's embarrassing," he said. "Don't get me wrong; we like U of M [the University of Michigan] and MSU [Michigan State University], and we need their help. But we got to take care of our own!" Another retiree voiced similar reservations. "It's sad," she said, "that there are all these white people coming in from the suburbs. Professionals [and] college students who pay their tuition by coming into the community to volunteer to pick up trash. The community should be ashamed. What will all these white outsiders think of black people?" For these residents, domesticating public works was a matter of pride. If the local government would not provide services, rather than rely on outside charity many residents tried to do at least some of the work themselves.

Provisional public workers had their limits. The mind game of incremental additions did not eliminate the physical labor involved. Residents usually worked only within a tight geographic radius around their homes. People with push mowers and shovels could not cover as much ground as neighbors with motorized equipment. Many residents pushed lawn mowers and snowblowers along sidewalks, but only a few would cross a street. Residents enjoyed living next to well-maintained property, but they had no legal claim to compensation for the work they performed or the value they added to those gray spaces, which discouraged larger investments. Dale,

Elena, and their neighbors mowed and shoveled anyway, but their atomized working methods did not fully counteract the effects of municipal cutbacks, and residents on high-vacancy blocks with more gaps than occupants were easily overwhelmed. These limits encouraged self-provisioners to collaborate to ease the workload and address larger problems.

» ELLISON'S PROVISIONAL LIGHTING POOL

Ellison, an Asian American computer programmer, bought his house when he graduated from college in 1978. Thirty-five years later, he and his wife still liked their house, and they enjoyed their neighborhood. But sometimes, he said, "we get really frustrated with the way things are in the city." He was concerned about falling property values and rising vacancy rates, but he felt those market considerations were beyond his and his government's control. Broken streetlights, he said, were another matter. "Our street has lost probably half its streetlights," Ellison told me. "They're not working. The one across the street from us hasn't worked [for years]." He blamed the municipality for the literal and symbolic darkness he faced on his block. "Sometimes I think, 'Oh my goodness, what are the politicians doing?' Sometimes we think, 'Maybe we want to throw in the towel.' But then we think, 'No, why would we want to do that? What we have here is worth fighting for.'"

Ellison was an active community volunteer. We met once while he was leading perspective homebuyers on an informal cycling tour of the neighborhood. We met again at a community fund-raising event, and his wife was on the board of their neighborhood association. Ellison relied on those civic activities to recruit new neighbors for vacant homes and raise money for youth summer programs. But the streetlight problem required a different kind of solution. "Most of the people leave their porch lights on all night," Ellison explained. "In fact, all of the people on the street leave their porch lights on."

Using porch lights to light up the night was an intentional, ubiquitous practice in many neighborhoods, something so prolific and matter-of-fact most residents described it as an afterthought. As Mara, the urban gardener, explained, "We don't have streetlights. OK. What is another way to keep your streets safe? Turn your own porch lights on." Residents in Dale's neighborhood made similar comments. One man, for instance, said the last functioning streetlight on his block had burned out about three years previously. He called the municipality "umpteenth times" asking for repairs, but since scrappers "stoled all the copper out of 'em," repairs were unlikely. In the meantime his neighbors began leaving their porch lights on all day and all night. "N— on the corner keeps it lit up," he said. "And the library [down the street] keeps it lit up. And my neighbors next door had the two big floodlights [installed] there. . . . At night, I can sit here and almost read a book from their lights."

Neighborhood associations like the one Ellison's wife joined encouraged residents to pool household lights in these ways. In a neighborhood association newsletter from 2012, one of Ellison's neighbors wrote, "It's easy and costs only pennies a night. [The utility company] DTE Energy's web calculator reveals that a fourteen watt Compact Florescent Light (*equivalent to a sixty watt incandescent bulb*)"—and available for free from the utility company—"left on for twelve hours a day costs $2.38 per month to operate. . . . I challenge all residents of A— [Street] to kick off the campaign and help lead the way by turning on those lights!" Even without organizational encouragement, most residents left their porch lights on as a taken-for-granted practice on their ever-darkening blocks.

A more formal, market-based solution to the lighting problem was technically available. Only 40 percent of the city's streetlights were operational in 2012 when the mayor announced plans to privatize the lighting authority. The private electrical company preparing to take ownership planned to reduce the streetlight grid to 20 percent of its original capacity to make the system more profitable. But company spokespeople promised residents, businesses, and community groups would always have the option of paying between $136 and $537 to turn on an extra pole on their blocks.[18]

Most residents avoided this solution because it was impractical in low-income and high-rental areas. If a dozen neighbors shared the cost, it was comparable to what many residents were already paying by leaving their porch lights on, but many residents on the darkest streets no longer had neighbors to help shoulder the cost. Also, although light poles put the light on the street where residents wanted it most, the company required residents to sign multiyear service contracts ranging from two to five years, which was impractical in areas with frequent resident turnover or for residents worried about their month-to-month financial stability. In the end I met only one resident who used the program, and she paid for the entire light herself.

Residents who wanted to avoid making long-term cash commitments to companies or neighbors preferred to make smaller, unstructured donations to the community lighting pool, instead. For many residents the fluidity of the porch light solution made it possible for them to participate. Leaving porch lights on involved no long-term expectation of resource sharing or reciprocity. It involved no legal contracts with mercenary service providers. It avoided potentially messy social entanglements, and it left residents in full control of their day-to-day household expenses. Opting in and out was as simple as flipping a switch. It was not a perfect solution. Porch lights provided less light and more uneven coverage than streetlights, and the strategy failed on high-vacancy blocks like Janet's where 85 percent of the homes were vacant or demolished. These limits were important, but the incremental, noncommittal nature of the porch light solution made it easier for people who were unlikely to join community organizations or sign service contacts to provisionally pitch in and help light up the night.

The porch light phenomenon represented an informal mode of resource pooling that occurred alongside other more structured civic programs. For instance, some block clubs and community organizations created shared institutions like tool lending libraries. These lending libraries were often modest—sometimes including only a few dozen rakes and shovels stored in residents' garages—but they were explicitly collective. Neighbors could borrow those tools according to community protocols, and the tools reverted to the community when the task was complete. Provisional resource pools followed a different logic. Residents shared their personal resources with neighbors, but those resources reverted back to private households once the project was complete. Even if residents pooled resources many times, they maintained full control over their tools and finances, and they could opt in and out without owing anyone an explanation.

Residents pooled resources like time, tools, and expertise with friends and neighbors to accomplish work they could not manage on their own. Connie, the barricading booby-trapper, for example, worked with two of her neighbors to install a homemade "Neighborhood Park" sign on a vacant residential lot where the local kids liked to play. Connie had construction experience, so she designed, carved, and painted the sign using wood and tools her neighbors had left over from past home improvement projects. She taught her neighbors how to mix and pour concrete, and they spent two weekends installing a concrete footing for their sign. The footing gave their sign a more official aesthetic than if they had simply nailed a painted shingle to a tree. They hoped this formal image would discourage people from vandalizing the kids' informal play space.

Meg, the deconstructionist, shared a similar story. She noticed the overgrown bushes in front of her adopted house were knocking down a fence, and she worried the neighborhood kids waiting for the school bus on that corner might get hurt. Meg had "every tool imaginable," she said, so she tried removing the bushes and fence herself, but she was not physically strong enough to finish the job. "The older gentleman across the street saw me fighting with this grass," she recalled, "and he came out." Using her tools and his muscles, they removed the fence and bushes, and they cleared the trash that had accumulated underneath. Another neighbor then joined them, boarding the building behind the fence and painting murals on the boards.

Some residents pooled cash, as well, but that was less common. One exception involved a group of Ellison's neighbors who rallied around the shared problem of dying trees after the emerald ash bore invaded and killed nearly every street tree on their blocks. Neighbors called the municipality to complain, but tree cutting crews never arrived, and dying trees began falling on cars and roofs. A few neighbors talking on the sidewalk one day decided that even though the municipality was nominally responsible, "there's no reason to wait until the city cuts these trees down" because "the city was in bad shape, even then. . . . So we said, 'Well, let's see if we can get somebody who will give us a deal on tree cutting if we do a lot.' So we did. We found a man who would cut down the biggest tree for $400, and then down [in cost per tree for] the smaller ones if we got X number of trees." The neighbors went door-to-door and convinced every resident within a three-block radius to pay the private contractor to do the work. Ellison's neighbor estimated this economy-of-scale approach reduced the price by at least 60 percent of what

Figure 8. Residents raking leaves at a neighborhood park. Photograph courtesy of the Grandmont Rosedale Development Corporation.

each household would have paid had they hired private contractors independently.

Most residents preferred to share time, tools, and labor instead of cash. As Mara explained, even in very low-income neighborhoods "everybody has something they can contribute," and "if everyone takes care of their own area, plus just a little bit more, then things will be all right." Ellison's neighbors who hired private contractors enjoyed greater economies of scale with longer-lasting results, but even there, residents usually relied on informal volunteerism and incremental labor to light up the night and clean litter from the streets. Pooling household resources was not a perfect solution, but provisional working methods made it possible for residents to address immediate problems while advocating for longer-term policy reforms, and it made it easier for residents to participate despite precarious circumstances and anxieties about making long-term commitments.

» CAMILLE'S PUBLIC DISPLAYS OF VOLUNTEERISM

"There was so much dumping," Camille said, referring to the garbage people illegally dumped on her street at night. "There was so much dumping. . . . From my garden all the way down to C— [Street] was loaded. I literally had to go on the news for the city to come out here and pick it up."

It was a warm summer day, and Camille and I were chatting in her edible playscape. An infant dozed in a stroller, and two more youngsters were picking berries. The street was spotless. At least one-third of the homes on Camille's block were vacant or already demolished, and a large abandoned municipal building stood fenced, boarded, and silent across the street. But there was no trash in sight.

"Did you use volunteers to get that cleaned up?" I asked. Her block club had received over ten thousand hours of volunteer labor the previous summer, mostly from suburban churches.

Camille shook her head, no. "It took me two days to clean all the debris," she explained. "I had at least five houses in front full of debris. You couldn't even see my garden for the debris."

The Department of Public Works collected household waste from 1874 until the city privatized trash collection in 2014. In the early 2010s when Camille was building her garden, municipal contractors collected small amounts of household waste on a weekly basis, and three or four times a year, usually during the summer, they drove special bulk collection vehicles around the city to collect larger household items. On those warm-weather days, contractors removed up to one cubic yard of nonbuilding material from the fronts of occupied homes. This service worked well for household-generated trash, but illegal dumping often included construction debris, exceeded one cubic yard, occurred year-round, and was concentrated in unoccupied spaces. Although the city had the equipment to collect that bulk waste, they did not automatically collect it as a standard operating procedure.

Before Camille and her volunteers could build the edible playscape, Camille faced the daunting challenge of removing the piles of illegally dumped trash that had accumulated over several years of neglect. A bulk trash collection date was approaching, so Camille and a neighbor spent several labor-intensive days hauling trash strewn across five vacant lots to the sidewalk. They stacked it in consolidated piles where the mechanical arm of the municipal dump truck could scoop it up and haul it away.

The bulk collection vehicle came and went, and the trash pile was still there. Camille was upset, and she began calling several local television stations to plead her case. "Channel Two came in," she recalled, "and Channel Four did a story." During her on-air interviews, Camille did not complain about systemic problems with municipal trash collection, and she did not characterize the municipality as a general trash collection agency. Instead, Camille said the city owned specialized equipment, and she said city officials had a moral responsibility not to provide universal services but to pitch in and use equipment to help residents like her who were working on their own to reduce blight. She showed the news cameras her trash piles, and she described the backbreaking work she did getting the trash ready for mechanized collection. The mayor's office responded by sending the trash crew back to collect the debris. Camille laughed remembering the incident, but she sounded more tired than triumphant.

Public displays of volunteerism were one of many self-provisioning tactics residents used to access scarce municipal resources. Camille and her neighbors recognized government offices had limited funds, and they knew employees exercised considerable discretion when deciding how to allocate that money. If Camille had just complained about illegal dumping on vacant lots, the mayor would probably not have responded, and the trash elsewhere in her neighborhood was not removed. But by showing physical evidence of her own hard labor, she fashioned herself into a deserving subject eligible to receive discretionary municipal aid.

Many residents developed personal friendships with service providers and offered gifts of cash and food to get extra work done on their blocks. One strategy involved asking contractors working nearby to do odd jobs on the fly. Beth, the resident recycler, explained how this worked. "I've bribed the guys fixing the sidewalks or the alley to do this and clean up that and take this with them, and fried green tomatoes are going over the back fence." Food, like homemade zucchini bread or fried okra made from backyard gardens, was an especially common form of currency in these on-the-fly transactions. Some residents also paid cash. One of Beth's neighbors told me she "personally paid a city worker" to vacuum the sewer in front of her house so her basement would stop flooding. Another neighbor paid a municipal landscaper to cut down a street tree "because the city wouldn't do anything about it." Residents were irritated about paying extra for this work, since they paid taxes for public services already, but while phone calls to city offices usually ended in frustration, on-the-fly transactions produced easy, immediate results.

Residents in neighborhoods like Dale's and Ellison's where more people had white-collar jobs were more likely to ask office workers for favors in advance instead of bartering with contractors in the streets. Also, since offering money to public officials sometimes looked suspicious, those residents used food and friendships instead of cash to get things done. For example, Ellen the foster owner used cookies to build personal relationships with municipal employees in the public works department. "I called that office maybe ten times in the last year for various things," she told me, laughing. "And [I've] gone down there a few times and took them a bunch of chocolate chip cookies one time. [The office manager] had got us this special bulk trash pickup," she explained. "A little bribery like that doesn't hurt at all." Ellen's use of the term "bribery" was intentionally playful, but the comment implied residents often chatted with office workers and gave them small tokens of appreciation to bump their way up the municipality's service priority ladder.

Resident activists recognized the value of name recognition and quid pro quo. A group of resident volunteers in Ellison's neighborhood, for example, organized a tour of the city's 911 emergency call center to learn how the center operated and to meet the people answering the phones. After the tour the neighbors decided to collect food donations for an employee appreciation buffet to thank them for their work and hospitality. I listened as the group had a lengthy conversation about whether to provide food once for the daytime workers or twice to also include the night shift. The augment that resolved the matter was one of self-interest. "We're doing this to represent ourselves," one of the residents said, "and we need to be represented twenty-four hours." They offered the buffet twice. They also decided to request healthy food donations, like soup or sandwiches instead of donuts, so switchboard operators would "feel good when taking our calls." These comments indicated residents hoped their food offerings would encourage city workers to remember the neighborhood fondly and perhaps give calls from their area a little extra attention.

Community leaders and church officials publicly encouraged these favor-currying practices. An especially salient example involved the African American director of a neighborhood community group who arranged for a panel of municipal, county, and state police officers to speak with area residents. During the meeting, standing in front of three long tables filled with officers in uniform, the director urged audience members to join block clubs and attend community meetings "to build personal relationships" with officers "so that the cops will respond more quickly when you call them, because they know you." He paused, and several residents shifted in their chairs, perhaps feeling the same discomfort I felt at the thought of emergency response being based on favoritism rather than need. "Maybe it shouldn't be that way," the director continued, "but it is that way." The officers behind him nodded solemnly, and the conversation moved on to other topics.

Residents used similar strategies to get access to nonprofit resources. Mara, for instance, often led politicians, reporters, and foundation representatives on tours of her neighborhood where she showed them the urban garden she planted, the vacant lots her neighbors adopted, and the murals neighborhood kids painted. On one such tour in 2011, she led a group of AmeriCorps volunteers that included the daughter of a wealthy family with one of the largest charitable foundations in the state. "And I showed them around the neighborhood," Mara said, "and I told them stories. And by the end, I had her in tears." Mara laughed good-naturedly as she recalled the personal bond she formed with the heiress. "She was crying. She was so funny. And she gets on the phone, and she calls her money man, and she goes, 'You get your ass over here and talk to this lady and give her what she wants!'" Mara laughed again. "And that was it. A week later, . . . they wrote me a $50,000 check." She used the money to pay local teenagers to board vacant homes.

These demonstrations of appreciation and volunteerism organized residents' access to collective resources. Previous generations of urban residents used the ideological trumpet of universal services to rally public support for greater government accountability in providing public works. But in the new market-oriented climate, demands for services as a right of citizenship carried little weight. Local governments still had resources, and they were still involved in service delivery, but they and their nonprofit partners were reinvented as supplemental service providers helping on a case-by-case basis as resources permitted. This historical inversion of the social contract between city residents and their local government meant self-provisioning was not only a response to government contraction. Public displays of volunteerism also became important tools helping communities access resources in a highly competitive environment.

» PROVISIONAL COLLABORATIONS AND PUBLIC DISPLAYS OF DESERVINGNESS

"I don't want to lie to you," Rosa told me as we sipped our tea. The neighborhood "is ugly. Is depressing. Is dirty. And I don't like it." She sighed, shaking her head. Rosa was embarrassed when her friends from Mexico visited her in Detroit. Her childhood city was crowded; the busses were slow; and she thought she was moving up in the world when she left. Things had not worked out that way. "Sometimes you think you walk in a trash can," she said. "Its awful to see. It's trash. You walk on trash."

Dale's lawn mowing, Ellison's porch lights, and Camille's news interviews were stunning acts of heroism—and routine acts of daily life—in disinvested neighborhoods. The work was physically taxing, and it required considerable emotional strength to dream of solving collective problems at the household scale. Feelings of futility and indignation were understandable but debilitating. "I used to help some groups," Rosa said. Her neighbors mowed abandoned lots, disguised vacant homes, built informal parks, and organized street cleanups. "But I haven't helped anyone lately. Some people become very indifferent or depressed."

Many informal public workers shared Rosa's sentiments. They recalled times when they took "little breaks" from self-provisioning because the constancy of need felt demoralizing. More often than not, those residents said their neighbors helped them reengage. Sitting at home, they would look out their windows and see neighbors plugging away with lawn mowers and trash bags. Eventually, as these sights rekindled their sense of hope, they would find their brooms, shovels, and rakes and go back to work.

The habits and mind games residents used to divide public works into small chunks and incorporate those tasks into daily routines helped people minimize the toll of self-provisioning. Without these provisional working methods, the effort to solve collective problems individually easily overwhelmed the emotional energy and financial resources residents could devote to the work. Government policies encouraged provisional public works not only by creating need through budget cuts but also by rewarding neighborhoods where residents publicly displayed their self-provisioned accomplishments. Government offices and their nonprofit partners identified residents who were active in the community, and they gave them financial aid and special services in return. It was difficult to scale-up household labor into an organized social movement, but without domestic volunteerism residents forfeited one of the only tools they had available to access the limited resources in their city.

The promise of municipal governing once embodied ideals of universal equity and public good. Those ideals were always utopian. Strong twentieth-century municipal governments helped whites and hurt minorities. But instead of pushing for more genuinely equitable services, neoliberal policy makers abandoned the ideal of universal services and embraced private delivery models based on market segmentation. That shift casts inequitable services as a rational market practice rather than an unethical social norm.[19] Cities are once again becoming places where residents are entitled to only the services they can afford or the amenities they can create with their own bare hands.

6

Policing Home Spaces

"When I first heard of Habitat, I used to think they gave people houses. But after being in the program, I found out they don't give you a house. You work for your house."

Estelle, a middle-aged African American stay-at-home mom, spent nine months in 2008 and 2009 logging sweat equity hours with Habitat for Humanity Detroit's home ownership program.

"What do you like most about the house?" I asked.

Estelle answered emphatically, "Zero percent interest on my mortgage!" She laughed. "That's what I like about the house." Estelle had owned a home before, but she lost it when the variable interest rate tripled. With the Habitat house, she said, "there won't be anyone telling me I got to leave."

Habitat for Humanity built one hundred new homes in Estelle's neighborhood between 2005 and 2013. They clustered those homes on six consecutive blocks on Detroit's east side. Because of the foundation's tight geographic work area, for Estelle joining the home ownership program meant agreeing to live in a very specific section of the city.

Estelle had lived on the west side for years, and she worried about moving east. She knew of the neighborhood, but she had never spent time there. "So they told us to drive around," she recalled, to see if she would feel comfortable living on one of those six blocks. "So we drove around, me and my daughter. And I thought, 'Oh my goodness.' Because when we moved into the area, a lot of the houses on L— [Street] weren't there. It was barren land." Estelle had misgivings, she said with a shutter, but her daughter encouraged her to commit.

"She was like, 'Ma, it is not about the neighborhood. It's about our house.' And I told her, I said, 'You're right.' Because I knew this was a great opportunity. There was no other way for us to get a home."

Shortly before moving day, Estelle had an encounter with a soon-to-be neighbor that gave her more confidence. "We need[ed] to go water the grass," she said, but "it was hard to get to M— [Street] when we stayed on the west side." She arrived after dark. "It was, like, eleven o'clock at night," she recalled, "and we were over at the house trying to water the grass. And we were in the back of the house. And the lady that lives directly behind us came out her back door and asked us, who were we? She was about to call the police. And I went, 'It's OK, it's OK, it's our house!' And she was like, 'You gotta call somebody!'" The neighbors knew the home was supposed to be empty. No one had told them she would be coming by, and the neighbors were ready to defend the house. After moving in, Estelle heard similar stories of neighborly attentiveness protecting residents from home invasions while they were at work or traveling. "I thought, 'They looking out. That's good!'"

Estelle's experience of being challenged by a watchful neighbor gave her confidence in her new community, and she designed her landscaping to promote those visual relationships. "We were going to build a privacy fence," she said, "but once we saw how they looked out for you, it was like, well, we don't want to put a privacy fence up, because then they can't see. My neighbor's got to be able to see my yard!" Estelle installed a fence to keep people from cutting through the yard and to protect her kids from stray dogs, but she chose chain link instead of solid boards to maximize the transparency between her yard and the now-trusted neighbor behind her.

Estelle's neighbor acted essentially as an informal security guard watching her street and creating a sense of safety on the block. She worked alongside more formal community policing programs. Police departments nationwide began encouraging residents to form neighborhood watch groups and volunteer security patrols in the 1960s, and merchants began using business improvement districts to hire private security guards in the 1970s.[1] These civic- and market-based alternatives to municipal policing gained renewed traction in Detroit during the Great Recession. The city's long slide into bankruptcy meant a shrinking operating budget for the Detroit Police Department. Officers prioritized their resources. They stopped responding to scrapping and vandalism in empty buildings so they could focus on dangerous crimes, but they still had trouble responding quickly enough to prevent break-ins and violence. These municipal short-falls encouraged residents like Estelle and her neighbors to find other ways to prevent nuisance and crime near their homes.

Some residents volunteered with formal community patrols, but many more—about a third of the people I interviewed (36 percent)—used informal, domestic strategies to keep an eye on their blocks. Like Estelle and her fence, these residents arranged curtains, vehicles, and vegetation to make their streets easier to see. They developed daily rituals that helped them become familiar with their environment and decide which activities were normal and which seemed suspicious. When residents saw something unusual, like a stranger in the backyard of an empty house at night, some neighbors confronted the stranger directly. But since face-to-face confrontations could be dangerous, many people developed indirect strategies using lights, sounds, and body language to challenge strangers at a distance. These practices helped residents put eyes on the street, parse what they saw, and make their eyes visible to others.

Residents often used the language of "eyes on the street" to describe their informal habits of watching. Urban activists like Jane Jacobs popularized the expression in the 1960s by asserting that everyday interactions among ordinary people in public spaces kept social behavior in check more effectively than aggressive police surveillance. Jacobs's description of the "street ballet" in her dense, white, working-class community in New York City showed residents and shopkeepers enforced unwritten codes of conduct that, she believed, prevented nuisance and crime.[2] Recent ethnographies from minority communities reinforce the importance of street life in establishing local social norms, although not all norms are positive. Street vendors in New York City, gang members in Philadelphia, and nosy neighbors in Los Angeles regulate peer-to-peer economies, organize youth violence, and reinforce gender roles through the street ballets on their blocks.[3] These routinized interactions in public space reinforce unwritten but well-established social codes that make environments predictable.

Reducing these interactions to eyes alone does violence to the rich complexity of the social interactions involved, and the assumption that daily interactions reduce crime is questionable. But the expectation that peer pressure through public visibility will enhance safety has nonetheless become a cornerstone of design-based approaches to community policing. Advocates of eyes on the street challenge gated communities and privatized public spaces that use exclusion to make spaces defensible. Instead, they encourage community groups, merchants, and city planners to increase the number of people and the range of activities in public spaces. Operable windows, plentiful seating, and food vendors that increase interactions in those spaces can create greater potential for observation and added pressure to conform. City planners often use these principles as guides when designing urban spaces in growing or revitalizing neighborhoods nationwide.[4]

Residents with limited resources who live in preexisting environments cannot easily rebuild infrastructure, and increasing foot traffic in shrinking cities is difficult. The logic of eyes on the street still applies, but residents adapt it to suit their circumstances. The domestic, shrinking-city version of eyes on the street in Detroit looked somewhat different from Jane Jacobs's account. Residents made small physical retrofits to their homes and streets to create observable landscapes. They developed rhythms and habits that routinized their interaction with public spaces and made them familiar with the usual activity on their blocks. They also developed spatial routines to show neighbors and strangers they were watching. These practices intersected with other security responses, like hired guards and community patrols, and residents moved easily between these formal and domestic realms.

Residents used informal surveillance to feel safer in their homes, but these self-provisioning acts also had other socially generative effects. Resident watchers used their eyes on the street to negotiate shared landscapes of belonging and exclusion. They challenged people who looked suspicious at a glance, and they welcomed people who could prove they had an externally authorized or ethically justified reason for being in the neighborhood. Resident watchfulness also generated shared expectations about mutuality. People expected to help neighbors at times of crisis, and to alleviate the anxiety of false alarms, they expected neighbors to notify them if they planned to deviate from their usual routines—for instance, by having a party, lending their car to a friend, or going out of town. I cannot say whether these practices reduced crime, but even in instances where crime persisted, resident watchfulness created a sense of environmental predictability that helped people negotiate their everyday lives.

» PUBLIC SAFETY IN DETROIT

Residents knew their city was infamous for crime. Media sources described Detroit as one of the most dangerous, violent, and murderous cities in the country. Atlanta, Orlando, St. Louis, Birmingham, Oakland, Memphis, and New Orleans had similar crime rates, but Detroit still emerged as a poster child for all things dystopian.[5] Friends, family members, and strangers living in nearby suburbs reinforced this message. School children returned home from summer camps and sailing clubs with stories about suburban kids asking them if they saw dead bodies at home. Older residents had adult children who moved to the suburbs and then would no longer visit them, "because they have the boogeyman idea about Detroit." Residents also described former schoolmates and childhood friends who refused to meet for lunches and parties on the Detroit side of the municipal boundary line and insisted Detroiters drive to the suburbs to socialize, instead. These everyday interactions underscored the public perception that being in Detroit was dangerous.

City residents said these outsider perceptions were wildly out of sync with their own life experiences. Rhonda, a middle-aged African American woman, was especially eloquent on this point. "There is crime. That's the reality," she said, "and then there's the perception of crime that is either out of sorts or people who are unrealistic." Residents said crime occurred everywhere, not just in Detroit. "I'm cautious," Rhonda explained. "If I lived in Chicago, I would probably be the same way." Only a handful of residents told me they often felt afraid, and even they said news reporters and suburban friends exaggerated the problems. As an antidote to Detroit's sensationalized reputation, residents like Rhonda made explicit decisions to keep their anxieties in check. "I don't think I'm living in a fantasy world, thinking, 'Oh, there's no crime.' Yeah, there is crime. And I'm cautious. . . . But I refuse to be afraid in my city."

Residents used everyday knowledge to contextualize their public safety concerns. For residents parks, bakeries, street trees, theater troupes, and friendships defined neighborhood character more than crime, but those characteristics rarely appeared in media reports. Residents in some areas were also familiar with the sympathetic personal histories that pushed friends and neighbors toward criminalized or violent acts that were troubling but understandable given the circumstances. Residents used this everyday knowledge to qualify risk and contain fear despite social messages of a dangerous Detroit.

Residents who criticized hyperbole and encouraged compassion still felt safety was an important local issue, especially since the Detroit Police Department was understaffed and losing resources. In 2010, at 32.1 officers per 10,000 residents, Detroit had marginally more officers per capita than other Rust Belt cities like Pittsburgh (28.4) and Buffalo (29.0), but cities with similar crime rates like Baltimore (46.3) and St. Louis (38.4) had more officers per capita and a greater institutional capacity to respond to complaints.[6] Detroit was also geographically larger than many peer cities, and its police department was downsizing. The police force shrank by 25 percent from 3,350 officers in 2009 to 2,500 officers in 2013. These combined factors meant that in 2012 Detroit police response times averaged fifty-eight minutes, compared with the national average of eleven minutes.[7]

Private guards and community policing represented two of the most media-publicized local responses to the dwindling municipal police force. In 2012 civic groups in at least eight neighborhoods hired off-duty officers carrying guns and wearing uniforms to patrol the streets on bicycles or in police department vehicles. These guards worked in relatively affluent areas where residents paid up to $360 and merchants paid up to $2,000 each year for the service.[8] They responded to nuisances like loitering and public drunkenness so that on-duty officers could focus on urgent calls about home invasions and violence. They also acted as visual symbols of police authority in the neighborhoods that hired them. Some residents hoped to make private security more affordable by encouraging more neighbors to share the cost, but it was still expensive for low-income residents, especially in sparsely populated areas.

Residents also organized volunteer patrols. Informal community patrols and neighborhood watches have a long history in Detroit. Residents in one neighborhood, for instance, had been operating a volunteer safety patrol for three decades. The Detroit Police Department began formalizing these volunteer groups in the early 2010s by training, certifying, regulating, and reimbursing them in an attempt to maintain service levels despite budget cuts. By 2013 the police department had certified twenty-five citizen patrol groups citywide, and they hoped to add three new patrols every year.[9] Certified patrols where most popular in the same higher-income areas where residents also hired private guards. These formal police responses supplemented—but did not replace—informal resident watchfulness.

A large consumer industry of household alarm systems, window bars, and security cameras also prospered in Detroit, although it received less media attention than hired guards and citizen patrols. Professional alarms and infrared cameras were popular in upper-income areas. Many residents used smart-phone technologies to receive alerts whenever sensors detected movement around their home. Residents on lower-income blocks who could not afford special equipment often used large dogs to keep people away or used scrap metal to reinforce the locks on ground-level doors and windows. These private acts of fortification reflected resident security concerns, but compared with other forms of resident watchfulness, they generated fewer collective negotiations over social norms in public spaces.

Some residents occasionally joked about wanting to see state or federal officers standing guard on every corner, but most people said they did not want to live in a militarized city and instead wanted a holistic response to their safety concerns. An African American community advocate summarized this perspective in a 2013 newspaper article. "Police can't be on every corner," she said. "You should be able to walk your dog, push kids in a stroller or use the parks. We don't want a handful of knuckleheads to take away our quality of life."[10] Comments like these emphasized the importance residents placed on building neighborhood ties and encouraging everyday interactions as an alternative to gating homes and militarizing streets. Residents still hired guards and set alarms, just in case, but they hoped informal habits of watchfulness would make them unnecessary.

›› EDNA'S OBSERVABLE LANDSCAPE

"The only house on this block that has a problem to it is this house over there," Edna said, pointing through her living room wall toward the house next door. "This house, to me, stayed a bad-luck house. The kids used to call it the Haunted House. I said, 'Why do you call it the Haunted House?' There was a murder there. First time in my life."

Edna held a photograph of neighborhood kids in her hand as we sat on her living room couch and flipped through old scrapbooks. It was early afternoon, but heavy curtains covered the front windows, and the only light in the room came from a dim electric floor lamp. Edna, a retired city employee, was seventy-six years old. She and her husband, Clarence, had lived in their house since the late 1970s when they became the third African American family to move onto the block.

"Clarence is sitting right here," Edna said, pointing to the couch as she continued her story. "He doesn't hear. He has hearing [loss]. He's sitting right here reading. I'm back there," in the kitchen, "doing something. And I thought, 'Oh, now, they're going to do the firecrackers right in front of the house!' . . . Next thing we know, neighbors are calling, 'Are you alright in there?' And Clarence said, 'Yeah, what's going on?' And they said, 'You didn't hear what happened?' I mean, this was like a gunfight. This was so many bullets. Those little cones all around in the front of our yard. The caution thing was tied to our porch!" Edna chuckled softly, shaking her head. "He's sitting right there, reading! All this is going on. Never heard a thing."

Edna shared this sad story with the same good humor she showed every time we spoke. She felt safe in general, she said, and confident her neighbors were looking out for her. She explained this by telling me about a time the neighbors closed her garage door to protect her valuables when she left it open by mistake. She described another instance when her neighbors stood in the street stopping traffic so she could slowly cross the road with her cane to visit a friend. And

Edna emphasized the importance of watching. After the Haunted House gunfight, she said, "we got very strong as far as our security in this area here. We operate on . . . what is that called . . . ." She paused, searching for words. "That police plan . . . the broken window theory from Boston. They're starting to do that. . . . They say, 'We're watching you.' My eyes are on you, too."

Edna was a self-described resident watcher, and she approached the task pragmatically. It was easier to be observant when the environment was orderly, she said, so on her block "it was like a gentleman's agreement that nobody parked on the street." Edna and her neighbors followed this implicit, unspoken rule for years. "We did that," she explained, "because that was our way of safety. If nobody was on the street and you saw a car with people sitting in it, *you know*!" The local convention of leaving the street clear was obvious to most neighbors, but it was less apparent to outsiders, and they enforced the rule informally. One family, Edna said, had not figured it out yet. "They've been here a couple years. They park on the street. They're the only ones you'll see parked on the street." That one car aside, the neighbors' habits of arranging cars in predictable patterns kept sight lines clear and made newcomers stand out.

Edna's cars, like Estelle's backyard fence, were part of a larger landscape of objects and plants carefully arranged to enhance the ability to put eyes on the street. Residents were especially likely to use brute-force methods to create sight lines around neglected gray spaces. A white block club president, for instance, decided to "open up" the landscape in response to "a mini–crime wave" on her block. She knocked on doors and recruited neighbors to remove debris, cut down large tree branches, and raze the shrubs to the ground around every vacant structure on their street. "It made a difference," she said. "We had lots of problems before, and now there are very few. There's nowhere to hide."

Residents were less heavy-handed with their own homes and instead combined their aesthetic tastes with their interest in watching. Lamar, an African American auto worker, for instance, bought a house with his wife in 2009 to live near his extended family. When moving in, before the boxes were fully unpacked, Lamar immediately rearranged all the plants in his front yard. "I don't like tall bushes," he said, "because people can hide behind tall bushes. So I took all the bushes out." Several homes on his block originally had dense foundation shrubs planted by doors and windows. Those evergreens became thick and tall if left untrimmed, and Lamar and his neighbors worried criminals or animals would hide there. Lamar dug them up and replaced them with visually delicate ornamental grasses planted off center and "out of eyeshot" from inside the house. "I can sit in this window and look out and see straight across the street, on the sides, all across," Lamar explained. "I just kept [the plants] really low, so I could see out from every direction if I needed to."

Other residents chose window treatments that created filtered views of the street. A few people, like a white woman in Edna's neighborhood, preferred to keep their windows "totally exposed. I keep my drapes open all the time," she told me. "I never, never, ever, ever, ever pull the drapes." The only exceptions were an hour she spent wrapping Christmas presents and an hour spent filing taxes. Otherwise, the curtains were open. This exposure helped her passively monitor the street without feeling paranoid. "I basically don't look out," she said. "But the fact that my windows are open . . . is a way of having eyes and ears [on the block]."

Edna took a very different approach to her windows. Transparency made Edna feel exposed and vulnerable. "When we first moved here," she said, "everybody kept their windows open and all. Because that's the way you lived in the white world. Where we lived, you didn't have people driving by and seeing where your library was and where the TV was and looking all through." Edna wanted some connections with the street. "We want people to know that we're here. The lights on and all." But when it came to direct views into the house, she wanted to shield herself from prying eyes. "Crooks think in a different way," she said. "It's, like, casing the place."

Other residents preferred screened views for similar reasons. They trusted some neighbors to have their backs, but they did not trust everyone, and they worried so-called problem neighbors let people use their homes as "watching spots," "exit routes," and "hiding places" when breaking into homes and cars. These residents wanted to create sight lines with the neighbors they trusted while blocking the views that put them at risk.

Residents like Connie, the barricading booby-trapper, solved this dilemma by hanging white curtains and sheets in front of their windows. Connie, like Edna, kept her curtains closed all the time.

When I visited her house, I initially felt fully screened from view, but the white color was light enough that Connie could discern the movement of shapes and shadows outside. Several times during our conversation, she noticed a change and jumped up to peak around the curtains or walk outside for a clearer view. When I asked Connie and other residents about their curtains, they described their ability to see through fabric as a specially honed skill. "It's not easy," Connie said. "You learn to detect movement." Connie also arranged her furniture so that she faced the front window when seated in her favorite chair, which helped her keep her eyes on the street.

Edna's heavy curtains prevented these filtered views, but she still wanted to see what was happening outside. "We have a camera now," she told me. "We finally had a camera put up so he can watch."

"A security camera?" I asked, surprised. Other residents in the neighborhood used closed-circuit cameras to keep an eye on things. Some residents also placed baby monitors or other remote sensors in nearby vacant homes so that they could look into those spaces without being physically present. But seventy-six-year-old Edna and her husband had not struck me as the technophile types.

"Um hmm," Edna said, nodding. "Our own [security camera]. So we can watch." Edna had trouble walking and climbing stairs, and she wanted to keep an eye on her husband when he took out the trash or left the house on errands. The camera let her watch him from her bedroom television set. Edna said she felt safe, but she did not take her safety for granted. She and many other residents used parking habits, window treatments, and hidden cameras to create the filtered sight lines that put eyes on the street and sustained their sense of well-being.

» CAMILLE'S HABITS OF WATCHFULNESS

"I'm not afraid of anything," Camille said, not even the drug dealers who had sent so many of her neighbors running to the suburbs. "Me and this little old lady named L—, . . . we literally was not afraid of anybody in this neighborhood. We walked day and night. We would let them know that we were the eyes and ears and we were watching them." Camille laughed, remembering their walks. "It just never fazed us how dangerous it was until now when I sit back and say, 'Oh, we got a lot of nerve!'"

Figure 9. Window treatments that enhance eyes on the street. Photograph by author.

"When was that?" I asked. I was sitting on a toddler-sized chair in the basement of Camille's house where she ran a state-subsidized childcare center.

"Oh, that was in the early '80s," Camille answered. "So I would like to say '85 through '90 that we literally patrolled. And the police department worked with us. We had a couple officers that gave us their personal number. So anytime we had a problem, we could personally get a police officer out here and take care of our problems that we were having."

"Did it help?"

Camille shrugged. She and her neighbor quickly realized their walks and phone calls "really didn't do anything. They would bust the house, and as soon as they raided the house, within an hour, they were open back up again." Camille kept walking anyway, every day for ten years, because it helped her become familiar with the neighborhood dynamics and avoid the fear of the unknown she felt paralyzed her neighbors. Walking was also an act of resistance that demonstrated her refusal to be intimidated. Camille said this environmental awareness and self-expression gave her the confidence to stay in her home and continue investing in her community.

Camille was one of many residents who self-consciously shaped their daily routines to put their eyes on the streets. Shaping observable landscapes helped, but people could see only so much from their windows, and they still had to decide whether what they saw was "normal." Daily routines, like Camille's walks, gave people a wider perspective on local norms. They also helped neighbors informally divvy up the watching workload and decide when to shift from passive awareness to active surveillance.

Camille investigated her neighborhood on foot, but other residents preferred to drive. Tony, a young African American barber, for instance, took a different route home from work every day. Some days, he would "fly by" his aunt's house. Other days, he drove past his brother's house. He rarely stopped to say hello. Instead, he drove by "just to look. Not to bug him and be like, 'Hey, man, What you doing?' . . . Still giving everybody their space. But more eyes." Tony's neighbor always followed the same route, but she said it sometimes took her a long time to get in or out of the neighborhood because she stopped so frequently to check on vacant buildings or scrutinize strangers she noticed through her windshield. These daily routines brought resident watchers away from home and created regular opportunities to put their eyes on the street.

Older residents who spent more time at home used their leisure activities and hobbies to study the activity on their blocks. Several retirees took coffee breaks on front porches or in front rooms around eight o'clock every morning and three o'clock in the afternoon, when young children were walking to and from school. They memorized which kids usually walked together so they could recognize if an unknown child was ever following them or bullying them.

Some residents in Camille's neighborhood were especially purposeful in their gaze. Mara, for instance, started a garden on a vacant lot that gave her a clear view of "an active crack house." Several other lots were available, but she wanted to use gardening as an excuse to discretely monitor the drug activity to help police officers make arrests. Mara was unusual. Most residents did not see themselves as guards or spies. They told me they were not looking for anything in particular. They were just self-consciously watching, and they developed daily habits that put them in positions to see what was happening.

Block clubs encouraged people to invent reasons to spend time outdoors. Neighborhood newsletters urged residents to "take along a flashlight, a cell phone, and the number for our neighborhood patrol, and step by step we will make this a more connected community." Organizational encouragement was important, but these practices remained fundamentally domestic. Residents following this advice met friends and neighbors for walks and bicycle rides simply to put more eyes on the street.

These daily routines became part of the sidewalk ballet bringing people into public spaces and establishing local norms, and many residents prided themselves on their expert knowledge of neighborhood street life. "There are lots of older people in this neighborhood who have been in the neighborhood a long time," one of Edna's neighbors told me. "People who are home a lot and who are familiar with the rhythm of daily life on the block. And several of them are great watchers. They don't have computers. But they can tell you which car should be in the neighborhood and which car shouldn't be in the neighborhood." Coffee breaks and daily walks helped residents create the mental maps of everyday life they used to differentiate between normal events and suspicious activity.

The residents making these mental maps approached the task with varying levels of rigor. Dale, the incremental lawn mower, said he was just "nosy. I try to make it my business to know who's coming and going on the block," he explained. "My mother's nosy, so I think I picked it up from her." Some of Dale's neighbors were more methodical. Lamar, for instance, had attended a police safety event that gave him an explicit vocabulary to systematize his observations. The police "had what they call a 'baseline,'" he told me. "You know what goes on in your neighborhood usually." He used his street as a hypothetical example. "There's no cars parked in front of my house at midnight. Never. . . . But we wake up, and we see four cars in front of here [and] another here across the street. Look out. Watch something. Look at something. . . . Because history tells us, something's not right. This is not the baseline. Watch those guys."

Resident watchers' cognitive maps customized their baselines to reflect individual concerns, and without discussing it, they fine-tuned their watchfulness to informally divvy up the workload. Edna studied the cars parked on her street after dark. Dale memorized his neighbors' work schedules and the faces of their regular guests. These residents also knew who else on their block was watching and when. Some neighbors were retired and kept an eye on things during the day. Other people, like Edna, kept watch late at night. "I have insomnia," Edna explained. "So I'm awake at night. [The neighbors] say, 'What happened last night? Did you see?' 'Cause I'm the only one on the street that's still awake." Janet, the defensive matchmaker, expected her brother to keep the lookout during the early morning hours. "He gets drunk and passes out around nine o'clock," she said, and "he might wake up around three o'clock in the morning and can't get back to sleep. So if I see him out and about with a flashlight checking around, I know it's OK for me to go to bed. P—'s up."

Residents used these cognitive maps to collaborate informally in watching the street and to decide whether activities seemed suspicious. Connie could not prevent house stripping just by watching the shifting shapes and shadows through her white-colored curtains, and Camille could not stop the drug trade just by walking the streets. But they could learn the unwritten codes of conduct for their environment, which helped them navigate their streets safely and take action to deter unwanted behavior.

» DERRICK'S VISIBLE GAZE

"On our particular block, all the neighbors are very close, and we just pretty much looked out for each other. So if we see anybody that looks strange," Derrick said, pretending to dial a telephone, "'We see somebody out there, what are they doing? They know you?' 'No.' 'They know you?' 'No.' 'OK, keep an eye out.' That kind of thing."

Derrick and I met for coffee at a McDonald's near his home. We discussed home remodeling projects and squatters and then discussed a theft that had occurred that morning. Derrick prided himself on being "a nosy neighbor," and he eagerly shared his ideas about neighborhood safety. "What people don't understand [is] they think being safe and secure involves a lot of work. But it doesn't. It involves something as simple as . . . [if] somebody pulls up on your block, you just open up the window. If somebody's doing something wrong, the last thing they want is somebody watching them." He paused. "You don't even have to be watching them," he added. "They pull up, they notice your window closed. Next thing they notice, your window's open, they're gone. Or whatever they were going to do, they stop doing."

"Have there been many incidents on your block?" I asked.

"No," he said, "only one." Before the "good squatter" moved in across the street, Derrick and his dinner guests noticed a utility van pulling into the driveway. "And I'm like, 'What? Who are these people?'" Derrick watched surreptitiously as the strangers got out and started shining their flashlights into the windows. "Well, we knew that real estate people normally don't come and do anything once it gets dark," he said, "so we knew it was suspicious." He opened his front door to let the light from his living room spill out into the night, and he and his guests lingered nonchalantly in the doorway, pretending to socialize. The van's driver noticed them and tried to diffuse the situation by saying his aunt owned the house and had sent him over to collect some things from inside. "And I said, 'What's your aunt's name?' He says, 'So-and-so. We been living over here for years. The neighbor next door knows.' And I said, 'OK, I want you to go next door, knock on her door, and let her know that you're taking some stuff out of the house. . . . You don't do it, I'm going to call the police.' . . . Of course, he ran back to his van, jumped in, and sped off." Derrick felt certain the men were scrappers, and he was proud his gaze had protected the home.

Public visibility was only one part of the sidewalk ballet, and Derrick's experience underlined that the social effect of being watched came as much from the social interactions that followed as from the act of surveillance. Watching might encourage self-regulation, but only if the people being watched recognized authority in the gaze. When residents in Detroit saw something suspicious, they could call the police, but people often told me they wanted to verify the threat first or they felt some quicker response was needed. Some residents, like Estelle's backyard neighbor, took direct action by rushing outside to confront strangers quickly and forcefully. Other residents, like Derrick, preferred indirect tactics, at least initially, because direct confrontation was risky.[11]

Derrick, like many other residents, made his eyes visible to the people he was watching. These residents opened doors, rearranged curtains, or stood on porches to let strangers know they were not alone. One of Derrick's neighbors told me she had recently seen a group of people walking in an unusual way on her street, and she suspected they might be casing the block. The woman grabbed the broom and dustpan she left by the front door exactly for these occasions, and she went outside and pretended to sweep her stoop. While outside, she said she just looked at the strangers, making sure to catch their eye, and then kept pretending to sweep until they seemed uncomfortable and left. Residents had a wide range of props they used in these types of circumstances. People pretended to water plants and change porch lights. Residents banged on doors while pretending to oil squeaky hinges, and they flipped through piles of junk mail they purposefully stored by their front doors.

Landscape props were important mediums in these performances. Make-work activities helped residents get a better look at what was going on outside, but the larger goal was to create changes in light, noise, and movement to attract people's attention and let strangers know they could be seen, even if the resident was not actively looking. These performances were intentionally indirect. As Derrick explained, "You don't even have to be watching them." Residents hoped reminding people they were exposed to public view would be enough to make them think twice before violating local norms.

Public displays of eyes on the street often sparked conversations between neighborhood watchers and the people they observed, and residents used those conversations to test the legitimacy of strangers. Cordial greetings like, "Hi, how are you?" and, "Are you looking for someone?" were polite phrases that carried the implied probe, "Who are you, and what are you doing here?" Residents lingered over these conversations to see whether newcomers could sustain their stories over time. Residents also asked for information they could verify with neighbors. If someone said they were hired to make repairs on a home, residents asked to see badges and paperwork, and they called their neighbors to see if the information checked out. Residents wrote down names and took discrete photographs of faces, cars, and license plates and then asked neighborhood watchers whether those people were part of the baseline. The best references

Figure 10. Residents watching the pedestrian activity on the street. Photograph by author.

came from other neighbors who looked out their doors and windows and gave the strangers the nod.

Most residents had experience on both sides of these interactions. Sometimes, they were the watchful neighbor, and other times, they were the stranger under investigation. Many people found those confrontations reassuring. Patrice, the opportunity matchmaker, for example, asked her nephew to help her clean the seven vacant homes she bought at auction. When he went to the homes, he said, "neighbors came out everywhere, like, 'Hey, how are you doing? What are you doing over here?' You know what I'm saying? They took interest." He appreciated these exchanges. "'Who are you?' That's nice. 'Thank you for coming over and letting me know that people have been watching the house.'"

Another resident had similar experiences while house hunting in 2008. Over a thousand vacant units were available in his neighborhood, and they came in many sizes, ages, materials, styles, and price points. But when inspecting homes, he said he looked for "block-level indicators that aren't obvious or aren't in usual real estate measures." He found what he was looking for when he arrived ten minutes early for an appointment with a real estate agent who was helping him inspect a long-vacant home. The front door was open, so he "poked his head inside" for a quick look around before returning to his car to wait. Within moments, he said, "there were neighbors knocking on my window, asking why I had been in the abandoned house and why I was sitting on their block. I found that encouraging." He bought the house on the spot.

Not everyone appreciated nosy neighbors who knocked on their doors, questioned their guests, and took photographs of their properties. But everyone who agreed to speak with me said polite confrontations were comforting. Being watched by protective neighbors was a sign people lived on a good street where neighbors had their backs.

When resident watchers could not verify the legitimacy of strangers, they sometimes confronted them, using the landscape to protect them and to make the confrontation as publicly noticeable as possible. The window shout was an especially common technique, where residents shouted challenges or threats through open windows at a safe distance from the suspicious person. Some residents ran outside and acted crazy by shouting and banging on anything that would make a loud noise. Residents directed these shouts and performances at the suspected person, but equally important, they hoped their exaggerated, noisy spectacles would encourage other neighbors to open their curtains and let the light spill out from their front doors. While strangers might ignore one resident watcher, residents felt fewer people would ignore several neighbors who made a show of watching together.

» LAMAR'S ALMOST-FORMAL SECURITY PATROL

Lamar was a tall, broad African American man in his thirties, and he could be very intimidating when he wanted to be. As a volunteer peewee football coach, he prided himself on giving kids structure in their lives. "I'm very stern," he told me. "I don't take no BS. I don't negotiate with kids. I'm that coach. You know, the coach you stay away from if you get in trouble." Lamar also had a generous, affable side that came through during our two-hour conversation at a suburban shopping mall during his lunch break. But his commanding stance demanded respect, and he seemed able to turn his charm on and off at will.

Lamar's no-nonsense attitude was most apparent when he described his two-year effort to organize a neighborhood security patrol, an effort that drew him into a turf battle with a competing patrol group Lamar believed was corrupt. Under the police department's citizen patrol program, the police chief could certify one patrol group per neighborhood. Official recognition came with training sessions and access to a citywide $270,000 pot of money used to reimburse volunteers for mileage and incidentals.[12] The police chief had already certified another resident in Lamar's neighborhood as the president of their official patrol, but Lamar and his neighbors believed that man was filing fraudulent paperwork to collect reimbursements.

Lamar's elderly neighbor, Gloria, was a resident activist who decided to challenge the suspect group. She first tried to join them by recruiting new members she trusted would perform legitimate patrols. "And they'd kind of box her out," Lamar said. "Not having meetings. Not telling her when the meetings were. And Gloria's a really sweet, sweet girl. She's so sweet. And I would see her get so emotionally upset about how they're doing." Gloria eventually decided to patrol the neighborhood informally on her own. One evening, while her neighbors gathered in a local church for their monthly community meeting, she put a small yellow light on the top of her car and drove through the streets. "And Gloria was driving around," Lamar said, "and some kids threw a brick at her window. . . . And they hit her. Her eye was busted open or some such stuff." Two years had passed since the incident, but Lamar's voice still strained in anger. "That's how I got involved," he said. "Mainly because of Gloria. And I'm seeing her frustration. And I said, that could be my mom. That could be anybody's mom. Just being ran over and disrespected. So I really took issue with that and got involved because of Gloria."

Lamar approached the problem patiently and directly. "Along with Gloria," he said, "I got a group of people together. And I said, since they don't want to let us in, we'll build our product. That's what I taught them. Packaging the product." I asked for more details.

"They don't have bylaws? We'll have bylaws. They don't have meeting minutes? We'll have meeting minutes. They don't have organized patrols? We'll have organized patrols on our own." Lamar kept working for several months and recruited thirty-three neighbors to join his patrol, but "the city," he said, "they're still overlooking our program."

Lamar was unfazed. He kept a detailed record of volunteers' names, the dates they patrolled, the routes they followed, the protocols they implemented, the incidents they reported, and the planning meetings they attended. Then, with his paperwork in hand and with a meeting scheduled with the deputy police chief, he confronted the competing patrol president. "And I say, 'Well, I hate to see you and your other people get arrested for taking money from the city for something you're not doing.'" Lamar went to the meeting with about twenty people in tow and spread his paperwork on the table. The other president, who attended the meeting with only his girlfriend, announced he no longer had time to run the patrol and resigned his certification.

Lamar's heroic effort to build a community patrol resonated, up to a point, with the growing citywide movement toward community policing. Residents in most neighborhoods organized patrols of various kinds. Some residents eagerly embraced the official police model. In Grandmont Rosedale, for instance, a resident volunteer proudly proclaimed, "This area has the best radio patrol in the city!" During a ride along with two middle-aged white women, I learned they usually had cars circulating through the neighborhood a few dozen hours each week. Participants passed police background checks and attended police-run training programs. They attached magnetic patrol signs to their cars while driving, and they were not allowed to carry guns. Residents traveled in pairs, and they communicated by radio with a third volunteer who acted as a base station while they were out.

"What are you looking for?" I asked.

"With the [magnetic] sign out," the driver replied, "we're just another indication to people that people are watching." She said she had never seen a crime in progress and patrolling was just another way to perform watchfulness. Her patrol partner nodded, saying she used her patrol time to check on vacant homes, document cases of vandalism, and verify government officials had delivered on promised services. The driver agreed. "For my perspective," she said, "this is just another version of being eyes and ears. So when I go out, I'm not looking for anything. I'm just being out."

News reporters investigating community policing praised this patrol group as an inspiring success story, but it was also an unusual case. It operated in a comparatively affluent neighborhood with a strong neighborhood association, low vacancy rates, and low crime rates. The residents often discussed safety in us/them terms, which imposed an imagined distance between the supposedly law-abiding local residents and the externalized criminal elements they hoped to control. These features encouraged patrol-style security solutions, since the risks seemed minimal and the neighborhood appeared united.

In other neighborhoods people faced different risks and had different perceptions of criminality, and those differences discouraged residents from joining formal patrols. Residents in high-vacancy areas said the scale of scrapping made a few scattered hours of volunteer patrols irrelevant. Residents were even more hesitant to get involved with robberies or violent crimes, and people living next door to scrappers and drug dealers said it was impossible to play the cop a few hours a week and then expect their neighbors not to challenge them during the rest of the month. In those contexts official signs, slow speeds, and deliberate gazes felt dangerous. "Radio patrols work better in higher-income areas, where incidents are more isolated," one man told me. "In our area I don't want to make myself a target."

Resident distrust of the police department also limited participation. Instead of seeing citizen patrols as a two-way partnership, residents like Lamar said officers were more interested in controlling the volunteers than responding to their concerns. Even after spending two painstaking years building a patrol, Lamar and his neighbors intentionally dragged their feet in getting certified themselves. Many volunteers would not agree to criminal background checks. Volunteers said they felt exploited, since citizen patrollers did not receive priority attention over other 911 callers and since officers refused their requests to patrol certain streets at certain times of day. Even the promise of money seemed suspect. "I don't want to take anything from you without you giving the specifics," Lamar said. "I'm not that smart, but I'm not that dumb." He laughed derisively. "What am I actually signing up for? If . . . I'm taking money from you, I'm at your mercy."

Residents who were interested in community policing but who

also worried about attracting unwanted attention still watched their streets, but they worked informally. The aesthetic of informal watching while pretending to sweep stoops and sort junk mail did not create the same sense of vulnerability as flashing lights and official patrol signs. Even residents who volunteered with citizen patrols often developed domestic surveillance strategies, as well, and they moved easily back and forth between official patrols and informal watching.

» STREET BALLETS OF RESIDENT WATCHFULNESS

Floretta, an elderly African American woman, lived in a well-kept two-story brick home with symmetrical windows, bright-green grass, and a cheery flower garden framing her front door. She loved that door. It had a large glass window in the center and a clear glass storm door in front. "It's not a security door," she told me proudly. "It's transparent!" Floretta went shopping for her door in the suburbs. When the salesman learned she lived in Detroit, he steered her toward their metal security doors. "I was so upset," she said. "I went to the manager and said this salesman was making a value judgment that my neighborhood [and] my street was not safe for me to live on." Her eyes glistened as she spoke. "I don't like the way they look," she added. "It sends a bad signal and indicates that the neighborhood is not safe." Floretta refused to be part of a landscape of fear. She bought a clear glass door, and she was proud of what that door said about her community. "I don't need a security door," she told me. "We look out for each other."

Political activists in other cities like Los Angeles, San Diego, and Seattle have argued fear has become a new organizing logic of urban space. Privatized public spaces and increased police surveillance are cornerstones of postindustrial reurbanization that caters to affluent, white consumer tastes. Cities also figure as prime potential battlegrounds and contact zones in the contemporary era of social inequality and international terrorism.[13]

These trends toward militarized space were visible in Detroit, especially in neighborhoods where public officials and private developers were consolidating their investments. But most Detroit residents lived far away from the artifice of scripted street ballets in private malls and privatized plazas. Instead, resident watchers arranged domestic props and daily routines to self-organize eyes on the street.

Detroit residents were not unique. Urban planner James Rojas, for instance, describes Latino residents in marginalized Los Angeles neighborhoods who bring streetscapes to life in similar ways. "What may look like random groups of people," he writes, "are actually sets of well-ordered interactions in which everybody has a role. Children play, teenagers hang out, the elderly watch. These roles enhance the street activity and provide security for families, neighbors, and friends."[14] These practices are informal but predictable, and residents use them to create landscapes of mutuality, surveillance, and belonging.

Floretta's street was not like the one James Rojas described. Floretta did not know her neighbors' names. They did not spend time talking on street corners, and they did not visit each other's homes. But her street still had a rhythm and a pattern residents knew how to read. Floretta noticed when a neighbor stopped arriving home at the usual time every day, and her neighbors noticed when the man's yard began looking unkempt. Without ever discussing it, they began taking turns disguising the newly vacant house and maintaining the yard. Floretta also knew which neighbors she could call to start a phone tree alert if something happened on the block. And she kept her front door transparent as a symbol physical fortifications were unnecessary, because the neighbors were paying attention. There had never been an incident on her block, she said, not even a burglary or a loud argument in the street. Their security was built into the landscape and the street ballet that sustained it, and that was the way Floretta liked it.

7

Producing Local Knowledge

≫ RESIDENT RESEARCHERS

One warm spring evening in 2013, several dozen residents gathered in a rented multipurpose room for a community meeting. The neighbors brought food from their homes and gardens and spent twenty minutes chatting over their potluck meal before getting down to business. As the formal conversation began, residents discussed their ideas about how to reduce litter, improve relations with the county sheriff's office, and reduce scrap metal theft. The conversation then turned to two residents who were completing a parcel-by-parcel survey of the neighborhood to identify which homes were occupied, vacant, or damaged and which lots were repurposed or overgrown.

A resident raised his hand and asked whether the volunteer surveyors were also collecting ownership information, which was notoriously difficult to find in Detroit. His question prompted a lively debate about the self-fashioned strategies of sleuthing and espionage residents used to locate absentee owners and encourage them to take responsibility for their property. Some people preferred searching government records. Others had more luck talking with longtime neighbors and following local gossip chains. These resident sleuths quickly began swapping stories about the tactics that had worked for them in the past, the ones that had failed, and the publicly accessible databases that had helped them the most.

I had observed similar conversation in other neighborhoods, and I knew people's favorite research methods changed from month to month. That spring, residents were especially intrigued with the Wayne County treasurer's website, which included a feature allowing people to pay property taxes online. With two clicks anyone could enter the anonymous site for free and collect basic tax information on any address in the county. The resident leading the meeting explained how it worked. "It's easy," she told her neighbors. "While you're in there pretending to pay your taxes, you can type in a street name with an address range, or with no numbers at all, and get a whole list of who owns what on your street."

The website was not perfect. Some owners were identified only as "taxpayer." The site did not include contact information, and the data was often about six months out-of-date. The database also contained inaccuracies that could last several years. For example, if an owner died without a will, as long as friends, relatives, or squatters kept paying the taxes county officials generally left the situation alone. These were important limits, but many residents still used the website as a starting point to find out who was responsible for the neglected spaces on their blocks.

Market disinvestment and government contraction made official record keeping difficult in Detroit, and many social groups took advantage of that confusion. Owners who walked away from their property without filing change-of-address forms could abandon their land without incurring fines for the zoning infractions that ensued. Squatters and scrappers could take over empty homes where no one could legally prove they did not belong. And suburban politicians could tell sensationalized stories that vilified Detroit and steered investment dollars toward the suburbs without having to substantiate their facts.

These abuses prompted residents to gather their own information about property ownership and community traits. About half of the residents I interviewed (47 percent) participated in some way. Resident sleuthing was not new. Residents said there had always been busybodies on their blocks, people who had "been in the neighborhood or on the street for forever" and who "knew everything there was to know" about the buildings and people around them. But the economic crisis, housing shuffle, and municipal bankruptcy of the late 2000s and early 2010s brought resident research to a heightened pitch.

Resident researchers often mimicked government protocols—for instance, by surveying entire neighborhoods and making systematic maps and databases that conformed to industry standards and gave their data added legitimacy in officials' eyes. Domesticating state knowledge production was not, however, a straightforward process. Data collection involved filtering information by ignoring some characteristics to bring patterns of interest to light.[1] Resident sleuths who disguised vacant homes and created observable streets recorded different types of information about building conditions and street activity than did government administrators. Residents also used the information in different ways—for instance, by asking absentee owners to donate their homes or by blackmailing them into cutting their grass. Similarly, alongside records of blight and crime, resident researchers publicized neighborhood assets and community accomplishments that challenged negative stereotypes of their city.

Organizations were crucial partners supporting resident research. Most informal researchers routinely interacted with community organizations that used surveys, maps, statistics, and photographs in grant applications and advocacy campaigns. Neighborhoods with strong community groups were also the areas where resident researchers collected the most information and explored the broadest range of questions. These organizations encouraged knowledge creation, and they used their professional networks to share resident-generated data with a broad audience.

Some private companies advertised research services to residents, but most of the people I spoke with avoided fee-based products. In the fall of 2012, for example, residents were excited about a newly founded technology company with the stated mission of "putting America online parcel by parcel."[2] The company collected publicly available information from many government and market sources, and it consolidated the data in a user-friendly, map-based website that allowed users to select any property of interest to see who was listed as the taxpayer of record. The website was initially very popular among resident researchers, but after beta testing the site, the company began charging membership fees of $25 for individuals and $1,000 for organizations. No one I spoke with said they were willing to pay for the publicly available data, and the free Wayne County treasurer's website became the new favorite.

Invisibility is not always a problem. Peer-to-peer economic exchanges through garage sales and neighborhood babysitting arrangements have been around for decades, and many marginalized residents in U.S. cities rely on informal economies to make ends meet. Invisibility is risky, since it comes with few protections against exploitation and abuse, but government-sanctioned hierarchies of class, race, and citizenship sometimes make formal, regulated markets more dangerous than informal alternatives.[3]

These tensions were evident in Detroit. For example, poor government record keeping inadvertently fueled the seizures of side lots and the creation of urban gardens that were technically illegal but that repurposed blight and strengthened community ties. But invisibility cut both ways, leaving gardeners and caretakers vulnerable to displacement.[4] Similarly, residents lacking the resources to keep their homes code compliant benefitted from limited environmental inspections, but those same code enforcement oversights also allowed slumlords to perpetuate gross violations that undercut neighborhood stability.

Knowledge about the city improved living conditions indirectly by creating stronger foundations for general activism. Resident researchers helped solve problems governments were not addressing or neighbors preferred to solve using different means. They helped community groups make more effective use of limited resources and coordinate self-provisioning among neighbors. Resident researchers and their organizational partners also challenged the negative stereotypes encouraging disinvestment in Detroit. These counternarratives did not reverse structural disinvestment, but it helped residents see their communities in a more hopeful light, which encouraged self-provisioning and other forms of activism.

» THE (UN)KNOWN CITY

Local knowledge has a tense relationship with legacies of centralized, standardized, Anglo-European statecraft. Governments can tax, conscript, and punish only the people they can find, and predicting future conditions is crucial to strategic decision making. Standardized laws about land, trade, and citizenship played an important role in the rise of modern nation states and in industrial-era urban growth. Zoning laws and building codes that reduced irregularities in street grids and land uses made service delivery more efficient and made real estate speculation more profitable. Parcel maps, deed registries, tax receipts, and residency laws created the paper trails urban administrators needed to locate residents in space and hold them accountable for taxes and property maintenance.[5]

Standardized environments and government records are important, but they are only one way people come to know a place. Photographers, novelists, advertisers, and journalists create images and narratives that inform public perceptions about what cities and neighborhoods are like. Physical details like architectural styles, building materials, and public art also communicate information about a city's development history, political priorities, and social hierarchies. Residents learn about places through direct experiences, as well; experiences they interpret through culturally specific—not universal—cognitive frames.[6] These overlapping and sometimes competing ways of knowing the world are always selective, inaccurate, and biased. These limits do not make one worldview inherently better or worse than another, but they do mean different modes of knowledge engender different capacities for action.

Detroit has the reputation of being both underdocumented and oversensationalized. Urban planners have said that compared with cities like Chicago and Cleveland, "Detroit is notoriously bad at keeping its property records up to date."[7] Market disinvestment and municipal contraction make this task especially difficult. Budget constraints discourage administrators from upgrading computer software to more powerful and accessible programs, and cash-strapped municipalities have trouble keeping pace with rapidly changing property markets.[8]

Record keeping is even harder when people have financial incentives to avoid municipal oversight. Residents who take over land without buying it are invisible from the municipality's perspective. Some of these residents would prefer to buy the land if they could find the owner and get a clean title, but others intentionally avoid formal ownership to avoid higher property taxes and maintenance liabilities. Absentee owners who walk away from property or who inherit property they do not want use their invisibility to avoid paying taxes and fines. These reluctant or hostile owners also use their invisibility to encourage government officials to foreclose on unwanted property, which transfers maintenance costs from private owners to the state.

Institutional and government actors exploit local knowledge gaps, as well. Banks that do not want to invest in Detroit's predominantly low-income communities of color use dubious property appraisal methods to justify refusing mortgage applications.[9] Similarly, politicians in neighboring counties use exaggerated statistics of vacancy and crime to steer new investment dollars away from the city and into the suburbs—for instance, by saying Detroit has forty square miles of vacant land, an unscrupulous but widely cited statistic that inaccurately counts nineteen square miles of parks, cemeteries, and landscaped boulevards as "vacant."[10] Detroit politicians play this game, too—for instance, by saying Detroit has 79,700 vacant housing units, a high number that nevertheless excludes the 33,000 abandoned housing structures that have holes in walls and roofs but are otherwise still standing.[11]

These elusive land practices and slippery statistics undermine efforts to stem disinvestment. It is difficult to answer factual questions such as how much land is empty and who is responsible for maintaining it. Public disagreement only intensifies over matters of opinion, like deciding how much money a house is worth and which structures should be demolished first. In this contested context, socially conscious investors trying to buy vacant property to interrupt cycles of decay spend months trying to locate elusive owners and obtain clear titles only to see the properties stripped and burned before the transaction is complete. Knowledge distortions also harm community organizations renovating housing—for instance, when banks using unfair market comparisons artificially deflate property value assessments and refuse to provide willing buyers with adequate mortgages.

Resident self-provisioners suffer, as well. Elena, the Latina stay-at-home mom whose husband mowed five city-owned lots, wanted to buy the lots to build a large vegetable garden. But after fourteen months of phone calls, officials were still unable to produce the necessary paperwork. "The city's giving me a hard time," Elena explained. "I tell them, 'It's on B— [Street].' And they're like, 'You need to have the address. If you don't have the address, we can't help you.' OK. So I basically have to argue with them to get them to help me. I'm like, 'I don't know the addresses, because there's no existing houses on there. What am I going to do, make up an address? I don't know. I just know it's on B— [Street] and P— [Street]. And I can tell you the address of the house next door to it, so maybe you guys can figure it out. You're the city. You should have the parcel numbers and all that.' And they're like, 'Well, you have to call so-and-so,' or 'so-and-so is taking care of it.' OK. 'So can I get so-and-so's number?' I get so-and-so's number. I get a voice mail. Full. I call [again]. I leave a message. They don't call me back." Elena sighed, shaking her head. "It's not working. It's really frustrating."

Experiences like Elena's reflected the limits of state-based record keeping in Detroit. Residents were used to thinking of the municipality as a repository of local knowledge, as it was during the twentieth-century period of centralized technocratic governing. But times had changed. City administrators in the early 2010s often expected residents to provide them with technical information like parcel numbers and owners' names rather than vice versa. This role reversal encouraged residents and community organizations to develop knowledge-making initiatives of their own. These initiatives shed new light on neighborhood conditions, helped residents access scarce government resources, and encouraged alternative forms of self-provisioning and activism.

» COMMUNITY-ORGANIZED MAPPING PROJECTS

The confusions, distortions, and evasions just described may give the impression of a fundamentally unknowable city, but this was not the case. Community-driven knowledge projects were under way in every neighborhood I studied, and residents used their self-made knowledge to address a wide range of local concerns. Community organizations were crucial in encouraging resident researchers and disseminating their findings. Organizations sometimes tried to replicate the comprehensive property databases municipal officials once assembled, but those groups encountered the same financial and practical problems government officials faced. Instead, the knowledge-making practices that gained the most traction were the ones that moved away from outdated visions of bird's-eye-view statecraft and instead responded to the situated priorities of local residents.

On the more formal end of the spectrum, nonprofit organizations like Data Driven Detroit completed citywide surveys and data analysis for government offices and charitable foundations. Their 2009 and 2014 property surveys, for instance, provided the most authoritative aggregate statistics on housing conditions and vacancy rates citywide.[12] Public officials with the Mayor's Office, Planning and Development Department, and Land Bank Authority routinely used that data to guide funding and policy decisions, as did private charities like the Skillman Foundation, Kellogg Foundation, Kresge Foundation, and Ford Foundation. These snapshots helped city leaders and their nonprofit partners shape long-term development and service agendas, but the tumultuous economy meant the information quickly became out-of-date. The surveys also excluded categories of information residents and community-based organizations wanted to know, such as who owned which buildings and which structures were associated with illegal activity.

To overcome these limits, many smaller organizations instigated mapping projects of their own. Emerging technology made this work easier but also contested. In 2012, for example, several community groups were excited the national nonprofit organization Code for America was considering developing an online "blexting" (blight texting) tool to allow volunteers with smart phones or tablets to submit property information online and have that data automatically entered into a citywide spreadsheet. One significant problem, though, was that Code for America was philosophically committed to open-source platforms, which meant their software and the maps it generated had to be made publicly accessible. This requirement undercut enthusiasm for the project because community organizations and the residents with whom they worked did not want to expose the vacancies neighbors worked so hard to disguise.[13]

Community organizations did not abandon the goal of real-time mapping and instead developed internal protocols they could complete and control independently. One especially comprehensive example from my field notes involved David, a white AmeriCorps volunteer who worked for a small community-based nonprofit. David was not from Detroit. He moved to Michigan in 2012, rented an apartment in the suburbs, and moved out of state the following year to take a job with an investment firm. Despite his transience, as a nonprofit employee David had access to more specialized software and charitable grants than most residents. During his brief stay, David was one of many nonprofit employees working to create local alternatives to the municipality's unreliable and outdated property databases.

The community organization where David worked was completing a community visioning process at the time. Large foundations required community groups to create these reports documenting neighborhood strengths, weaknesses, and development priorities as a prerequisite for funding and logistical support. David's organization convened a special housing working group as part of the process, and that group asked the organization to make weekly property surveys a top priority. I played a minor role in jump-starting the project by connecting a university internship coordinator with a local business donor who helped the community organization hire a summer intern for David's office. The intern recruited volunteers to survey over six thousand properties in the neighborhood. Those volunteers assigned every building a series of numbers to indicate whether it was occupied and to describe its physical condition.

"How many volunteers did you have?" I asked.

"I'd say that there were maybe twenty volunteers," David replied. The paid intern also did a lot of the work himself. "So if there was no volunteers one day, he might just go out and spend a few hours just walking up and down the streets."

With the survey pages in hand, David entered the data into a centralized spreadsheet and used a pilot version of a free online Google software program to create a password-protected map showing neighborhood conditions. "So just by looking," he said, pointing at a color-coded housing map on his computer screen, "you can know these blue ones are in good condition, these green ones are in fair condition, the yellow ones are in poor condition, and the red ones are in need of demo[lition]. Or let's say I went on to lawn condition," he said with a click of his mouse. "Over the summer we had a mow-a-thon where we went out and tried to mow up these yards." He zoomed in. "Maybe there's a block where it's really bad, six or eight properties in a row that need to be mowed. So it can make an easy way of saying, 'OK, we can focus here today.'" He panned to another view. "Or maybe it's just one lot, and we can say, 'Alright, we have one lot here. Between you six neighbors, can we work out a way of having one of you neighbors mowing it every two weeks?'"

David presented a filtered version of the map at a public community meeting to great applause. The next day, his AmeriCorps term expired, and he moved to Indiana. He told me he hoped the mapping project would continue after he left, since getting the base map established was so labor intensive. But the organization lacked the funding to hire a dedicated person to update the map on a weekly basis or to coordinate a response to the pictures that emerged. These challenges underscored the lingering question of whether community organizations had the resources to sustain intensive data collection and whether the information they generated helped solve local problems. In the meantime resident researchers had ample reason to instigate additional research projects of their own and to adapt their working methods to align with other self-provisioning goals.

» EARL, THE NEIGHBORHOOD SURVEYOR

"There's no light," Earl said, scrutinizing the house through his windshield. "Some foot traffic. It looks like somebody's been driving up in here or something. Like maybe they park their cars there." He shook his head. "Doesn't look like anybody's living in there. But sometimes you can't always tell." Earl was dictating. I wrote his comments on a piece of paper and added a fresh form to the clipboard as he rolled the car forward to the next house. "I see cars in the driveway sometime," he said. "They got one of the Courville [municipal trash cans]. They do have foot traffic goin' in from yesterday [after the snowfall]. And some car traffic going in. So I'm assuming somebody's there." I wrote it down, and he rolled forward. "Now, what I think is still vacant is this house," he said. "I think the neighbors drive up," putting tire tracks in the driveway to disguise vacancy. "I don't know if this is occupied now or not. But I'd put it as 'unknown.'" I wrote it down. He rolled the car forward. Three houses done, nearly one thousand to go.

Earl was a soft-spoken African American man and former public school district employee. After retiring he became an active volunteer with his neighborhood association. "I just work all the time," he told me. "I don't serve in an official capacity. But as a volunteer you gotta treat it just like a job, even though you're not gettin' paid." We met during a task force meeting of resident volunteers who were working to reduce vacancy-related blight in their neighborhood. At that meeting the group decided to survey the six-thousand-plus housing structures in their area to identify how many homes were vacant and which of them showed signs of decay or vandalism. The volunteers divided the streets among themselves, and I offered to help Earl on his round, since his usual patrol partner was out of town. A few weeks later, with fresh snow on the ground and a stack of xerox paper in our laps, we sat in Earl's car visually inspecting hundreds of homes, one by one.

Resident volunteers in other neighborhoods made similar maps. They usually toured the streets on foot with markers and colored pens, making notes on preprinted copies of digital street maps. One such informal surveyor explained how it worked. "It involves having an eye for whether the windows and siding are intact and in good condition," she said, "and spotting open spots in the walls" where people, animals, or rain could get inside. She and her survey partner assigned each property a color code based on its occupancy status and physical condition. The nonprofit organization Data Driven Detroit then helped them digitize the information on a base map that made their notes look more official and made the information easier to distribute to key decision makers.

These maps helped residents secure grants and municipal services. Municipal demolition campaigns in 2012 and 2013, for instance, asked for "community input" in deciding which structures to raze, but administrators gave residents only a couple weeks to submit their feedback. "It's always like that with government," Mara, the gardening social reformer, complained. "By the time we hear about it and they say they want community input, the money is already over." Community groups with credible-looking, resident-generated, comprehensive surveys and maps could submit those documents as "systematic, up-to-date data that the city or state would trust," which helped them get money otherwise spent somewhere else.

Resident property surveys were less common than other self-provisioning strategies, like disguising vacant homes and mowing city-owned lots, but they were more comprehensive and strategic. Documenting housing conditions across several blocks or entire neighborhoods covered a larger geographic terrain. Resident surveyors standardized their working methods, and they recorded data on locally shared logs and maps. Many residents kept detailed files on individual problem properties, as well, but larger surveys created more complete records of the surrounding environment.

Surveying involved time spent away from home with no immediately tangible benefit, so usually only resident volunteers connected with local organizations attempted the work. Organizations

Figure 11. Residents discussing neighborhood land use with neighbors. Photograph courtesy of Neighbors Building Brightmoor.

encouraged resident surveyors by explaining how the organizations could use the data for strategic decision making. Organizations also helped volunteers streamline the workload by educating residents about what to look for, providing pens and photocopying support, and connecting residents with citywide nonprofits that synthesized the findings. Organizations also connected residents with donors, administrators, and politicians who could act on the data they generated.

Only a few residents completed surveys independently. One of Earl's neighbors, for example, an African American retiree, was frustrated with the bulk waste on her block. She took a pad of paper and surveyed every commercial property on a nearby cross street, making a list of addresses where shopkeepers were improperly storing debris. She repeated the survey for the residential properties on her street, and she gave both lists to municipal code enforcement officers for follow-up. Another resident, an older white man in Earl's volunteer group, was concerned about rats, so he and a neighbor "went on a campaign to canvas the entire neighborhood and try and assess what the situation was." They visually surveyed several blocks around their homes, identifying potential food sources and nest locations, and they passed the information along to the city.

Whether working alone or in groups, domesticating mapmaking involved important shifts in the information collected and the actions that followed. Resident surveyors like Earl made notes about bulk waste in front yards, snow accumulating on sidewalks, and structurally damaged front porches, just as municipal code enforcement officers would do. But Earl also noted whether he saw footprints in the snow, a clue to whether the house was vacant. He scrutinized roofs to identify which homes needed new occupants most urgently to avoid costly water damage. Earl also recorded the names and phone numbers on every rental sign, security plaque, and foreclosure notice he saw, creating his own paper trail he and other residents could use to trace absentee owners and request property maintenance in the future.

Resident surveyors also approached "unknowns" differently than did city inspectors. Environmental officers issuing citations used municipal records to identify owners. If that information was inaccurate—for instance, if the owner had died or the mailing address was incorrect—the court officer hearing those cases automatically dismissed the citations. Officers could write new tickets if they found updated information, but they were limited to official sources. Earl, by contrast, used the local memory of longtime neighbors to find out who owned what and where they lived. Whenever he saw a building he was unsure about, he asked me to make a note for him to "check with some of the neighbors. I try to meet one or more neighbors on each block," he explained, "and get to know them and get their phone numbers and stuff. I can call. We can share information." This local knowledge was not valid in court, but it helped him and his neighbors find elusive owners and informally encourage them to change their practices.

» CONNIE, THE COMMUNITY-SANCTIONED EXTORTIONIST

Connie, the barricading booby-trapper, believed the best way to solve trenchant problems was to find mutually agreeable solutions. The problem, though, was residents in her neighborhood found little common ground with the absentee owners and landlords she felt were responsible for the disinvestment around her. The trick, she said, was to reframe the question so reluctant parties would decide it was in their best interest to "do the right thing." Connie called it "shaming." Another word might be "blackmail."

Connie used this strategy with her own landlord after one of the two furnaces in her basement exploded. "It was building up gas and wasn't voiding," she said. She tried to repair it, but the pilot light from the water tank caught the gas on fire, and the furnace blew up in her face. "I think I had a slight concussion from the back blast," she said laughing. "I wasn't quite right for a couple of days."

Connie called her landlord to negotiate his response. Reflecting on the conversation, she told me she explained to him why he wanted to pay to have the second furnace inspected. "Since I've been here," she said, recalling her side of their conversation, "you've never had any of these units inspected. And I know you're not registered with the city of Detroit. I'm not trying to create all kinds of financial grief and make you pay the fee every year to have your property inspected [or to have] lead paint inspected when there's no children in the house. But," she added, "given that one furnace just blew up in my face, we're going to have a safety inspection of the second furnace." The implication was clear. Either the landlord could pay for the inspection, or she would alert the city to his illegal rental operation and he would have to start paying for rental licenses and lead paint tests. She got the furnace inspection.

On another occasion, Connie used this strategy to convince a "slum landlord" to evict "problem" tenants on her block. "We got into the landlords stuff," she said. "We told him his whole history and how he was money laundering for the drug operation in exclusively renting to them. And [we said] that we were going to do informational pickets at his pizzeria and his car wash and let all the residents know. Or," she added, "he could not rent." She knew landlords had trouble finding qualified tenants, and she did not promise him someone better would come along. Instead, given the severity of the problems the residents were facing, she wanted him to walk away from the property and let the community take it over. "You can keep on doing what you're doing," she told him, "and all your customers will know. Or you can take this operation off our street." He terminated the rental agreement. The evicted tenants were angry. They broke into the house and squatted there for a few days. When they eventually left, Connie boarded the house, and the city demolished it a couple years later.

Connie's strategy of threatening to share sensitive information illustrated how residents used all sorts of pressure points to address problems of nuisance and blight. Only the most fortunate residents felt they could turn to the municipality for help. Earl's neighbor who surveyed her street and gave the information to code enforcement officers was one such resident. "It does work," she said. Even though the city was officially bankrupt, "there's been a gradual cleaning up around the neighborhood. It takes seven to ten days for them to get out and issue a citation. But it does work."

For other residents, asking municipal officials for help was a luxury they could not afford. One group of Latino residents I met on the street explained the problem clearly. The three homeowners were part of an extended family who bought rundown homes on the same block and renovated them by hand. Their relatively well-maintained properties contrasted sharply with several intermixed vacant structures that had large holes in their roofs and walls and extensive vandalism visible from the sidewalk. Frustrated with the decay, one of the men called the city and asked code enforcement officers for help. A few days later, the responding officer issued citations for the dilapidated buildings, but he also fined the complainer for not having a rain gutter on his roof and the man's sister for using an unpainted board to patch a hole in her siding.

The neighbors were irate. The man who called the officer for help called him a "blatant henchman fining everyone up and down the street." He added, indignantly, "as though my house was the problem!" He described the hours of manual labor he spent renovating his home, transforming the once-decaying building into a fairly immaculate house. He emphasized the absurdity of caring about a rain gutter in the middle of winter when it did not rain. His sister nodded, adding she had intentionally delayed repairing the hole in her siding because she wanted to save money to replace all the siding at once. They felt the city was ungrateful for their efforts and unable to distinguish between genuine blight and issues of taste.

Conversations like these underscored the risks involved in asking officials for help. Many low-income residents living in non–code compliant property did not want to invite officials to tour their blocks. Residents who were afraid officers might arrest or deport them or their neighbors also avoided making formal complaints. Some disaffected residents simply believed formal citations made no difference. "This is the city's response," one man told me, showing me a photograph he had taken of a municipal blight violation notice stapled to the front door of a falling-down house. "Posting this sign that no owner will ever see, fining someone they'll never be able to locate." For these residents, Connie reasoned, if they wanted land-lords and absentee owners to change their behaviors, the residents would have to make it happen themselves.

Some residents "pestered" owners, which sometimes worked. A white woman in Earl's neighborhood, for instance, was concerned about a dying tree on the vacant property next door. It took several months of searching to find the Idaho-based management company responsible for the home and several more months of phone calls to get them to take action. "I called them," she said, "and I harassed them. I pestered them every day. The file was here. When I got up every morning, it was like going to the office. I picked it up. I called them. I said, 'What are you going to do about this tree? It has to be removed.' Finally, after three or four months, they came. They did re-move the tree." The management company eventually honored her re-quest, but it took a significant amount of time and energy on her part.

Most residents who asked owners and managers to maintain property felt ignored or rebuffed. The woman who patched her sid-ing with an unpainted board, for example, used the local memory of older residents on her block to find the man who owned the van-dalized house next door. She called him on the phone, she recalled, "to tell him that he had citations" and to ask him "to come out and clean the property up and do the mowing. And he just laughed." The memory of his derisiveness brought tears to her eyes. Other hos-tile owners verbally intimidated the neighbors who complained and threatened them if they called the police. Most often, absentee own-ers passively ignored residents' requests, or the token assistance they offered made no lasting improvement.

Connie, the blackmailing booby-trapper, was unique in her un-flinching, creative approach to these seemingly intractable problems. Not long after threatening one landlord on her block with an infor-mational picket, she convinced another absentee owner to improve his property maintenance. She was frustrated with the deteriorating quality of a nearby vacant house, and she traced its owner to an up-scale suburb outside Detroit. The owner refused her initial request to improve maintenance and make basic repairs, so Connie made an "informational flier" containing a photograph of the house and a note reading, "This is what your neighbor is doing in Detroit." She distributed the flier to his neighbors in the suburbs. As a strategy, she said, "shaming the owner into doing the right thing works really well in finally getting them to fix up, or to sell."

Like Connie, many residents searched for informal pressure points to encourage reluctant owners to contribute to neighborhood upkeep. Some residents searched property databases to see whether the people who owned vacant units on their block also owned active rental properties elsewhere they could threaten with code inspections unless the owner addressed their maintenance concerns. Some people who volunteered with neighborhood associations threatened to print the names and addresses of people with code violations in association newsletters unless the owners fixed the problems within a certain number of days. Other residents searched tax records to see if foreclosure proceedings were likely, which helped them decide whether to continue pushing for owner involvement or start planning for the property's future reuse.

These practices emphasized the importance of creative information exchange in encouraging neighborhood upkeep. Pestering managers and blackmailing owners were negative, short-term interactions, but they solved certain problems. They also existed alongside a more general trend of resident efforts to document their neighborhood and, when possible, publicize community strengths and inspire neighborhood pride.

» DEBORAH, THE NEIGHBORHOOD PUBLICIST

"People who don't know about Detroit or who have never visited," Deborah said, "when they come to our neighborhood, . . . they were like, 'This is Detroit? You mean this is outside Detroit!'" Deborah was thinking especially about her kids' college-aged friends who visited from North Carolina and Washington, D.C. "I said, 'No, this is Detroit!' People are just taken back because what they see on TV doesn't match the reality of the variety of homes and neighborhoods that we have." Deborah paused, breathing deeply. "Of course, we have some horrible blight areas," she said, "and we don't have to go but a half a minute from here to see that. But I think the challenge that we have is letting people know that there are a variety of options here."

Deborah was an African American woman in her fifties, and she worked for a community organization a few blocks from her home. She had lived in her house for over thirty years and wanted to downsize. "I don't really need a house as big as I have right now, just for me and my husband," she said, but it was not a good time to sell. The vacant house next door was on the market for $39,000. "That's a disgrace," Deborah said, shaking her head. "At one time, our home was valued at almost $300,000. So that's so scary. I'm not giving my house away for no $39,000."

Deborah described the property market as a public relations problem. She was confident in the architectural quality of the neighborhood. Her house had four bedrooms, three-and-a-half baths, and two fireplaces. "They don't make homes like that anymore." Deborah also liked the neighborhood's high-quality landscaping. "Our grass is like carpet, in the front and the back." The challenge, from her perspective, was to get the word out and let people know high-quality homes in well-maintained areas existed in Detroit. Young adults with high living costs in places like Boston and San Francisco were her prime audience. "They come here, and they see our homes, and they see what the prices are. 'Oh my god!' It's something they have more appreciation for, I think, than a lot of Detroiters [who] take a lot of it for granted."

Residents like Deborah emphasized the importance of sharing positive images and "normal" stories to counter the maelstrom of negative media sensationalizing Detroit and to bring new people and resources onto their blocks. On a recent trip to the state capital in Lansing, Deborah brought along photographs and brochures of homes in her area to share with her state representative's office. "They were looking at the literature with their mouths hanging open," she said. "'Are these pictures of homes in Detroit?' I went, 'Oh my god!'" She rolled her eyes. "Those are the kinds of things that just really makes you angry, and also disappointed that people just have the most negative view. That's not *all* that's here. There's other things that are going on in Detroit. They're not *all* blight, and they're not *all* falling down." She laughed unhappily. For her, showing people the positive side of Detroit was as much about overcoming injustice as it was about combating ignorance. "Somebody's marketing strategy is to make Detroit not look so great," she said, "because the suburbs . . . . What's the point of having all that urban sprawl if Detroit is *all that*?"

Many residents citywide made a point of "telling the good," but people framed those narratives differently depending on their context. Deborah's approach reflected her life experiences in a comparatively stable neighborhood with culturally valued period architecture and household incomes sufficient to maintain high standards of maintenance and landscaping. Her insistence on recognizing neighborhood variety implied that some parts of Detroit genuinely embodied the blight, vandalism, and violence the media described but that not every neighborhood was like that. Deborah's critique differentiated her neighborhood from the rest of the city, setting it up as an exception to the rule.

For residents living in neighborhoods where people had fewer resources to spend on bent-grass lawns, double-fireplace homes, and strong neighborhood associations, it was more difficult to argue the absence of blight. Camille and Mara, for instance, lived in one of Detroit's most heavily abandoned neighborhoods where residents were turning neglected spaces into gardens and art pieces. Their physical environment all too easily provided evidence of the blight that was nearly absent from Deborah's street, but that blight did not stop them from publicizing community strengths. On the contrary, sharing positive images despite evidence of decay was central to resident researchers' strategies of neighborhood empowerment.

Community newsletters and resident-authored editorials illustrated this process. Widely publicized government and media reports often described neighborhoods like Camille's and Mara's using statistical counts of the number of people who were minorities, unemployed, disabled, impoverished, alcoholic, and on welfare. These categories—applied without reference to the history of socially produced inequality—contributed to dubious denouncements of marginalized residents as drains on collective resources.[14]

Resident activists wrote articles countering these portrayals. One such article in a neighborhood newsletter described the fictitious Mrs. Jones, a stand-in for the average neighborhood resident, who the author conceded was ill, poor, and black but whose identity was not defined by those characteristics. "Mrs. Jones is the person who neighbors go to when they are in trouble. She listens, counsels, feeds them fried chicken and uses her old donated car to bring them to the ER."

Another resident wrote a similar editorial that appeared in the *Detroit Free Press*. The author criticized the newspaper for publishing photographs that made his neighborhood "look as if it's all an empty wasteland. There are vacant lots and abandoned houses," he wrote, "but there are also many examples of how neighborhood organizations . . . have repurposed those properties into gardens and pocket parks and gathering spaces and places of art. When will those efforts be recognized and celebrated?"[15]

The differences between Deborah's neighborhood and Mara's meant residents in areas like the latter did not have the same ability as those in the former to distance themselves from discourses of blight, so they used different strategies when "telling the good." These differences were important, but their narratives intersected in residents' shared assertion that disinvestment and social problems were only one part of Detroit's story. Their communities had strengths that went unreported, and many residents became self-proclaimed publicists sharing positive messages about their city. They took photographs of community strengths. They generated statistics that measured neighborhood vitality. They led reporters, city council members, and foundation donors on show-and-tell tours. And they made brochures and scrapbooks that preserved a record of success and illustrated it for outsiders.

Resident researchers were strategic in the positive information they collected, building on personal experiences to challenge misinformation that harmed their communities. Deborah, for example, did not believe media reports that crime in Detroit was rampant. "Once we started doing some homework and some research," she told me, "we actually found out that our [neighborhood] crime rate was actually lower than some of the surrounding [suburban] areas like Redford and Livonia. But of course, nobody was talking about that." Deborah also refused to believe every urban school was failing. Her kids had attended public schools, and they received scholarships to elite universities. She wanted potential homebuyers to know their kids could have similar opportunities, so she made a list of dozens of

Detroit schools that received high statewide rankings, and she gave that list to local neighborhood associations to include in their real estate promotional packets.

Another group of residents made a similar information packet to give to judges who might have stigmas about Detroit. These residents worried that authorities with negative views of the city would treat victims of crime inside Detroit as less deserving of government protection than suburban victims. They wrote a cover letter to go with their self-generated photographs, statistics, and descriptions of neighborhood strengths, and they gave copies to judges hearing criminal cases connected to their community. The goal, one woman told me, was "to influence sentencing so the judge will be less likely to let the criminal walk or will go to the higher end of the sentencing guidelines bracket rather than the lower end." These documents combined positive images of place with visions of an organized, engaged citizenry who deserved state protection.

Residents also self-generated numbers and statistics to underscore the scale of community accomplishments. One resident's standard show-and-tell tour of her neighborhood included "fifty gardens, parks, and points of interest," which came out to "two-and-a-half projects per block." Another resident counted the twenty-five years he and his neighbors spent demolishing 113 abandoned homes, as well as the 15,500 pounds of nails, 15,470 sheets of plywood, and 21,000 gallons of paint they used to secure vacant structures. Another man counted the sixty vacant buildings he boarded in two years. Residents counted the four dumpsters of 20,000 tons of trash 156 outside volunteers cleaned from public spaces during large volunteer events, as well as the 372 trash bags seventy neighborhood residents filled during smaller cleanups and the 483 neighborhood residents who adopted vacant homes. These statistics quantified volunteerism, and the numbers provided a direct counterpoint to state-generated statistics of vacancy, dependency, and blight.

Residents shared this information with neighbors to boost morale and encourage more people to self-provision the city. Organizations helped, as well, by hosting award banquets and neighborhood parties where residents could share their information with each other and with the press. Residents honored unsung heroes at these events. They displayed before-and-after photographs of adopted homes

Figure 12. Resident volunteer showing neighborhood accomplishments to city officials, potential donors, and researchers. Photograph courtesy of Neighbors Building Brightmoor.

and repurposed lots. Organizations also printed programs for these events that put resident-generated data into a more official format with a longer shelf life. These positive stories, photographs, numbers, and archives painted a positive picture of Detroit that recentered negative discourses of blight and crime and promoted uplifting images of high-quality living environments and vibrant communities.

» SLEUTHS, PUBLICISTS, AND THE POWER OF LOCAL KNOWLEDGE

Phrases like *local knowledge* and *situated awareness* emphasize the incomplete nature of public information. States and markets generate some knowledge, but the worldviews they describe are always partial. They focus on some characteristics, ignore others, and may say very little about how the world came to be that way. Community activists with different experiences and agendas produce other—often competing—knowledge claims that help marginalized groups challenge institutional oppression and engender new capacities for action.[16]

These esoteric theories would probably not surprise resident researchers like Earl, Connie, and Deborah. They knew maps, surveys, and statistics looked objective, and they knew photographs and personal details made that data feel real. But numbers lied, maps obscured, and photographs were cropped. Earl, Connie, and Deborah did not challenge the validity of those mediums of communication, but they were determined to challenge the partial worldviews those sources portrayed as universal truth. Instead of mapping the city every five years, they toured their blocks every week. Alongside government databases, they valued local memories and gossip. And instead of counting only problems, they also counted solutions. Their intimate modes of knowing shaped the way they approached their city and the self-provisioning strategies that emerged.

Local knowledge was not neutral. It was as partial and political as the institutional facts it challenged. The primary difference was less about accuracy and more about utility. Bird's-eye views aggregated lumpy information into clean, standardized measures officials could use to guide broad policies and outsiders could use to denigrate Detroit. Resident research, however, helped neighbors maintain the spaces markets ignored. It helped them hold absentee owners accountable that governments could not find. It helped residents recruit new neighbors, reduce physical blight, and predict future risks. It also helped residents bring more municipal and charitable resources into their communities. This local knowledge did not automatically reverse long-standing regional prejudices and structural inequalities. But as an act of self-representation, it did create opportunities for residents to see their neighborhoods in a hopeful light that encouraged residents to reinvest, physically and emotionally, in their community.

Conclusion

Triumphs of Hope over Reason

In March 2014 the cash-strapped Detroit Water and Sewerage Department began cutting water service to 350 residential customers per day. The department was $90 million in debt. The residents were mostly low-income minorities who owed at least $150 in utility fees or whose bills were at least two months overdue. Commercial and industrial facilities with debts in the tens of thousands were unaffected. Many families received no notification before their service was terminated. Renters suffered when negligent landlords failed to pay their bills on time. Parents and teachers instructed children to keep quiet about service interruptions because the state's Child Protective Services program could remove children from homes that lacked running water. By the end of October, an estimated 27,000 households had experienced service interruptions, and the Water and Sewerage Department was disconnecting between 1,500 and 3,000 new households every week. A year later in September 2015, tensions remained high as antishutoff activist groups faced budget shortfalls and as the city moved forward with plans to terminate water service to an additional twenty to twenty-five thousand households.[1]

Inadequate water and sewer service is a significant global problem, but until recently, it was extremely rare in industrialized countries. Municipal governments built public water and sewer systems in most large U.S. cities during the late nineteenth and early twentieth centuries to protect industrial investors and their workers from disruptive fires and diseases. These national trends were evident in Detroit, where city leaders purchased their first public waterworks in 1835, opened the world's then-largest water filtration plant in 1923, and built the nation's third-largest water department by the century's end.[2] These physical projects created the impetus to transform the size and role of local governments. Small private municipalities that coordinated trade and business interests before this sanitation movement were reinvented as public municipalities with large bureaucracies, new economic capabilities, and the legal authority to implement general health and safety projects.[3]

Despite these historical gains, the problem of living without running water is resurfacing in many industrialized countries. When authorities in England and Wales partially privatized their water infrastructure in the mid-1990s, vulnerable social groups who could not afford to pay rising prices experienced service interruptions and health problems until the government resumed control in the early 2000s. Similar events occurred in Berlin, Atlanta, and New Orleans over the following decade, and cash-strapped governments enacted water-privatization measures in Spanish, Greek, Portuguese, and Italian cities during the Great Recession. When water cutoffs came to Detroit in 2014, protestors in Dublin organized solidarity marches to underscore the rising transnational concern about preserving affordable access to life-sustaining services across Europe and North America.[4]

Activists in Detroit responded to the water cuts with a combination of public protests, relief efforts, and legal interventions. From May through August, protestors organized weekly demonstrations in front of the water department and city hall at which they demanded restored services and moratoriums against future cutoffs. Their protests attracted national media attention. Activists from other states came to Detroit and created grassroots organizations like the Detroit Water Brigade to collect donations of cash and bottled water for affected households. These organizations also negotiated payment plans to get water services restored more quickly.[5]

Activists filed lawsuits, but those legal challenges inadvertently reinforced the water department's position. Since the city was in bankruptcy, elected officials like the mayor and city council members had no legal authority to intervene in the water department's operations. The federal judge overseeing the bankruptcy proceedings eventually heard the case. In September he ruled that although water was a necessary ingredient to sustaining life and although living without water did irreparable harm, Detroit could not afford revenue shortages and Detroit residents did not have a fundamental right to free or affordable water—or, for that matter, affordable shelter, food, or medical care.[6] The decision prompted a visit from United Nations officials who issued a statement saying that disconnecting water services due to lack of payment and lack of means to pay constituted a human rights violation. Despite this international criticism, the water shutoffs continued.[7]

The water crisis in Detroit illustrates a new threshold in the making of cities without services. In these cities residents are consumers not entitled citizens, and local governments are responsible for advancing economic growth not coordinating collective needs. Affluent households that can afford services get them, and cash-poor residents do not. Similar trends affected public works, transportation, lighting, emergency response, and social services, but the water cuts brought these issues to a heightened pitch by creating public health risks that have not existed in U.S. cities for over a century. This resurgence of cities without services reinforces the precariousness of contemporary life, a precariousness that encourages self-provisioned alternatives to the markets and governments that are failing to meet people's most basic everyday needs.

》 FRAGMENTED URBAN GOVERNANCE

Urban planning ideology in the late nineteenth and early twentieth centuries compared cities to human bodies. In these metaphors neighborhoods, parks, roads, and pipes were like internal organs and arteries that performed specialized tasks for the benefit of the organic whole. These metaphors garnered widespread support for strong municipalities and universal services. Coordinated road development and centralized infrastructure created economies of scale that benefitted investors and residents alike. And land use laws that physically separated noxious industries and large factories from residential neighborhoods improved public health outcomes.[8]

In recent decades, however, the city-as-body metaphor has fallen out of favor. One problem was that constructing specialized neighborhoods had unintended effects. For example, homogeneous residential suburbs fueled racial segregation, automobile dependency, social isolation, obesity, and global warming. City builders also misused these metaphors of a collective unity when advocating for urban development projects that benefitted white residents and promoted downtown business interests at the expense of minority communities. These negative outcomes eroded public trust in technocratic city planning methods, and they tainted the utopian rhetoric of an imagined public good.[9]

Instead of responding with political movements to build more genuinely inclusive publics, neoliberal advocates abandoned the metaphor of a social whole and embraced the rhetoric of home rule. In Detroit, for instance, the metropolitan area continues to grow, but the central city and its sprawling suburbs do not have a political mechanism for integrated decision making. Even within the city limits, municipal governing has devolved to the point where individual neighborhoods no longer look like constitutive parts of a unified city. As centralized services disappear, residents become more dependent on local volunteers and small community organizations that manage property markets, public works, and public safety within narrowly defined subneighborhood boundaries.

Advocates of neoliberal governance use the rosy rhetoric of flexible markets and grassroots governance to cast these splintering cities in a positive light. But by definition market segmentation means people with resources have access to high-quality services while low-income residents do not. Government devolution also leaves residents free to respond to global economic processes but lacking the collective clout needed to enact structural reforms.[10]

During the Great Recession, Detroit residents responded to disinvestment in various ways. Some people moved and bought their way into better-served neighborhoods. African Americans leaving Detroit for the suburbs found improved living conditions and expanded life opportunities.[11] Relocating was especially important because politically conservative suburban voters derailed other potential solutions like regional taxation, job training, and drug treatment alternatives to mass incarceration. The political failure of collective alternatives left residents more dependent on individual decisions like relocation. But since racially motivated disinvestment could quickly produce the same social problems in the suburbs residents had hoped to leave behind in the city, the benefits of relocating were often fleeting, and the collective problem of disinvestment remained unresolved.[12]

Some residents who stayed in Detroit got organized and created formal community groups to manage devolved urban governance more effectively. Residents with stable incomes and professional work histories were especially well equipped to write grant applications for external funding, hire private contractors to perform public works, and lobby government officials to amend existing laws. These activities propped up failing real estate markets and replicated miniaturized versions of municipal governments at the neighborhood scale. Other residents organized alternative social movements that intentionally moved away from the formal institutional practices that had not served them well. These residents used gray spaces to support informal economies, racial autonomy, and social reciprocity.

Alongside these relocation decisions and civic responses, many residents adjusted their everyday practices and began using household labor and domestic resources to manage gray space and improve public works. These residents intervened in real estate markets by recruiting new neighbors, disguising vacant homes, and adopting abandoned lots. They used their brooms, shovels, lawn mowers, and trash bags to maintain public streets and neighborhood parks. They repurposed blight on other people's property. They monitored street activity to keep each other safe. And they used local knowledge and public displays of volunteerism to bring outside resources to their communities. These residents worked alongside formal community organizations, and their practices were especially significant, since market reforms and citizenship entitlements were not forthcoming.

» THE SELF-PROVISIONED CITY

The social movement response to Detroit's domestic water cuts in 2014 represented a flashpoint of political activism against the backdrop of constant, mundane practices residents used to prevent crisis. Most residents who were behind on their bills owed a few hundred dollars, but several hundred residential addresses had debts of five thousand dollars or more. Those were usually vacant homes where scrappers stealing pipes had left the municipal water gushing into empty basements. Those leaks generated millions of dollars of public debt.[13] Intentionally or otherwise, residents who recruited new neighbors, disguised empty buildings, and kept watch over their blocks protected the city from spiraling debts and wasteful public expenses.

These self-provisioning acts were not integrated social movements. Compared with the collective activism of groups like the Detroit Water Brigade, residents' everyday interventions in property markets and public works might look small, haphazard, and disorganized. However, whereas a few hundred protestors marched in front of city hall during one summer season, several thousand residents had been using their everyday routines to shore up markets and improve public services for years. These self-provisioning acts did not protect residents' legal rights to water, but neither did demonstrations and lawsuits. Instead, resident self-provisioners organized people in space, organized access to resources, and organized the moral geographies of the city.

Markets—and the government policies that frame them—usually organize people in space. But in Detroit markets were creating patterns of vacancy instead of occupancy. Informal matchmakers, foster owners, and neighborhood publicists intervened in empty spaces. They prevented them from deteriorating, and they pulled people from other areas to fill those voids. Markets still mattered, and these practices did not fully counteract structural forces of disinvestment. But self-provisioning nonetheless created new logics of kinship clustering, social idealism, and reciprocity that helped explain settlement patterns and the uneven distribution of vacancy.

Self-provisioning also mediates residents' access to shared resources. The neoliberal trend toward market-based governing means resident consumers with limited resources are increasingly dependent on charitable donations for basic needs. Residents who could show city officials and foundation leaders physical evidence of volunteerism framed themselves as deserving recipients of scarce resources. Residents who worked as unpaid volunteers surveying neighborhoods, cleaning trash, and maintaining parks expected to receive higher-quality services in exchange for their work. In the competitive environment of scarce grants and dwindling government funding, self-provisioning became about much more than solving a local problem. It became leverage. Self-provisioning was a tool residents used to bring resources to their blocks that otherwise went somewhere else.

Resident-led practices that organized people in space and mediated access to resources created normative expectations about who deserved those spaces and support. Gray spaces were not passive environments sitting idle while the urban prairie filled in. Instead, they were conflict zones where people competed for resources and advanced social goals. Neighbors made personal judgments about who belonged in gray space, what activities could occur there, and what methods of control were ethically justified. These practices generated moral dilemmas because the most effective strategies for controlling and reusing gray space were often technically illegal and sometimes dangerous. Residents negotiated these dilemmas through on-the-ground interactions that generated new, contested, and constantly evolving moral geographies.

Self-provisioning was politically open-ended. Some matchmakers, sleuths, and posturban visionaries used self-provisioning to challenge the status quo and build alternative communities—for instance, by using abandoned lots to support food justice or peer-to-peer exchanges. But self-provisioning was not inherently revolutionary. Residents who recruited new neighbors, collected trash from public streets, and watched over their blocks often did this work to keep formal markets functioning, reinforce normative behavioral expectations, and maintain the image of municipal authority.

Self-provisioning was also a collaborative endeavor not an insular practice. It involved residents from many racial and economic backgrounds who worked together to solve shared problems. Friends, family members, and neighbors cooperated to fill homes, board structures, patrol streets, and circulate information. They borrowed strategies, ideologies, and discourses from national social movements and regional civic organizations, and their work influenced those groups' responses to urban decline.

These self-provisioning practices reworked social ties among neighbors. The work sometimes produced mutual dependencies—for instance, between matchmakers and their recruits or among neighbors who informally divvied up the workload of lighting the night and watching the street. These practices set limits and boundaries to reciprocity—for example, when residents maintained provisional working methods that protected them from long-term obligations even when formalized solutions were technically available. These social interactions reworked community relationships and social expectations among neighbors.

The partial domestication of urban governing and collective problem solving was a socially produced phenomenon not a natural or inevitable outcome of disinvestment. Government leaders and civic organizations encouraged residents to self-provision. They provided manuals with detailed instructions about how to do the work. They organized small grant programs to help residents accomplish daunting tasks and streamline working methods. They also toured neighborhoods to learn about self-provisioning, and they incorporated that knowledge into institutional visions of what the future of Detroit could look like. This government and civic encouragement helped self-provisioning become more widespread and have a larger impact on collective life.

Alongside this intentional encouragement, frustrating encounters with markets and governments fueled self-provisioning. Code enforcement officers ticketed residents who asked for help. Absentee owners ignored or intimidated neighbors who demanded accountability. And government reports cataloged everything that was wrong with Detroit. Those discouraging interactions motivated residents to find other ways to solve local problems and define their identities, ways that did not involve government or market intermediaries.

Whenever and however an individual resident decided to start self-provisioning, the everyday practices that emerged had significant effects on Detroit. Collective stewardship was a process of devolved urban governance. It was fragmented, disorganized, and reactionary, but it was also widespread and continuous. These practices reworked community identities as people took charge of gray space and inscribed it with new forms, functions, and ethics. These socially generative acts reworked the logics of life and space in the neoliberal city.

» STRENGTHENING WEAPONS OF THE WEAK

The same year Detroit residents lost access to running water, residents in Seattle saw deep cuts in their county bus service, residents in the Lyons suburb of Chicago lost one-third of their police officers, and residents across Pennsylvania organized fund-raisers to prevent public libraries from closing.[14] The struggle to keep municipal services operational is not new. The challenge is emblazoned in places like St. Louis with its "ghostly landscape of vacant houses, boarded-up storefronts, and abandoned factories" and in San Bernardino, where "years of fiscal purging" have reduced the city "to a rump administration" with emergency response services and nothing more.[15]

Within this evolving national landscape of cities without services, collective self-provisioning is one of many responses pushing against austerity. Resident interventions in property markets and public works are a politics of practice not protest. The people doing this work do not know each other and do not work in organized collectives, but they develop similar responses to shared challenges. Social movement scholars use phrases like "social non-movements" and "movements without marches" to describe these politics of practice.[16] Self-provisioning the city involves those types of small, distributed practices that when carried out by large numbers of people, rework social norms.

In Detroit the shared problem of market disinvestment and government contraction created generalized risks and hardships. Residents expressed skepticism over their elected officials' ability to change Detroit's circumstances, and the imagined perpetrators of disinvestment—the white-flight residents, the long-lost factory owners, and the conservative state voters—were far away. In this context where political rallies and outright defiance offered few immediate benefits, many residents channeled energy into everyday practices. These fragmented, mundane acts did not lead to quick structural reforms, but they were personally meaningful and reworked the logic of the city.

These traits indicate that self-provisioning in response to disinvestment is a weapon of the weak.[17] Detroit has a long history of social movement activism around labor unions, race relations, and urban redevelopment.[18] That history is important, but despite that legacy urban decline accelerated during the Great Recession, and many residents expressed the belief that railing against the wind was ineffective. So residents recruited new neighbors, disguised vacant housing, repurposed abandoned lots, performed public works, policed neighborhood streets, and generated local knowledge. These practices reshaped local landscapes, but they were indirect forms of struggle, disconnected from the political economic infrastructure that could have given everyday practices more meaningful structural significance.

Acknowledging this weakness is important in an era of home-rule politics and romantic notions of community governance. Saying self-provisioning has positive benefits does not imply residents who do not form their own miniature tax districts or spend their leisure time shoveling public sidewalks and boarding vacant homes are to blame for the blight that exists in their communities. Civic activism and unpaid volunteerism are difficult to sustain, and many residents in precarious circumstances do not have the time, money, skills, health, or confidence to do the work. Stories of self-provisioning are inspiring because they show people in difficult circumstances still have agency, but it would be politically irresponsible to say people's capacity to live with hardship justifies market and government neglect.

The challenge is not to get rid of self-provisioning because it is a weak weapon but rather to strengthen it by connecting it with other modes of activism. For instance, if devolved urban governance is a political reality, then consistent, robust grant programs can give residents greater opportunities to make meaningful improvements. Similarly, if block clubs had legal mechanisms to take temporary control of neglected spaces without incurring prohibitive maintenance costs or legal liabilities, then residents could collaborate more formally to secure gray space and negotiate community standards. Instead of conceptualizing self-provisioning as an alternative to civic activism and municipal authority, these types of policies could reinforce the interconnections across these nested scales of governing.

Supporting self-provisioning does not alleviate the need for structural reform. Grant programs and community capacity building help residents navigate difficult circumstances, but structural reforms like regional taxation, national antiracism training, and policies that limit the growth of social inequality are nonetheless crucial to ongoing social justice goals. Residents can adopt vacant buildings, but that should not decenter calls for greater owner accountability. Neighbors can mow vacant lots and sweep public streets, but that does not mean communities should perform public works indefinitely. Self-provisioning is a weak weapon, but every weapon is needed in a context where precariousness is rising nationwide. Residents often turn to self-provisioning because too few politically viable alternatives exist. It helps, but it also underscores the need for meaningful, organized, collective responses against neoliberal capitalism and market-based governing.

» LEAVING DETROIT

One of the last formal interviews I completed for this book was with an African American man who was born and raised in Detroit and became an energetic member of Detroit's city council. Sitting in his high-rise downtown office building, he discussed his approach to government.

"My entire life in the city," he said, "I've seen a constant downward slide. You've got pockets of good stuff here and there that's happening. But overall, you've seen this." The councilman made a downward motion with his arm. "But you can't just turn it like you would an Indy car. It's more of a freighter." He made a slow sweeping motion with his arm. "It slowly turns. It slowly turns. And you go in the backyard and plant some stuff. Yup," he said, looking at his arm, "it's still turning. And you go back and put some stuff on the stove. And you look. Yup, still turning. But sooner or later, you look, and the freighter's turning in the opposite direction. That's what this feels like."

The councilman's description of urban governing as a series of domestic chores is an especially apt analogy for the post-Fordist city where things like cooking and backyard gardening have assumed new roles in economic development and community building. These practices merge seamlessly with the growing informal economy. Residents prepare food in their kitchens to sell on the streets. They rent rooms to reduce expenses, and they polish nails and repair cars for cash in their living rooms and driveways. Using home spaces as sites of production is not new, but mid-twentieth-century labor laws, zoning ordinances, and public safety nets pushed those practices to the margins. This is no longer the case. Many residents are once again self-provisioning, and home spaces are once again not only sites of informal economies but also places of informal governance. As municipal services degrade, self-provisioning residents move beyond the confines of their private homes. They shovel public streets, survey neighborhood blight, adopt vacant homes, and re-purpose nearby lots to control their neighborhoods and shape the city's future.

The city councilman expressed humility and respect for these grassroots practices, even as he acknowledged the desperation that fueled them. The city had been in decline for decades, and government solutions failed to fully stem the fall. "I think now," he said, "folks get that the government is not the solution. It's really community based, the solutions are. Folks are thirsty for it now. It's a thirst for, 'How do we play a role in making it better?'"

Other residents have characterized self-provisioning as "the triumph of hope over reason" and "an embrace of optimism over evidence." With their words ringing in my ears, I asked the city councilman the inevitable question, "Will it work?"

He took a deep breath, sighed, and then said, "It hasn't been as difficult as I thought it was going to be. Now, can it sustain itself? I'm going to try to make sure that it does."

Acknowledgments

First, I thank the University of Michigan's Society of Fellows for their financial support for the researching and writing of my manuscript.

This book would not have been possible without the Detroit residents in Brightmoor, Grandmont Rosedale, Morningside, and Springwells Village who shared time and experiences with me. To preserve your privacy, I am not listing you by name, but you know who you are, and I thank you. You taught me a lot, and the best parts of this book come from you.

Many organizations graciously facilitated this research. Thanks go to Brightmoor Alliance, Bridging Communities, Department of Administrative Hearings, Engine House 33, Grandmont Rosedale Crime Prevention Task Force, Grandmont Rosedale Development Corporation, Grandmont Rosedale Vacant Housing Task Force, Grandmont #1 Neighborhood Improvement Association, Michigan Community Resources, Minock Park Block Club, MorningSide Community Organization, Motor City Blight Busters, Neighbors Building Brightmoor, North Rosedale Park Civic Association, Office of City Council Member James Tate, Office of State Representative Alberta Tinsley-Talabi, Office of State Representative Rashida Tlaib, Springdale Woodmere Block Club, U-SNAP-BAC, Habitat for Humanity Detroit, and Urban Neighborhood Initiative.

Scholars and faculty at the University of Michigan provided support and guidance for this book. My thanks go to the members of the Michigan Society of Fellows Humanities Working Group and the Michigan Society Junior Fellows for providing immeasurable encouragement. Several faculty members from the Taubman College of Architecture and Urban Planning provided detailed feedback on early ideas and drafts. Thanks go to Margaret Dewar, June Manning

Thomas, Martin Murray, Scott Campbell, Eric Dueweke, Lucas Owen Kirkpatrick, Lesli Hoey, and Suzanne Lanyi Charles.

Several students assisted with this project. I thank Meagan Elliott for recruiting interviewees and arranging opportunities to share the emerging work with activists and scholars. Students from the University of Michigan Undergraduate Research Opportunity Program helped process the data. Thanks go to Andrea, Florence, Kashira, Teryn, and Stephanie.

University of Michigan staff played important supporting roles. Thanks go to Linda Turner with the Michigan Society of Fellows and Barbara Tietjen with the Taubman College of Architecture and Urban Planning for managing funding and logistics, Rebecca Sestili for her sage publishing advice, Rebecca Price for locating useful library materials, the Sand Lab for providing data support, and Lisa Holland for her survey advice.

I thank Jason Weidemann and his editorial team at the University of Minnesota Press for their advice and support. Jason's detailed comments on research focus and writing style significantly improved the quality of this book. My thanks go to the anonymous reviewers who provided feedback on the research.

Conversations and idea exchanges with academic colleagues enriched the quality of this book. A modified portion of the material in chapter 3 previously appeared in the *International Journal of Urban and Regional Research* as "Guerrilla-Style Defensive Architecture in Detroit." I also presented material in this book to several academic audiences in 2013 and 2014. The comments and questions I received from those audiences influenced my manuscript's development. Conference audiences included attendees at several annual meetings of the Association of American Geographers, the Urban Affairs Association, the University of Michigan's symposium on Turbulent Urbanism, and the University of Michigan's Detroit School Lecture Series. Additional University of Michigan audiences included the Michigan Society of Fellows and the Urban and Regional Planning Program. Financial support for these presentations came from the Michigan Society of Fellows and the Taubman College of Architecture and Urban Planning.

At the personal level, I thank Jen for her unfailing encouragement and insights. And my deepest gratitude goes to Cora, Charlie, and Ross. This project is for you.

Notes

INTRODUCTION

1. All the names in this book are pseudonyms.
2. Yiftachel, "Critical Theory and Gray Space."
3. For example, see Herscher, *Unreal Estate Guide to Detroit.*
4. Galster, *Driving Detroit*; Hackworth, *Neoliberal City*; Mallach, *Stabilizing Communities*; Sugrue, *Origins of the Urban Crisis.*
5. Mast, *Detroit Lives*; Orr and Stoker, "Urban Regimes and Leadership in Detroit," 51; Ryan, *Design after Decline*; Thomas and Blake, "Faith-Based Community Development."
6. SEMCOG, *2010 Census Data.*
7. Hackworth, "Urban Crisis, Relationality, and Detroit."
8. Detroit Works, *Detroit Future City.*
9. Bomey et al., "Detroit Becomes Largest U.S. City"; Dolan, "Record Bankruptcy for Detroit"; Rushe, "Detroit Becomes Largest US City."
10. For more on the history of racial segregation, see Farley et al., *Detroit Divided*; Sugrue, *Origins of the Urban Crisis*; Thomas, *Redevelopment and Race.* For additional information about resident experiences of discrimination, see Bates and Fasenfest, "Enforcement Mechanisms Discouraging Black-American Presence"; Galster and Godfrey, "By Words and Deeds"; Rose, "Captive Audience."
11. Brookings Institution, "State of Metropolitan America"; Data Driven Detroit, *State of the Detroit Child*; Reich, "Income Inequality Ruined Detroit"; U.S. Census Bureau, "2010 Surveys: Race" and "Surveys: Population."
12. Dewar, "What Helps or Hinders Nonprofit"; Shaw and Spence, "Race and Representation in Detroit's."
13. Several factors mediate the local effects of disinvestment, including socioeconomic composition, housing characteristics, geographic proximities, community activism, and local patronage relationships. The relative importance of these factors remains unclear.
14. See Table 2 for coding information.

1. DO-IT-YOURSELF CITIES

1. Kneebone, *Growth and Spread*, 3; Mallach, *Laying the Groundwork for Change*, 3; McKernan et al., "Disparities in Wealth Accumulation"; United Nations, *Global Social Crisis*, 27–29.

2. Brady, "Facing Budget Gap"; Cooper, "Going to Extremes"; Goode, "Crime Increases in Sacramento"; Peck, "Pushing Austerity," 2.

3. Roy, "Who Is Dependent on Welfare?"

4. Davey, "Private Boom amid Detroit's"; Lowrey, "Pay Still High at Bailed-Out"; Williams, "Drop Dead, Detroit!"

5. Brady, "Facing Budget Gap"; Cooper, "Going to Extremes"; Crawford, "Reviving Clayton Bus Service"; Goode, "Crime Increases in Sacramento"; Lawson and Sorensen, "When Overwhelming Needs Met."

6. U.S. Census Bureau, "Geography: 2010 census."

7. For an overview of the "shrinking cities" literature, see Beauregard, "Urban Population Loss in Historical"; Martinez-Fernandez et al., "Shrinking Cities"; Oswalt, *International Research*; Rienets, "Shrinking Cities."

8. Harris, *Building a Market*; Lawson, *City Bountiful*; Nicolaides, *My Blue Heaven*.

9. Mukhija and Loukaitou-Sideris, *Informal American City*; Nicolaides, *My Blue Heaven*; Wiese, *Places of Their Own*.

10. Gandy, *Concrete and Clay*; Gregory, *Black Corona*; Lipman and Mahan, *Holding Ground*; Small, *Villa Victoria*; Stack, *All Our Kin*; Susser, *Norman Street*.

11. Doussard, *Degraded Work*; Gowan, *Hobos, Hustlers, and Backsliders*; Mukhija and Loukaitou-Sideris, *Informal American City*.

12. Patillo, *Black on the Block*, 150.

13. Dilger et al., "Privatization of Municipal Services"; Segal, "Georgia Town Takes"; Streitfeld, "City Outsources Everything."

14. Adams, *Markets of Sorrow*; Dolhinow, *Jumble of Needs*; Herbert, "Trapdoor of Community"; Irazábal and Neville, "Neighbourhoods in the Lead."

15. Chase et al., *Everyday Urbanism*; Herscher, *Unreal Estate Guide*; Mele, *Selling the Lower East Side*; Rojas, "Enacted Environment"; Stevens, "German 'City Beach.'"

16. Swyngedouw and Kaika, "Making of 'Glocal' Urban Modernities."

17. McGirr, *Suburban Warriors*; Nicolaides, *My Blue Heaven*.

18. Yiftachel, "Critical Theory and Gray Space."

19. Einhorn, *Property Rules*; Frug, *City Making*; Gillette, *Camden after the Fall*; Nicolaides, *My Blue Heaven*.

20. Garb, *City of American Dreams*; Nicolaides, *My Blue Heaven*; Wiese, *Places of Their Own*.

21. Garb, *City of American Dreams*; Nicolaides, *My Blue Heaven*; Wiese, *Places of Their Own*.

22. Beauregard, *When America Became Suburban*; Jackson, *Crabgrass Frontier*; Self, *American Babylon*.

23. Einhorn, *Property Rules*; Frug, *City Making*.

24. Brechin, *Imperial San Francisco*; Gandy, *Concrete and Clay*; Nicolaides, *My Blue Heaven*; Weiss, *Rise of the Community Builders*.

25. Rusk, *Cities without Suburbs*.

26. Harvey, *Brief History of Neoliberalism*; Harvey, "From Managerialism to Entrepreneurialism"; Peck and Tickell, "Neoliberalizing Space"; Tabb, *Long Default*.

27. Bakker, *Uncooperative Commodity*; Graham and Marvin, *Splintering Urbanism*; Harvey, *Brief History of Neoliberalism*; Leitner et al., *Contesting Neoliberalism*; Peck and Tickell, "Neoliberalizing Space"; Purcell, *Recapturing Democracy*.

28. Cohen, "CDCs Can Help Detroit"; Eikenberry and Kluver, "Marketization of the Nonprofit Sector"; González, "Construction of the Myth"; Hackworth and Akers, "Faith in the Neoliberalisation"; Martin, "Nonprofit Foundations and Grassroots Organizing"; Reese, "Matter of Faith."

29. Anderson, "Dissolving Cities"; Maher et al., "Hard Times Spread for Cities"; Peck, "Pushing Austerity"; Plumer, "Detroit Isn't Alone."

30. Gillette, *Camden after the Fall*; Gordon, *Mapping Decline*.

31. Herbert, *Citizens, Cops, and Power*; Small, *Villa Victoria*.

32. Cresswell, "Moral Geographies"; Matless, *Landscape and Englishness*.

33. Cheng, *Changes Next Door to the Diazes*; Enke, *Finding the Movement*; Mitchell and Staeheli, "Clean and Safe."

34. Chase et al., *Everyday Urbanism*; Mukhija and Loukaitou-Sideris, *Informal American City*; Rojas, "Enacted Environment"; Shyong, "Too Young for Tai Chi."

35. Data Driven Detroit, *Detroit Residential Parcel Survey*; Detroit Blight Removal Task Force, *Every Neighborhood Has a Future*, 15; Detroit Works, *Detroit Future City*, 98, 211; Mallach, *Facing the Urban Challenge*.

36. Cohen, "CDCs Can Help Detroit"; Hackworth and Akers, "Faith in the Neoliberalisation"; Herbert, "Trapdoor of Community"; Purcell, "Urban Democracy and the Local Trap."

2. SEEKING NEW NEIGHBORS

1. Castells, *City and the Grassroots*; Sassen, *Global City*; Smith, *New Urban Frontier*.

2. Lipman and Mahan, *Holding Ground*; Smith, *Gaining Ground*. See also the Dudley Street Neighborhood Initiative website, http://www.dsni .org/. For a similar account of residents who self-organized neighborhood recovery efforts in post-Katrina New Orleans, see Adams, *Markets of Sorrow, Labors of Faith*; Irazábal and Nevil, "Neighbourhoods in the Lead."

3. Osman, *Invention of Brownstone Brooklyn*. For another similar case study, see Mele, *Selling the Lower East Side*.

4. Elliott, "We Need to Ask."

5. Sugrue, *Origins of the Urban Crisis*; U.S. Census Bureau, "Surveys: Population."

6. Detroit Foreclosure Prevention, *Community Stabilization and the Impact*; Detroit Works, *Detroit Future City*.

7. Despite nominally low home prices, the full cost of living in Detroit is actually comparatively high because tax rates, insurance rates, and transportation costs are unusually high. Affordability is also a problem because many residents have very low incomes. See Darden, "Detroit."

8. Sugrue, "Dream Still Deferred."

9. As Sugrue explains, these opportunities are often pyrrhic, since white flight and disinvestment easily creates the same characteristics of segregation and decay that black buyers hope to escape through relocation.

10. Dolan, "Detroit Mayor Scales Back"; Saulny, "Razing the City to Save"; Wilgoren, "Detroit Urban Renewal without the Renewal."

11. The resident sometimes said six homes and other times said eight homes. I did not have the opportunity to verify with her which number she intended.

12. Maps and descriptions of Neighborhood Stabilization Programs in Detroit are available from the City of Detroit Planning and Development Department website at http://www.detroitmi.gov/How-Do-I/Obtain-Grant-Information/NSP-Information.

13. This information is based on my personal interviews with organization leaders. See also Crain's Detroit Business News, "Charities in Detroit Area See More Donated Homes."

14. Cwiek, "Worlds Largest Property Auction"; Lewis, "No Property Left Behind"; Loveland Technologies, "Grandmont Rosedale 2012 Tax Auction"; Muller, "What Can Be Done With."

15. Arreola, "Picture Postcard Mexican Housescape"; Fogelson, *Fragmented Metropolis*; Jackson, *Crabgrass Frontier*; Mele, *Selling the Lower East Side*; Osman, *Invention of Brownstone Brooklyn*.

3. PROTECTING VACANT HOMES

1. Data Driven Detroit, *Detroit Residential Parcel Survey*; Detroit Blight Removal Task Force, *Every Neighborhood Has a Future*, 15.

2. Linn, "Encouraging Residential Blotting."

3. See also Mallach, *Laying the Groundwork for Change*.

4. Chase et al., *Everyday Urbanism*; Holston, *Insurgent Citizenship*; Hou, *Insurgent Public Space*; Shyong, "Too Young." See also Bayat, *Life as Politics*.

5. Bayat, *Life as Politics*; Beckett and Herbert, *Banished*; Mitchell, *Right to the City*.

6. Newman, *Defensible Space*.

7. Interview with organization director. See also Michigan Community Resources, "Michigan Community Resources Awards $50,000."

8. Newman, "Defensible Space," 150.

9. Newman, "Defensible Space."

10. Newman, "Defensible Space," 149.

11. Carmona et al., *Public Places, Urban Spaces*, 51.

12. Mitchell, *Right to the City*; Kaplan and Kaplan, "Alternatives to Fear"; Merry, "Defensible Space Undefended."

13. SEMCOG, *2010 Census Data for City*; see Table 1 for neighborhood-specific information.

14. Raleigh and Galster, "Neighborhood Disinvestment, Abandonment and Crime Dynamics."

15. Hackney, "Detroit Mayor Dave Bing Pledges."

16. McGraw, "Exclusive"; Satyanarayana and Bell, "Gov. Rick Snyder's Plan."

17. Gallagher, "Next Detroit Blight Removal Site"; Reindl, "One of Detroit's Largest."

18. Sack, *Human Territoriality*.

4. REPURPOSING ABANDONMENT

1. Hackney, "Living with Murder."

2. Olasky, "Brightmoor Fighters." See also Gallagher, "Acres of Barren Blocks"; McMillan, "Urban Farmers' Crops Go."

3. Millington, "Post-industrial Imaginaries."

4. Detroit Long Term, *Detroit Future City*, 98.

5. Gallagher, "Acres of Barren Blocks"; Gallagher, *Reimagining Detroit*; Green and Gopal, "Detroit Survival Depending on Destruction"; Saulny, "Razing the City to Save"; Wilgoren, "Detroit Urban Renewal without the Renewal."

6. Detroit Long Term, *Detroit Future City*; Green and Gopal, "Detroit Survival Depending on Destruction"; Saulny, "Razing the City to Save"; Wilgoren, "Detroit Urban Renewal."

7. Bennet, "Tribute to Ruin Irks Detroit."

8. Carey, "On the Edge of Bankruptcy."

9. Daniels, "Advocates Attack Blight by Salvaging"; Greenovation TV, *Deconstruction Detroit*.

10. A pole barn is a barn without a foundation. From a city planning perspective, it is a temporary structure, and so the builders do not need a construction permit.

11. Herscher, *Unreal Estate Guide to Detroit*; Hurewitz, *Bohemian Los Angeles*; Shaw, "Place of Alternative Culture"; Swyngedouw and Kaika, "Making of 'Glocal' Urban Modernities."

12. The literature on countercultural movements citywide indicates urban agriculture and food justice movements citywide included many projects and organizations started by African Americans for African Americans. But among self-provisioners in the neighborhoods I studied, whites disproportionately figured as organization leaders and countercultural activists.

13. Nelson, "Affordable Urban Canvas."

14. See also Arens, "Heidelberg Project."

15. Herscher, "Detroit Art City"; Pesca, "Detroit Artists Paint Town Orange"; Rich, "Ice House Detroit"; Runk, "Ice House Detroit."

16. For additional information, see the following organization websites: CatherineFergusonAcademy.org; CSKDetroit.org; DetroitAgriculture.net; DetroitBlackFoodSecurity.org; DetroitFoodPolicyCouncil.net; GreeningOfDetroit.com.

17. Conners, *Urban Roots*; Dworkin and Moore, *We Are Not Ghosts*; White, "Sisters of the Soil." See also Alkon, *Black, White, and Green*; Archambault, "Greening of Brightmoor"; Carey, "On the Edge of Bankruptcy"; McMillian, "Urban Farmers' Crops"; Signer, "How Food Is Revitalizing Detroit"; Timm, "Urban Farming Takes Hold"; Whitford, "Can Farming Save Detroit?"

18. Li, *Will to Improve*.

19. See also Daniels, "Advocates Attack Blight by Salvaging"; Greenovation TV, *Deconstruction Detroit*.

5. DOMESTICATING PUBLIC WORKS

1. Corburn, *Toward the Healthy City*; Melosi, *Effluent America*; Rabinow, *French Modern*.

2. For information on these developments in Detroit, see Daisy, "Detroit Water and Sewerage Department"; Department of Public Works, "About Us"; Franklin and Wood, *History of Lighting in Detroit*; Public Lighting Department, "About Us." For information on similar developments in other large U.S. cities, see Brechin, *Imperial San Francisco*; Fogelson, *Fragmented Metropolis*; Gandy, *Concrete and Clay*; McWilliams, *California*; Melosi, *Sanitary City*.

3. Frug, *City Making*; Einhorn, *Property Rules*; Nicolades, *My Blue Heaven*.

4. Massey and Denton, *American Apartheid*; Sugrue, *Origins of the Urban Crisis*.

5. Rusk, *Cities without Suburbs*.

6. Brookings Institution, "State of Metropolitan America"; Data Driven Detroit, *State of the Detroit Child*; Reich, "Income Inequality Ruined Detroit." For more on the history of racial segregation, see Boyle, *Arc of Justice*; Farley et al., *Detroit Divided*; Martin, "Crossing the Line"; Sugrue, *Origins of the Urban Crisis*; Thomas, *Redevelopment and Race*. For more on present-day discrimination, see Bates and Fasenfest, "Enforcement Mechanisms Discouraging Black-American Presence"; Galster and Godfrey, "By Words and Deeds"; Williams, "Drop Dead, Detroit"; Rose, "Captive Audience?"

7. Oosting, "Michigan's $6.2B 'Raid' on Revenue"; Spangler and Helms, "Report"; Urahn, *America's Big Cities in Volatile.*

8. Detroit Board of Realtors, "Average Home Price in Detroit." See also the Zillow real estate website, "Detroit Home Prices and Values," updated September 30, 2014, http://www.zillow.com/detroit-mi/home-values/.

9. MacDonald and Wilkinson, "Half of Detroit Property Owners."

10. Detroit Works, *Detroit Future City.*

11. Detroit Works, *Detroit Future City.*

12. Helms, "Detroit Mayor Bing Rounds Op"; Williams, "For Some Detroit Services."

13. Bukowski, "Detroit Founded Health Dept"; Greene, "Care for Poor Grows Heavier." For information about similar trends in other cities, see Tabb, *Long Default*; Tabb, *Restructuring of Capitalism in Our Time.*

14. Cwiek, "Orr Looks to Private Sector"; Helms and Guillen, "Kevin Orr"; Nichols, "Detroit Announces First Phase"; Watson, "More Drastic Service Cuts Hit."

15. Christoff, "Half of Detroit's Streetlights"; Detroit Works, *Detroit Future City*; Eligon, "Detroit Threatens to Cut Water"; Guillen, "Protestors Claim Detroit Water Shutoffs"; Helms and Guillen, "Kevin Orr."

16. Archambault, "Main Street Detroit Takes Shape"; Laitner, "Many Detroiters Take Safety."

17. Williams, "For Some Detroit Services."

18. Prices ranged by wattage and lamp type. For more information, see Khouri, "Rate Book for Electric Service."

19. Graham and Martin, *Splintering Urbanism.*

6. POLICING HOME SPACES

1. Hoyt and Gopal-Agge, "Business Improvement District Model"; Mukhija and Loukaitou-Sideris, *Informal American City,* 102.

2. Jacobs, *Death and Life of Great,* 50–54.

3. Anderson, *Code of the Street*; Duneier, *Sidewalk*; Rojas, "Enacted Environment."

4. For a summary of these debates, see Carmona et al., *Public Places*

Urban Spaces, 51. See also Duany et al., *Smart Growth Manual*; Whyte, *Social Life of Small Urban Spaces*.

5. Christie, "Most Dangerous U.S. Cities"; Katz and Bradley, "Detroit Project"; Kurtzleben, "11 Most Dangerous U.S. cities"; Sauter et al., "Most Dangerous Cities in America."

6. Maciag, "Law Enforcement Officers per Capita."

7. Bialik, "Detroit Police Response Times"; Christoff, "Detroit Citizens Protect Themselves." Important to note, response times are not the only measure of emergency response effectiveness, and by 2014 the mayor's office announced average response times had been reduced to just over seventeen minutes.

8. Christoff, "Detroit Citizens Protect Themselves"; Laitner, "Many Detroiters Take Safety."

9. Christoff, "Detroit Citizens Protect Themselves"; Dolan, "Detroit District Rents Police"; Hackney, "Living with Murder"; Laitner, "Many Detroiters Take Safety."

10. Christoff, "Detroit Citizens Protect Themselves."

11. For example, in August 2013 a resident challenged two men he believed were pushing a stolen car into the driveway of a vacant home, presumably to dismantle it for parts. Gunfire was exchanged, and the resident was wounded.

12. Christoff, "Detroit Citizens Protect Themselves."

13. Beckett and Herbert, *Banished*; Davis, *Ecology of Fear*, 357–422; Davis, "Fortress Los Angeles"; Graham, *Cities under Siege*; Mitchell and Staeheli, "Clean and Safe."

14. Rojas, "Enacted Environment," 279.

7. PRODUCING LOCAL KNOWLEDGE

1. Scott, *Seeing Like a State*.

2. Loveland Technologies, "About Loveland Technologies."

3. Mukhija and Loukaitou-Sideris, *Informal American City*; Simone, *For the City yet to Come*.

4. Pothukuchi, "Urban Agriculture and Food Networks."

5. Mitchell, *Colonising Egypt*; Rabinow, *French Modern*; Scott, *Seeing Like a State*; Scott, *Art of Not Being Governed*. See also Haraway, "Situated Knowledges"; Jasanoff, *States of Knowledge*; Pickles, *History of Spaces*.

6. Arreola, "Picture Postcard Mexican Housescape"; Corburn, *Street Science*; Henderson, *California and the Fictions of Capital*; Mason, *Once and Future New York*; Mele, *Selling the Lower East Side*; Schorske, "Ringstrasse, Its Critics"; Stratigakos, *Woman's Berlin*.

7. Armborst et al., "Improve Your Lot," 48.

8. These observations are based on interviews with the office managers of two state representatives. See also Dewar, "Selling Tax-Reverted Land"; Weber, "Informal Ownership and the Shrinking."

9. These dynamics were especially apparent in an interview with the director of the Grandmont Rosedale Development Corporation and in organizational newsletters dated March 2012 and December 2012, downloaded from the organization's website at http://www.grandmontrosedale.com. See also Green, "Detroit Homes Rot as Appraisals."

10. For more on this dispute, see Davidson, "Detroit Has Tons of Vacant"; Detroit Works, *Detroit Future City*, 11; Gallagher, "With So Much Space"; Williams, "Drop Dead, Detroit!"

11. Detroit Works, *Detroit Future City*, 211; Raleigh and Galster, "Neighborhood Disinvestment, Abandonment and Crime," 23.

12. Data Driven Detroit, *Detroit Residential Parcel*; Detroit Blight Removal Task Force, *Every Neighborhood Has a Future.*

13. Code for America eventually abandoned the project and developed a public transit app instead.

14. For a critique of these tendencies, see Gregory, *Black Corona*; Massey and Denton, *American Apartheid.*

15. Bill Hickey, letter to the editor, *Detroit Free Press*, April 7, 2012.

16. Braun, "Buried Epistemologies"; Corburn, *Street Science*; Haraway, "Situated Knowledges"; Leitner et al., *Contesting Neoliberalism.*

CONCLUSION

1. Barrabi, "Detroit Water Crisis"; Eligon, "Detroit Threatens to Cut Water"; Kielburger and Kielburger, "Access to Water Is No"; Lambert, "U.S. Bankruptcy Judge Allows Detroit"; Mitchell, "In Detroit, Water Crisis Symbolizes"; NAACP, "Detroit Water Shutoff Crisis"; Ramirez, "Detroit Urged to Tie Water Bills"; Russell, "Detroit Water Assistant Funds."

2. Daisy, "Detroit Water and Sewerage Department"; DWSD, "History of DWSD."

3. Corburn, *Toward the Healthy City*; Melosi, *Effluent America*; Schultz and McShane, "To Engineer the Metropolis." For more on the global perspective, see Barlow and Clarke, *Blue Gold*; Swyngedouw, *Social Power and the Urbanization*; World Health Organization, *Meeting the MDG Drinking Water.*

4. Bakker, *Uncooperative Commodity*; Barlow, *Blue Future*; Harrison, "Irish Water"; Jehl, "As Cities Move to Privatize"; Mitchell, "In Detroit, Water Crisis Symbolizes"; Rayasam, "Who Should Control Our Water?"

5. Abbey-Lambertz, "How Detroit's Water Crisis"; Barrabi, "Detroit Water Crisis"; Mitchell, "In Detroit, Water Crisis Symbolizes."

6. Cwiek, "Judge Rules There's No Guaranteed"; Lessenberry, "Judge's Ruling Doesn't Mean He"; Mitchell, "In Detroit, Water Crisis Symbolizes"; NAACP, "Bankruptcy Judge Denies Motion."

7. Associated Press, "Groups Discuss Detroit Water Shutoffs"; Barrabi, "Detroit Water Crisis"; "UN Officials Criticise Detroit Water."

8. Corburn, *Toward the Healthy City*; Melosi, *Effluent America*; Rabinow, *French Modern*.

9. Corburn, *Toward the Healthy City*; Hurley, *Environmental inequalities*; Massey and Denton, *American Apartheid*; Self, *American Babylon*.

10. Harvey, *Brief History of Neoliberalism*.

11. Bullard, *Black Metropolis in the Twenty-First Century*; Darden, "Detroit."

12. Sugrue, "Dream Still Deferred."

13. Kurth, "Empty Detroit Homes Accrue Millions."

14. Brill, "First Wave of Metro Bus"; NBC Chicago 5 News, "Lyons Cuts One-Third of Police"; Nussbaum, "Pennsylvania Libraries Feeling Pressures."

15. Gordon, *Mapping Decline*; Peck, "Pushing Austerity."

16. Bayat, *Life as Politics*, 15–26; Levenstein, *Movement without Marches*.

17. Scott, *Weapons of the Weak*.

18. Mast, *Detroit Lives*; Smith, *Dancing in the Street*; Thomas, *Redevelopment and Race*; Thompson, *Whose Detroit?*

Bibliography

Abbey-Lambertz, Kate. "How Detroit's Water Crisis Is Part of a Much Bigger Problem." *Huffington Post,* August 19, 2014. http://www.huffingtonpost.com/2014/08/19/detroit-water-shutoffs_n_5690980.html.

Adams, Vincanne. *Markets of Sorrow, Labors of Faith: New Orleans in the Wake of Katrina.* Durham, N.C.: Duke University Press, 2013.

Alkon, Alison H. *Black, White, and Green: Farmers Markets, Race, and the Green Economy.* Athens: University of Georgia Press, 2012.

Anderson, Elijah. *Code of the Street: Decency, Violence, and the Moral Life of the Inner City.* New York: W. W. Norton, 2000.

Anderson, Michelle W. "Dissolving Cities." *Yale Law Journal* 121 (2011): 1364.

Archambault, Dennis. "The Greening of Brightmoor." *Model Media,* September 14, 2010. http://www.modeldmedia.com/features/greenbrightmoor910.aspx.

———. "Main Street Detroit Takes Shape." *Model Media,* July 26, 2005. http://www.modeldmedia.com/features/mainstreet.aspx.

Arens, Robert, "The Heidelberg Project." In *Shrinking Cities,* edited by Philipp Oswalt, 450–55. Ostfildern-Ruit, Germany: Hatje Cantz Publishers, 2006.

Armborst, Tobias, Daniel D'Oca, and Georgeen Theodore. "Improve Your Lot!" In *Cities Growing Smaller,* edited by Karina Pallagst, 45–64. Cleveland: Cleveland Urban Design Collaborative, 2008.

Arreola, Daniel. "The Picture Postcard Mexican Housescape." In *Landscape and Race in the United States,* edited by Richard Schein, 113–26. New York: Francis and Taylor, 2006.

Associated Press. "Groups Discuss Detroit Water Shutoffs with UN Experts." *Detroit Free Press,* October 19, 2014. http://www.freep.com/story/news/local/michigan/detroit/2014/10/19/detroit-water-shutoffs-united-nations/17585855/.

Bakker, Karen J. *An Uncooperative Commodity: Privatizing Water in England and Wales.* Oxford: Oxford University Press, 2003.

Barlow, Maude. *Blue Future: Protecting Water for People and the Planet Forever.* New York: New Press, 2013.

Barlow, Maude, and Tony Clarke. *Blue Gold: Global Water Wars*. DVD. Directed by Sam Buzzo. Irvine, Calif.: Purple Turtle Films, 2008.

Barrabi, Thomas. "Detroit Water Crisis: Shutoffs Resume after Month-Long Moratorium." *International Business Times*, August 27, 2014. http://www.ibtimes.com/detroit-water-crisis-shutoffs-resume-after-month-long-moratorium-45-percent-water-bills-1670990.

Bates, Tim, and David Fasenfest. "Enforcement Mechanisms Discouraging Black-American Presence in Suburban Detroit." *International Journal of Urban and Regional Research* 29, no. 4 (2005): 960–71.

Bayat, Asef. *Life as Politics: How Ordinary People Change the Middle East*. Stanford, Calif.: Stanford University Press, 2013.

BBC News. "UN Officials Criticise Detroit Water Shutoffs." *BBC News*, October 20, 2014. http://www.bbc.com/news/world-us-canada-29697767.

Beauregard, Robert, "Urban Population Loss in Historical Perspective: United States, 1820–2000." *Environment and Planning A* 41 (2009): 514–28.

———. *When America Became Suburban*. Minneapolis: University of Minnesota Press, 2006.

Beckett, Katherine, and Steve Herbert. *Banished: The New Social Control in Urban America*. Oxford: Oxford University Press, 2009.

Bennet, James. "A Tribute to Ruin Irks Detroit." *New York Times*, December 10, 1995. http://www.nytimes.com/1995/12/10/us/a-tribute-to-ruin-irks-detroit.html.

Bialik, Carl. "Detroit Police Response Times No Guide to Effectiveness." *Wall Street Journal*, August 2, 2013. http://online.wsj.com/news/articles/SB10001424127887323997004578642250518125898.

Bomey, Nathan, Brent Snavely, and Alisa Priddle. "Detroit Becomes Largest U.S. City to Enter Bankruptcy." *USA Today*, December 3, 2013. http://www.usatoday.com/story/news/nation/2013/12/03/detroit-bankruptcy-eligibility/3849833/.

Boyle, Kevin. *Arc of Justice: A Saga of Race, Civil Rights, and Murder in the Jazz Age*. New York: Macmillan, 2007.

Brady, Jeff. "Facing Budget Gap, Colorado City Shuts Off Lights." *National Public Radio*, February 14, 2010. http://www.npr.org/templates/story/story.php?storyId=123691065.

Braun, Bruce. "Buried Epistemologies: The Politics of Nature in (Post)colonial British Columbia." *Annals of the Association of American Geographers* 87, no. 1 (1997): 3–31.

Brechin, Gray. *Imperial San Francisco: Urban Power, Earthly Ruin*. Berkeley: University of California Press, 2006.

Brill, Linda. "First Wave of Metro Bus Service Cuts Begins Saturday." *NBC King 5 News*, September 26, 2014. http://www.king5.com/story/news/local/2014/09/26/metro-bus-service-cuts-begin-saturday/16248051/.

Brookings Institution. "State of Metropolitan America: Detroit-Warren-

Livonia, MI." Brookings Institution, 2011. http://www.brookings.edu/about/programs/metro/stateofmetroamerica/profile?fips=19820#/?fips=19820&viewfips=19820C&subject=8&ind=75&year=2010&geo=city.

Bukowski, Diane. "Detroit Founded Health Dept. in 1825." *Voice of Detroit,* May 21, 2012. http://voiceofdetroit.net/2012/05/21/detroit-founded-health-dept-in-1825-it-previously-ran-3-hospitals-including-detroit-general-5-clinics-physician-home-visit-services/.

Bullard, Robert D., ed. *The Black Metropolis in the Twenty-First Century: Race, Power, and Politics of Place.* Lanham, Md.: Rowman and Littlefield, 2007.

Carey, Nick. "On the Edge of Bankruptcy, Detroit Focuses on Salvaging What It Still Has." *Financial Post,* February 19, 2013. http://business.financialpost.com/2013/02/19/on-the-edge-of-bankruptcy-detroit-focuses-on-salvaging-what-it-still-has/.

Carmona, Matthew, Steve Tiesdell, Tim Heath, and Taner Oc. *Public Places, Urban Spaces: The Dimensions of Urban Design.* 2nd ed. Oxford: Architectural Press, 2010.

Castells, Manuel. *The City and the Grassroots: A Cross-Cultural Theory of Urban Social Movements.* Berkeley: University of California Press, 1983.

Chase, John, Margaret Crawford, and John Kaliski, eds. *Everyday Urbanism.* Exp. ed. New York: Monacelli Press, 2008.

Cheng, Wendy. *The Changes Next Door to the Diazes: Remapping Race in Suburban California.* Minneapolis: University of Minnesota Press, 2013.

Christie, Les. "Most Dangerous U.S. Cities." *CNN Money,* January 23, 2013. http://money.cnn.com/gallery/real_estate/2013/01/23/dangerous-cities/.

Christoff, Chris. "Detroit Citizens Protect Themselves after Police Force Decimated." *Bloomberg News,* May 30, 2013. http://www.bloomberg.com/news/2013-05-31/detroit-citizens-protect-themselves-after-police-force-decimated.html.

———. "Half of Detroit's Streetlights May Go Out as City Shrinks." *Bloomberg News,* May 24, 2012. http://www.bloomberg.com/news/2012-05-24/half-of-detroit-s-streetlights-may-go-out-as-city-shrinks.html.

Cohen, Rick. "CDCs Can Help Detroit, but They Can't Replace City Hall." *Nonprofit Quarterly,* July 2, 2012. http://www.nonprofitquarterly.org/policysocial-context/20644-cdcs-can-help-detroit-but-they-cant-replace-city-hall.html.

Conners, Leila. *Urban Roots.* DVD. Santa Monica, Calif.: Tree Media Foundation, April 2011.

Cooper, Michael. "Going to Extremes as the Downturn Wears On." *New York Times,* August 6, 2010. http://www.nytimes.com/2010/08/07/us/07cutbacksWEB.html?pagewanted=all.

Corburn, Jason. *Street Science: Community Knowledge and Environmental Health Justice.* Cambridge, Mass.: MIT Press, 2005.

———. *Toward the Healthy City: People, Places, and the Politics of Urban Planning*. Cambridge, Mass.: MIT Press, 2009.

Crain's Detroit Business News. "Charities in Detroit Area See More Donated Homes." *Crain's Detroit Business News*, December 5, 2011. http://www.crainsdetroit.com/article/20111205/FREE/111209963/charities-in-detroit-area-see-more-donated-homes.

Crawford, Johnny. "Reviving Clayton Bus Service Isn't Simple." *Atlanta Journal-Constitution*, September 17, 2013. http://www.ajc.com/news/news/transportation/reviving-clayton-bus-service-isnt-simple/nZzFP/.

Cresswell, Tim. "Moral Geographies." In *Cultural Geography: A Critical Dictionary of Key Concepts*, edited by David Sibley, Peter Jackson, and Neil Washbourne, 128–34. London: I. B. Tauris, 2005.

Cwiek, Sarah. "Judge Rules There's No Guaranteed Right to Detroit Water Service without Paying Bills." *Michigan Radio*, September 29, 2014. http://michiganradio.org/post/judge-rules-theres-no-guaranteed-right-detroit-water-service-without-paying-bills.

———. "Orr Looks to Private Sector for Help with Detroit Water Department Mess." *Michigan Radio*, March 21, 2014. http://michiganradio.org/post/orr-looks-private-sector-help-detroit-water-department-mess.

———. "World's Largest Property Auction: Wayne County Finishes First Round." *Michigan Radio*, September 24, 2012. http://michiganradio.org/post/worlds-largest-property-auction-wayne-county-finishes-first-round?utm_referrer=http%3A//m.michiganradio.org/%23mobile/9210%3Futm_medium%3Dreferr.

Daisy, Michael, ed. "Detroit Water and Sewerage Department: The First 300 Years." Detroit Water and Sewerage Department website, 2001. http://www.dwsd.org/pages_n/history.html.

Daniels, Serena M. "Advocates Attack Blight by Salvaging Building Material." *Detroit News*, May 10, 2012. http://www.detroitnews.com/.

Darden, Joe. "Detroit: Differential Disinvestment, Demographic Change, and the Geography of Opportunity as an Alternative for Social Mobility." Paper presented at Learning from Detroit: Turbulent Urbanism in the 21st Century, Ann Arbor, Mich., May 2014.

Data Driven Detroit. *Detroit Residential Parcel Survey*. Detroit: Data Driven Detroit, 2010. http://datadrivendetroit.org/projects/detroit-residential-parcel-survey/.

———. *State of the Detroit Child*. Detroit: Data Driven Detroit, 2011. datadrivendetroit.org/web_ftp/Project_Docs/DETKidsDrft_FINAL.pdf.

———. *2012 Data Profile: Grandmont Rosedale*. Detroit: Data Driven Detroit 2012. http://datadrivendetroit.org/projects/lisc-bsc/grandmont-rosedale/.

———. *2012 Data Profile: Springwells Village*. Detroit: Data Driven Detroit, 2012. http://datadrivendetroit.org/projects/lisc-bsc/springwells-village/.

Davey, Monica. "A Private Boom amid Detroit's Public Blight." *New York*

Times, March 4, 2013. http://www.nytimes.com/2013/03/05/us/a-private-boom-amid-detroits-public-blight.html.

Davidson, Kate. "Detroit Has Tons of Vacant Land. But Forty Square Miles?" *Changing Gears,* April 18, 2012. www.changinggears.info.

Davis, Mike. *Ecology of Fear: Los Angeles and the Imagination of Disaster.* New York: Macmillan, 1998.

———. "Fortress Los Angeles: The Militarization of Urban Space." In *Variations of a Theme Park: The New American City and the End of Public Space,* edited by Michael Sorkin, 154–80. New York: Hill and Wang, 1992.

Department of Public Works. "About Us." City of Detroit website, 2014. https://www.detroitmi.gov/DepartmentsandAgencies/DepartmentofPublicWorks/AboutUs.aspx.

Detroit Blight Removal Task Force. *Every Neighborhood Has a Future, and It Doesn't Include Blight.* Detroit: Detroit Blight Removal Task Force, 2014. http://report.timetoendblight.org/.

Detroit Board of Realtors. "Average Home Price in Detroit: 1994–2009." *Encyclopedia Britannica* blog, May 19, 2009. http://www.britannica.com/blogs/wp-content/uploads/2009/05/detroit.jpg.

Detroit Foreclosure Prevention and Response Initiative. *Community Stabilization and the Impact of the Foreclosure Crisis in Detroit: Progress toward Recovery: June 2008–December 2011.* Detroit: Detroit Foreclosure Prevention and Response Initiative, 2011. http://www.foreclosuredetroit.org/pages/Research___Reports___Foreclosure_Detroit.

Detroit Works Long Term Planning Steering Team. *Detroit Future City: Detroit Strategic Framework Plan.* Detroit: Detroit Works Long Term Planning Steering Team, 2012. http://detroitworksproject.com/.

Dewar, Margaret. "Selling Tax-Reverted Land: Lessons from Cleveland and Detroit." *Journal of the American Planning Association* 72, no. 2 (2006): 167–80.

———. "What Helps or Hinders Nonprofit Developers in Reusing Vacant, Abandoned, and Contaminated Property?" In *The City after Abandonment,* edited by Margaret Dewar and June Manning Thomas, 174–96. Philadelphia: University of Pennsylvania Press, 2012.

Dilger, Robert J., Randolph R. Moffett, and Linda Struyk. "Privatization of Municipal Services in America's Largest Cities." *Public Administration Review,* 1997, 21–26.

Dolan, Matthew. "Detroit District Rents Police: Merchants Hire Off-Duty Officers to Stem Lesser Crimes City Can't Afford to Pursue." *Wall Street Journal,* April 8, 2013. http://online.wsj.com/news/articles/SB10001424127887323916304578407662589454102.

———. "Detroit Mayor Scales Back His Overhaul Plan, for Now." *Wall Street Journal,* June 29, 2011. http://online.wsj.com/news/articles/SB10001424053111903635604576474391532014276.

————. "Record Bankruptcy for Detroit." *Wall Street Journal*, July 19, 2013. http://online.wsj.com/articles/SB10001424127887323993804578614144173 709204.

Dolhinow, Rebecca. *A Jumble of Needs: Women's Activism and Neoliberalism in the Colonias of the Southwest*. Minneapolis: University of Minnesota Press, 2010.

Doussard, Marc. *Degraded Work: The Struggle at the Bottom of the Labor Market*. Minneapolis: University of Minnesota Press, 2013.

Duany, Andres, Jeff Speck, and Mike Lydon. *The Smart Growth Manual*. New York: McGraw-Hill, 2010.

Duneier, Mitchell. *Sidewalk*. New York: Macmillan, 1999.

Dworkin, Mark, and Jessica C. Moore. *We Are Not Ghosts*. DVD. Seattle, Wash.: Moving Images Video Project, 2012.

DWSD. "History of DWSD." Detroit Water and Sewerage Department website, 2014. http://www.dwsd.org/pages_n/history.html.

Eikenberry, Angela M., and Jodie D. Kluver. "The Marketization of the Nonprofit Sector: Civil Society at Risk?" *Public Administration Review* 64, no. 2 (2004): 132–40.

Einhorn, Robin L. *Property Rules: Political Economy in Chicago, 1833–1872*. Chicago: University of Chicago Press, 2001.

Eligon, John. "Detroit Threatens to Cut Water Service to Delinquent Customers." *New York Times*, March 25, 2014. http://www.nytimes.com/2014/03/26/us/detroit-threatens-to-cut-water-service-to-delinquent-customers.html.

Elliott, Meagan. "We Need to Ask: Is Gentrification Happening in Detroit?" *Model Media*, December 13, 2011. http://www.modelmedia.com/features/gentrifyfeature1211.aspx.

Enke, Anne. *Finding the Movement: Sexuality, Contested Space, and Feminist Activism*. Durham, N.C.: Duke University Press, 2007.

Farley, Reynolds, Sheldon Danziger, and Harry J. Holzer. *Detroit Divided*. New York: Russell Sage Foundation, 2000.

Fogelson, Robert. *The Fragmented Metropolis: Los Angeles, 1850–1930*. Los Angeles: University of California Press, 1993 (1967).

Franklin, Drew, and Kate Wood. *A History of Lighting in Detroit*. New York: Illuminating Engineering Society of North America, 2005. www.iesna-mi.org/DOCUMENTS/pdf_history.pdf.

Frug, Gerald E. *City Making: Building Communities without Building Walls*. Princeton, N.J.: Princeton University Press, 1999.

Gallagher, John. "Acres of Barren Blocks Offer Chance to Reinvent Detroit." *Detroit Free Press*, December 15, 2008. http://www.freep.com/article/20081215/NEWS01/812150342.

————. "Next Detroit Blight Removal Site." *Detroit Free Press*, January 20, 2014. http://www.freep.com/article/20140120/BUSINESS06/301200065/pulte-blight-brightmoor-gilbert.

———. *Reimagining Detroit: Opportunities for Redefining an American City.* Detroit: Wayne State University Press, 2010.

———. "With So Much Space, So Few Options." *Detroit Free Press,* April 1, 2012. http://www.freep.com/article/20120401/NEWS01/204010467/With-so-much-space-so-few-options-Detroit-s-vast-vacant-lots-are-a-burden.

Galster, George. *Driving Detroit: The Quest for Respect in the Motor City.* Philadelphia: University of Pennsylvania Press, 2012.

Galster, George, and Erin Godfrey. "By Words and Deeds: Racial Steering by Real Estate Agents in the U.S. in 2000." *Journal of the American Planning Association* 71, no. 3 (2005): 251–68.

Gandy, Matthew. *Concrete and Clay: Reworking Nature in New York City.* Cambridge, Mass.: MIT Press, 2003.

Garb, Margaret. *City of American Dreams: A History of Home Ownership and Housing Reform in Chicago, 1871–1919.* Chicago: University of Chicago Press, 2005.

Gillette, Howard. *Camden after the Fall: Decline and Renewal in a Post-industrial City.* Philadelphia: University of Pennsylvania Press, 2005.

González de la Rocha, Mercedes. "The Construction of the Myth of Survival." *Development and Change* 38, no. 1 (2007): 45–66.

Goode, Erica. "Crime Increases in Sacramento after Deep Cuts to Police Force." *New York Times,* November 3, 2012. http://www.nytimes.com/2012/11/04/us/after-deep-police-cuts-sacramento-sees-rise-in-crime.html?pagewanted=all&_r=0.

Gordon, Colin E. *Mapping Decline: St. Louis and the Fate of the American City.* Philadelphia: University of Pennsylvania Press, 2008.

Gowan, Teresa. *Hobos, Hustlers, and Backsliders: Homeless in San Francisco.* Minneapolis: University of Minnesota Press, 2010.

Graham, Stephen. *Cities under Siege: The New Military Urbanism.* London: Verso, 2010.

Graham, Stephen, and Simon Marvin. *Splintering Urbanism: Networked Infrastructures, Technological Mobilities, and the Urban Condition.* London: Routledge, 2001.

Green, Jeff. "Detroit Homes Rot as Appraisals Stopping Sales." *Bloomberg News,* August 9, 2013. http://www.bloomberg.com/news/2013–04–09/detroit-homes-rot-as-appraisals-stopping-sales-mortgages.html.

Green, Jeff, and Prashant Gopal. "Detroit Survival Depending on Destruction of Housing." *Bloomberg News,* May 30, 2013. http://www.bloomberg.com/news/2013–05–30/detroit-survival-depends-on-speed-of-destruction.html.

Greene, Jay. "Care for Poor Grows Heavier for Downtown Hospitals." *Crain's Detroit Business,* August 4, 2008. http://www.crainsdetroit.com/article/20080804/SUB/808040340/care-for-poor-grows-heavier-for-downtown-hospitals#.

Greenovation TV. *Deconstruction Detroit: Putting People to Work Instead of Bulldozers.* Videocassette (VHS). Detroit: WARM Training Center, 2011.

Gregory, Steven. *Black Corona: Race and the Politics of Place in an Urban Community.* Princeton, N.J.: Princeton University Press, 1999.

Guillen, Joe. "Protestors Claim Detroit Water Shutoffs Unfair to Residential Customers." *Detroit Free Press,* May 30, 2014. http://www.nytimes.com/2014/03/26/us/detroit-threatens-to-cut-water-service-to-delinquent-customers.html?_r=0.

Hackney, Suzette. "Detroit Mayor Dave Bing Pledges a Demolition Blitz." *Detroit Free Press,* June 27, 2012. http://www.freep.com/article/20120627/NEWS05/206270377/Detroit-Mayor-Dave-Bing-pledges-a-demolition-blitz-1500-homes-in-90-days.

———. "Living with Murder: Detroit Neighborhoods Push Back against Criminals." *Detroit Free Press,* November 15, 2011. http://www.freep.com/article/20111115/NEWS01/111150394.

Hackworth, Jason. *The Neoliberal City: Governance, Ideology, and Development in American Urbanism.* Ithaca: Cornell University Press, 2007.

———. "Urban Crisis, Relationality, and Detroit." Paper presented at Learning from Detroit: Turbulent Urbanism in the 21st Century, Ann Arbor, Mich., May 2014.

Hackworth, Jason, and Joshua Akers. "Faith in the Neoliberalisation of Post-Katrina New Orleans." *Tidschrift voor Economische en Sociale Geografie* 102, no. 1 (2009): 39–54.

Haraway, Donna. "Situated Knowledges: The Science Question in Feminism and the Privilege of Partial Perspective." *Feminist Studies* 14, no. 3 (1988): 575–99.

Harris, Richard. *Building a Market: The Rise of the Home Improvement Industry, 1914–1960.* Chicago: University of Chicago Press, 2012.

Harrison, Shane. "Irish Water: How the Dublin Government Are Struggling with Water Charges." *BBC News,* October 30, 2014. http://www.bbc.com/news/world-europe-29798331.

Harvey, David. *A Brief History of Neoliberalism.* Oxford: Oxford University Press, 2005.

———. "From Managerialism to Entrepreneurialism: The Transformation in Urban Governance in Late Capitalism." *Geografiska Annaler. Series B. Human Geography,* 1989, 3–17.

Helms, Matt. "Detroit Mayor Bing Rounds Up Donations to Keep 51 City Parks Open." *Detroit Free Press,* April 24, 2014. http://www.freep.com/article/20130424/NEWS01/304240065/50-parks-stay-open-Bing.

Helms, Matt, and Joe Guillen. "Kevin Orr: City to Get Out of Lighting, Transfer Service to DTE." *Detroit Free Press,* June 27, 2013. http://www.freep.com/article/20130627/NEWS01/306270119/DTE-Energy-Detroit-Public-Lighting.

Henderson, George. *California and the Fictions of Capital*. New York: Oxford University Press, 1999.

Herbert, Steve. *Citizens, Cops, and Power: Recognizing the Limits of Community*. Chicago: University of Chicago Press, 2006.

———. "The Trapdoor of Community." *Annals of the Association of American Geographers* 95, no. 4 (2005): 850–65.

Herscher, Andrew. "Detroit Art City: Urban Decline, Aesthetic Production, Public Interest." In *The City after Abandonment*, edited by Margaret Dewar and June Manning Thomas, 117–49. Philadelphia: University of Pennsylvania Press, 2012.

———. *The Unreal Estate Guide to Detroit*. Ann Arbor: University of Michigan Press, 2012.

Holston, James. *Insurgent Citizenship: Disjunctions of Democracy and Modernity in Brazil*. Princeton, N.J.: Princeton University Press, 2008.

Hou, Jeffrey, ed. *Insurgent Public Space: Guerrilla Urbanism and the Remaking of Contemporary Cities*. London: Routledge, 2010.

Hoyt, Lorlene, and Devika Gopal-Agge. "The Business Improvement District Model: A Balanced Review of Contemporary Debates." *Geography Compass* 1, no. 4 (2007): 946–58.

Hurewitz, Daniel. *Bohemian Los Angeles: And the Making of Modern Politics*. Berkeley: University of California Press, 2008.

Hurley, Andrew. *Environmental Inequalities: Class, Race, and Industrial Pollution in Gary, Indiana, 1945–1980*. Chapel Hill: University of North Carolina Press, 1995.

Irazábal, Clara, and Jason Neville. "Neighbourhoods in the Lead: Grassroots Planning for Social Transformation in Post-Katrina New Orleans?" *Planning Practice and Research* 22, no. 2 (2007): 131–53.

Jackson, Kenneth T. *Crabgrass Frontier: The Suburbanization of the United States*. Oxford: Oxford University Press, 1987.

Jacobs, Jane. *The Death and Life of Great American Cities*. New York: Random House, 1961.

Jasanoff, Sheila, ed. *States of Knowledge: The Co-production of Science and the Social Order*. London: Routledge, 2004.

Jehl, Douglas. "As Cities Move to Privatize Water, Atlanta Steps Back." *New York Times*, February 10, 2013. http://www.nytimes.com/2003/02/10/us/as-cities-move-to-privatize-water-atlanta-steps-back.html.

Kaplan, Stephen, and Rachel Kaplan. "Alternatives to Fear: Review of Oscar Newman's *Defensible Space*." In *Humanscape: Environments for People*, 308–21. Ann Arbor, Mich.: Ulrichs Books, 1977.

Katz, Bruce, and Jennifer Bradley. "The Detroit Project: A Plan for Solving America's Greatest Urban Disaster." *New Republic*, December 9, 2009. http://www.newrepublic.com/article/metro-policy/the-detroit-project.

Khouri, N. A. "Rate Book for Electric Service." DTE Electric Company website, February 6, 2013. https://www2.dteenergy.com/.

Kielburger, Craig, and Marc Kielburger. "Access to Water Is No Longer Just a Third World Problem." *Huffington Post*, August 7, 2014. http://www.huffingtonpost.ca/craig-and-marc-kielburger/water-access-problem_b_5658442.html.

Kinder, Kimberley. "Guerrilla-Style Defensive Architecture in Detroit: A Self-Provisioned Security Strategy in a Neoliberal Space of Disinvestment." *International Journal of Urban and Regional Research* 38, no. 5 (2014): 1767–84.

Kneebone, Elizabeth. *The Growth and Spread of Concentrated Poverty, 2000 to 2008–2012.* Washington, D.C.: Brookings Institution, July 31, 2014. http://www.brookings.edu/research/interactives/2014/concentrated-poverty#/M10420.

Kurth, Joel. "Empty Detroit Homes Accrue Millions in Water Bills." *Detroit News*, September 12, 2014. http://www.detroitnews.com/article/20140912/METRO01/309120033.

Kurtzleben, Danielle. "The 11 Most Dangerous U.S. Cities." *U.S. News*, January 24, 2011. http://www.usnews.com/news/slideshows/the-11-most-dangerous-us-cities.

Laitner, Bill. "Many Detroiters Take Safety into Their Own Hands with Neighborhood Patrols." *Detroit Free Press*, October 21, 2012. http://www.freep.com/article/20121021/NEWS01/310210188/Many-Detroiters-take-safety-into-their-own-hands-with-neighborhood-patrols.

Lambert, Lisa. "U.S. Bankruptcy Judge Allows Detroit Water Shutoffs to Continue." Reuters, September 29, 2014. http://www.reuters.com/article/2014/09/29/us-usa-detroit-water-idUSKCN0HO1DS20140929.

Lawson, Laura. *City Bountiful: A Century of Community Gardening in America.* Berkeley: University of California Press, 2005.

Lawson, Laura, and Janni Sorensen. "When Overwhelming Needs Met Underwhelming Prospects: Sustaining Community Open Space Activism in East St. Louis." In *Insurgent Public Spaces: Guerrilla Urbanism and the Remaking of Contemporary Cities*, edited by Jeffery Hou, 255–66. New York: Routledge, 2010.

Leitner, Helga, Jamie Peck, and Eric S. Sheppard, eds. *Contesting Neoliberalism: Urban Frontiers.* New York: Guilford Press, 2007.

Lessenberry, Jack. "Judge's Ruling Doesn't Mean He Was Unsympathetic to Those Facing Water Shutoffs." *Michigan Radio*, September 30, 2014. http://michiganradio.org/post/judge-s-ruling-doesn-t-mean-he-was-unsympathetic-those-facing-water-shutoffs.

Levenstein, Lisa. *Movement without Marches: African American Women and the Politics of Poverty in Postwar Philadelphia.* Chapel Hill: University of North Carolina Press, 2009.

Lewis, Mathew. "No Property Left Behind." *Model Media*, December 4, 2012. http://www.modeldmedia.com/features/noproprecap1112.aspx.

Li, Tanya. *The Will to Improve: Governmentality, Development, and the Practice of Politics.* Durham, N.C.: Duke University Press, 2007.

Linn, Robert. "Encouraging Residential Blotting on the Lower East Side of Detroit." *Leap Detroit*, April 22, 2011. https://sites.google.com/site/leapdetroit/.

Lipman, Mark, and Leah Mahan. *Holding Ground: The Rebirth of Dudley Street.* DVD. Blooming Grove, N.Y.: New Day Films, 1996.

Loveland Technologies. "About Loveland Technologies." Loveland Technologies website, 2012. http://makeloveland.com/#about.

———. "Grandmont Rosedale 2012 Tax Auction." Loveland Technologies website, 2012. https://makeloveland.com/2015/neighborhoods/2916#.

Lowrey, Annie. "Pay Still High at Bailed-Out Companies, Report Says." *New York Times*, January 28, 2013. http://www.nytimes.com/2013/01/29/business/generous-executive-pay-at-bailed-out-companies-treasury-watchdog-says.html.

MacDonald, Christine, and Mike Wilkinson. "Half of Detroit Property Owners Don't Pay Taxes." *Detroit News*, February 21, 2013. http://www.detroitnews.com/article/20130221/METRO01/302210375.

Maciag, Mike. "Law Enforcement Officers per Capita for Cities, Local Departments." *Governing*, August 30, 2012. http://www.governing.com/gov-data/safety-justice/law-enforcement-police-department-employee-totals-for-cities.html.

Maher, Kate, Bobby White, and Valerie Bauerlein. "Hard Times Spread for Cities." *Wall Street Journal*, August 10, 2012. http://online.wsj.com/news/articles/SB10000872396390444900304577581162498135058.

Mallach, Alan. *Facing the Urban Challenge: The Federal Government and America's Older Distressed Cities.* Washington, D.C.: Brookings Institution, 2010. http://www.brookings.edu/~/media/research/files/papers/2010/5/18-shrinking-cities-mallach/0518_shrinking_cities_mallach.

———. *Laying the Groundwork for Change: Demolition, Urban Strategy, and Policy Reform.* Washington, D.C.: Brookings Institution, 2012. http://www.brookings.edu/research/papers/2012/09/24-land-use-demolition-mallach.

———. *Stabilizing Communities: A Federal Response to the Secondary Impacts of the Foreclosure Crisis.* Washington, D.C.: Brookings Institution, 2009. http://www.brookings.edu/research/reports/2009/02/foreclosure-crisis-mallach.

Martin, Deborah G. "Nonprofit Foundations and Grassroots Organizing: Reshaping Urban Governance." *Professional Geographer* 56, no. 3 (2004): 394–405.

Martin, Megan. "Crossing the Line: Observations from East Detroit, Michigan USA." *Qualitative Social Work* 6, no. 4 (2007): 465–75.

Martinez-Fernandez, Cristina, Ivonne Audirac, Sylvie Fol, and Emmanuèle Cunningham-Sabot. "Shrinking Cities: Urban Challenges of Globalization." *International Journal of Urban and Regional Research* 36, no. 2 (2012): 213–25.

Mason, Randall. *The Once and Future New York: Historic Preservation and the Modern City.* Minneapolis: University of Minnesota Press, 2009.

Massey, Douglas S., and Nancy Denton. *American Apartheid: Segregation and the Making of the Underclass.* Cambridge, Mass.: Harvard University Press, 1993.

Mast, Robert, ed. *Detroit Lives.* Philadelphia: Temple University Press, 1994.

Matless, David. *Landscape and Englishness.* London: Reaktion Books, 1998.

McGirr, Lisa. *Suburban Warriors: The Origins of the New American Right.* Princeton, N.J.: Princeton University Press, 2002.

McGraw, Bill. "Exclusive: Snyder Plans to Send Bulldozers and Cops to Three Detroit Neighborhoods." *Deadline Detroit,* July 13, 2012. http://www.deadlinedetroit.com/articles/1171/exclusive_snyder.

McKernan, Signe-Mary, Caroline Ratcliffe, Eugene Steuerle, and Sisi Zhang. "Disparities in Wealth Accumulation and Loss from the Great Recession and Beyond." *American Economic Review* 104, no. 5 (2014): 240–44.

McMillan, Tracie. "Urban Farmers' Crops Go from Vacant Lot to Market." *New York Times,* May 7, 2008. http://www.nytimes.com/2008/05/07/dining/07urban.html?pagewanted=all&_r=0.

McWilliams, Carey. *California: The Great Exception.* Berkeley: University of California Press, 1949.

Mele, Christopher. *Selling the Lower East Side: Culture, Real Estate, and Resistance in New York City.* Minneapolis: University of Minnesota Press, 2000.

Melosi, Martin. *Effluent America: Cities, Industry, Energy, and the Environment.* Pittsburgh: University of Pittsburgh Press, 2001.

———. *The Sanitary City: Urban Infrastructure in America from Colonial Times to the Present.* Baltimore: John Hopkins University Press, 2000.

Merry, Sally E. "Defensible Space Undefended: Social Factors in Crime Control through Environmental Design." *Urban Affairs Review* 16, no. 4 (1981): 397–422.

Michigan Community Resources. "Michigan Community Resources Awards $50,000 in Grants to Detroit Community Organizations." Press release, December 18, 2013. http://www.mi-community.org/file/documents/Fall-2013-Safe-Grant-Awards.pdf.

Millington, Nate. "Post-industrial Imaginaries: Nature, Representation, and Ruin in Detroit, Michigan." *International Journal of Urban and Regional Research* 37, no. 1 (2013): 279–96.

Mitchell, Bill. "In Detroit, Water Crisis Symbolizes Decline, and Hope: As Poor Residents Strain to Pay Bills, Neighbors and Activists Step Up."

National Geographic, August 22, 2014. http://news.nationalgeographic. com/news/special-features/2014/08/140822-detroit-michigan-water-shutoffs-great-lakes/.

Mitchell, Don. *The Right to the City: Social Justice and the Fight for Public Space.* New York: Guilford Press, 2003.

Mitchell, Don, and Lynn Staeheli. "Clean and Safe? Property Redevelopment, Public Space, and Homelessness in Downtown San Diego." In *The Politics of Public Space,* edited by Setha Low and Neil Smith, 143–75. New York: Francis and Taylor, 2006.

Mitchell, Timothy. *Colonising Egypt.* Berkeley: University of California Press, 1991.

Mukhija, Vinit, and Anastasia Loukaitou-Sideris, eds. *The Informal American City: Beyond Taco Trucks and Day Labor.* Cambridge, Mass.: MIT Press, 2014.

Muller, David. "What Can Be Done with Detroit's Thousands of Empty Properties?" *MLive,* November 29, 2012. http://www.mlive.com/business/ detroit/index.ssf/2012/11/what_can_be_done_with_detroits.html.

NAACP. "Bankruptcy Judge Denies Motion to Suspend Detroit Water Shutoffs." NAACP website, September 29, 2014. http://www.naacpldf.org/ press-release/bankruptcy-judge-denies-motion-suspend-detroit-water-shutoffs.

———. "Detroit Water Shutoff Crisis." NAACP website, July 21, 2014. http:// www.naacpldf.org/case-issue/detroit-water-shutoff-crisis.

NBC Chicago 5 News. "Lyons Cuts One-Third of Police Force: Union." *NBC Chicago 5 News,* April 11, 2014. http://www.nbcchicago.com/news/local/ Union-Lyons-Lays-Off-One-Third-of-Police-Force-254870831.html.

Nelson, Gabe. "Affordable Urban Canvas: Artists Scoop Up Cheap Houses to Start Enclaves." *Crain's Detroit Business,* August 23, 2009. http://www.crainsdetroit.com/article/20090823/FREE/308239972/ affordable-urban-canvas-artists-scoop-up-cheap-houses-to-start.

Newman, Oscar. "Defensible Space: A New Physical Planning Tool for Urban Revitalization." *Journal of the American Planning Association* 61, no. 2 (1995): 149–55.

———. *Defensible Space: Crime Prevention through Urban Design.* New York: Collier Books, 1973.

Nichols, Darren A. "Detroit Announces First Phase of Privatized Garbage Pickup." *Detroit News,* May 1, 2014. http://www.detroitnews.com/ article/20140501/METRO01/305010132#ixzz338ScINOm.

Nicolaides, Becky M. *My Blue Heaven: Life and Politics in the Working-Class Suburbs of Los Angeles, 1920–1965.* Chicago: University of Chicago Press, 2002.

Nussbaum, Matt. "Pennsylvania Libraries Feeling Pressures of Continued

Funding Cuts." *Pittsburgh Post-Gazette*, June 28, 2014. http://www.post-gazette.com/local/region/2014/06/29/Local-libraries-feeling-pressures-of-continued-funding-cuts/stories/201406290083.

Olasky, Susan. "Brightmoor Fighters." *WORLD*, March 9, 2013. http://www.worldmag.com/2013/02/brightmoor_fighters.

Orr, Marion E., and Gerry Stoker. "Urban Regimes and Leadership in Detroit." *Urban Affairs Review* 30 (1994): 48–73.

Oosting, Jonathan. "Michigan's $6.2B 'Raid' on Revenue Sharing? See How Much Local Communities Have Lost since 2003." *MLive*, March 18, 2014. http://www.mlive.com/lansing-news/index.ssf/2014/03/michigans_62b_raid_on_revenue.html.

Osman, Suleiman. *The Invention of Brownstone Brooklyn: Gentrification and the Search for Authenticity in Postwar New York*. Oxford: Oxford University Press, 2011.

Oswalt, Phillip, ed. *Shrinking Cities*. Vol. 1, *International Research*. Ostfildern-Ruit, Germany: Hatje Cantz Press, 2005.

Patillo, Mary. *Black on the Block: The Politics of Race and Class in the City*. Chicago: University of Chicago Press, 2007.

Peck, Jamie. "Pushing Austerity: State Failure, Municipal Bankruptcy and the Crises of Fiscal Federalism in the USA." *Cambridge Journal of Regions, Economy and Society* 7, no. 1 (2014): 17–44.

Peck, Jamie, and Adam Tickell. "Neoliberalizing Space." *Antipode* 34, no. 3 (2002): 380–404.

Pesca, Mike. "Detroit Artists Paint Town Orange to Force Change." *National Public Radio*, December 7, 2006. http://www.npr.org/templates/story/story.php?storyId=6592634.

Pickles, John. *A History of Spaces: Cartographic Reason, Mapping and the Geo-Coded World*. London: Routledge, 2004.

Plumer, Brad. "Detroit Isn't Alone: The U.S. Cities That Have Gone Bankrupt, in One Map." *Washington Post*, July 18, 2013. http://www.washingtonpost.com/blogs/wonkblog/wp/2013/07/18/detroit-isnt-alone-the-u-s-cities-that-have-gone-bankrupt-in-one-map/.

Pothukuchi, Kami. "Urban Agriculture and Food Networks in Detroit: A Resource for a Shrinking City?" Paper presented at Learning from Detroit: Turbulent Urbanism in the 21st Century, Ann Arbor, Mich., May 2014.

Public Lighting Department. "About Us: History." City of Detroit website, 2014. http://www.detroitmi.gov/DepartmentsandAgencies/PublicLighting/AboutUs.aspx.

Purcell, Mark. *Recapturing Democracy: Neoliberalization and the Struggle for Alternative Urban Futures*. New York: Routledge, 2008.

———. "Urban Democracy and the Local Trap." *Urban Studies* 43, no. 11 (2006): 1921–41.

Rabinow, Paul. *French Modern: Norms and Forms of the Social Environment.* Chicago: University of Chicago Press, 1995.

Raleigh, Erica, and George Galster. "Neighborhood Disinvestment, Abandonment and Crime Dynamics." Paper presented at the 44th Urban Affairs Association conference, San Antonio, Tex., March 2014.

Ramirez, Charles. "Detroit Urged to Tie Water Bills to Income." *Detroit News,* September 2, 2015. http://www.detroitnews.com/story/news/local/ detroit-city/2015/09/01/water-affordability-detroit-bills/71554188/.

Rayasam, Renuka. "Who Should Control Our Water?" *New Yorker,* December 9, 2013. http://www.newyorker.com/business/currency/who-should-control-our-water.

Reese, Laura A. "A Matter of Faith." *Economic Development Quarterly* 18, no. 1 (2004): 50–66.

Reich, Robert. "Income Inequality Ruined Detroit." *Salon,* July 22, 2013. http://www.salon.com/2013/07/22/income_inequality_ruined_detroit_partner/.

Reindl, J. C. "One of Detroit's Largest Private Blight-Cleanup Blitzes Gets Underway in Brightmoor." *Detroit Free Press,* July 1, 2013. http://www.freep.com/article/20130701/NEWS01/307010121/Detroit-Blight-Authority-Brightmoor-cleanup.

Rich, Sarah. "Ice House Detroit." *Dwell,* February 10, 2010. http://www.dwell.com/interviews/article/ice-house-detroit.

Rieniets, Tim. "Shrinking Cities: Causes and Effects of Urban Population Losses in the Twentieth Century." *Nature and Culture* 4, no. 3 (2009): 231–54.

Rojas, James. "The Enacted Environment." In *Everyday America,* edited by Chris Wilson and Paul Groth, 275–92. Berkeley: University of California Press, 2003.

Rose, Daniel J. "Captive Audience? Strategies for Acquiring Food in Two Detroit Neighborhoods." *Qualitative Health Research* 21, no. 5 (2011): 642–51.

Roy, Ananya. "Who Is Dependent on Welfare?" #GlobalPOV Project video, 13:32. http://blumcenter.berkeley.edu/globalpov/.

Runk, David. "Ice House Detroit." *Huffington Post Business,* October 27, 2009. http://www.huffingtonpost.com/2009/10/27/ice-house-detroit-artists_n_335031.html.

Rushe, Dominic. "Detroit Becomes Largest US City to File for Bankruptcy in Historic 'Low Point.'" *Guardian,* July 18, 2013. http://www.theguardian.com/world/2013/jul/18/detroit-formally-files-bankruptcy.

Rusk, David. *Cities without Suburbs.* Washington, D.C.: Woodrow Wilson Center Press, 1993.

Russell, Kim. "Detroit Water Assistance Funds are Running out of Money." *WXYZ Detroit,* August 20, 2015. http://www.wxyz.com/news/region/detroit/detroit-water-assistance-funds-are-running-out-of-money.

Ryan, Brent. *Design after Decline: How America Rebuilds Shrinking Cities.* Philadelphia: University of Pennsylvania Press, 2013.

Sack, Robert David. *Human Territoriality: Its Theory and History*. Cambridge: Cambridge University Press, 1986.

Sassen, Saskia. *The Global City: New York, London, Tokyo*. Princeton, N.J.: Princeton University Press, 2001.

Satyanarayana, Megha, and Dawson Bell. "Gov. Rick Snyder's Plan Would Raze Abandoned Houses in Detroit." *Detroit Free Press*, July 14 2012. http://www.freep.com/article/20120714/NEWS01/207140400/Gov-Rick-Snyder-to-send-in-wrecking-ball-to-raze-eyesores-in-Detroit-neighborhoods.

Saulny, Susan. "Razing the City to Save the City." *New York Times*, June 20, 2010. http://www.nytimes.com/2010/06/21/us/21detroit.html?pagewanted=all.

Sauter, Michael B., Douglas A. McIntyre, Ashley C. Allen, Alexander E. M. Hess, and Lisa Ne. "The Most Dangerous Cities in America." *NBC News*, June 17, 2012. http://www.nbcnews.com/business/most-dangerous-cities-america-832351.

Schorske, Carl E. "The Ringstrasse, Its Critics, and the Birth of Urban Modernism." In *Fin-De-Siecle Vienna: Politics and Culture*, 24–115. New York: Random House, 1961.

Schultz, Stanley K., and Clay McShane. "To Engineer the Metropolis: Sewers, Sanitation, and City Planning in Late-Nineteenth-Century America." *Journal of American History*, 1978, 389–411.

Scott, James C. *The Art of Not Being Governed: An Anarchist History of Upland Southeast Asia*. New Haven, Conn.: Yale University Press, 2009.

———. *Seeing Like a State: How Certain Schemes to Improve the Human Condition Have Failed*. New Haven, Conn.: Yale University Press, 1998.

———. *Weapons of the Weak: Everyday Forms of Peasant Resistance*. New Haven, Conn.: Yale University Press, 2008.

Segal, David. "A Georgia Town Takes the People's Business Private." *New York Times*, June 23, 2012. http://www.nytimes.com/2012/06/24/business/a-georgia-town-takes-the-peoples-business-private.html?pagewanted=all.

Self, Robert. *American Babylon: Race and the Struggle for Postwar Oakland*. Princeton, N.J.: Princeton University Press, 2003.

SEMCOG. *2010 Census Data for City of Detroit Neighborhoods*. Detroit: Southeast Michigan Council of Governments, 2011. http://library.semcog.org/InmagicGenie/DocumentFolder/2010CensusDataDetroitQuickFacts.pdf.

Shaw, Kate. "The Place of Alternative Culture and the Politics of Its Protection in Berlin, Amsterdam and Melbourne." *Planning Theory and Practice* 6, no. 2 (2005): 149–69.

Shaw, Todd C., and Lester K. Spence. "Race and Representation in Detroit's Community Development Coalitions." *Annals of the American Academy of Political and Social Science* 594 (2004): 125–42.

Shyong, Frank. "Too Young for Tai Chi?" *Los Angeles Times*, October 26, 2012. http://articles.latimes.com/2012/oct/26/local/la-me-line-dancers-20121026.

Signer, Rachel. "How Food Is Revitalizing Detroit." *Dowser*, May 29, 2012. http://dowser.org/how-food-is-revitalizing-detroit/.

Simone, AbdouMaliq. *For the City Yet to Come: Changing African Life in Four Cities*. Durham, N.C.: Duke University Press, 2004.

Small, Mario Luis. *Villa Victoria: The Transformation of Social Capital in a Boston Barrio*. Chicago: University of Chicago Press, 2004.

Smith, Llewellyn M. *Gaining Ground: Building Community on Dudley Street*. DVD. Boston: Vital Pictures, 2012.

Smith, Neil. *The New Urban Frontier: Gentrification and the Revanchist City*. London: Routledge, 1996.

Smith, Suzanne E. *Dancing in the Street: Motown and the Cultural Politics of Detroit*. Cambridge, Mass.: Harvard University Press, 2009.

Spangler, Todd, and Matt Helms. "Report: Detroit Bankruptcy Caused by State Cuts, Shrinking Tax Base, Not Long-Term Debt." *Detroit Free Press*, November 20, 2013. http://www.freep.com/article/20131120/NEWS01/311200115/detroit-bankruptcy-debt-revenue-sharing-cuts.

Stack, Carol B. *All Our Kin: Strategies for Survival in a Black Community*. 1975. Reprint, New York: Basic Books, 1997.

Stevens, Quentin. "The German 'City Beach' as a New Approach to Waterfront Development." In *Transforming Urban Waterfronts: Fixity and Flow*, edited by Gene Desfor, Jennifer Laidley, Quentin Stevens, and Dirk Schubert, 235–56. London: Routledge, 2011.

Stratigakos, Despina. *A Woman's Berlin: Building the Modern City*. Minneapolis, University of Minnesota Press: 2008.

Streitfeld, David. "A City Outsources Everything. Sky Doesn't Fall." *New York Times*, July 19, 2010. http://www.nytimes.com/2010/07/20/business/20maywood.html?ref=business&_r=0.

Sugrue, Thomas J. "A Dream Still Deferred." *New York Times*, March 26, 2011. http://www.nytimes.com/2011/03/27/opinion/27Sugrue.html?_r=0.

———. *The Origins of the Urban Crisis: Race and Inequality in Detroit*. Princeton, N.J.: Princeton University Press, 1996.

Susser, Ida. *Norman Street: Poverty and Politics in an Urban Neighborhood*. Updated ed. New York: Oxford University Press, 2012.

Swyngedouw, Eric. *Social Power and the Urbanization of Water: Flows of Power*. Oxford: Oxford University Press, 2004.

Swyngedouw, Erik, and Maria Kaika. "The Making of 'Glocal' Urban Modernities." *City* 7, no. 1 (2003): 5–21.

Tabb, William. *The Long Default: New York City and the Urban Fiscal Crisis*. New York: Monthly Review Press, 1982.

———. *The Restructuring of Capitalism in Our Time*. New York: Columbia University Press, 2012.

Thomas, June Manning. *Redevelopment and Race: Planning a Finer City in Postwar Detroit*. Baltimore: Johns Hopkins University Press, 1997.

Thomas, June Manning, and Reynard N. Blake Jr. "Faith-Based Community

Development and African American Neighborhoods." In *Revitalizing Urban Neighborhoods*, edited by Dennis Keating, Norman Krumholz, and Philip Star, 131–43. Lawrence: University Press of Kansas, 1996.

Thompson, Heather A. *Whose Detroit? Politics, Labor, and Race in a Modern American City*. Ithaca, N.Y.: Cornell University Press, 2004.

Timm, Jane C. "Urban Farming Takes Hold of Blighted Motor City." *MSNBC*, September 10, 2013. http://www.msnbc.com/morning-joe/urban-farming-takes-hold-blighted-motor.

U.S. Census Bureau. "Geography: 2010 Census Urban and Rural Classification and Urban Area Criteria." https://www.census.gov/geo/reference/ua/urban-rural-2010.html.

———. "Surveys: Population" for 1960, 2000, and 2010. *Social Explorer.* www.socialexplorer.com.

———. "2010 Surveys: Race." *Social Explorer.* www.socialexplorer.com.

United Nations. *The Global Social Crisis: Report on the World Social Situation 2011*. New York: UN Department of Economic and Social Affairs, 2011. http://undesadspd.org/ReportontheWorldSocialSituation/2011.aspx.

Urahn, Susan, ed. *America's Big Cities in Volatile Times*. Washington, D.C.: Pew Charitable Trusts, 2013. http://www.pewstates.org/research/reports/americas-big-cities-in-volatile-times-85899511780.

Watson, Debra. "More Drastic Service Cuts Hit Detroit Public Transportation." *International Committee of the Fourth International*, May 1, 2012. http://www.wsws.org/en/articles/2012/05/ddot-m01.html.

Weber, Matthew. "Informal Ownership and the Shrinking City: The Role of Local Policies and Practices." Paper presented at the 44th Urban Affairs Association conference, San Antonio, Tex., March 2014.

Weiss, Marc. *The Rise of the Community Builders: The American Real Estate Industry and Urban Land Planning*. New York: Columbia University Press, 1987.

White, Monica M. "Sisters of the Soil: Urban Farming as Resistance in Detroit." *Race/Ethnicity: Multidisciplinary Global Contexts* 5, no. 1 (2011): 13–28.

Whitford, David. "Can Farming Save Detroit?" *CNN Money*, December 29, 2009. http://money.cnn.com/2009/12/29/news/economy/farming_detroit.fortune/.

Whyte, William H. *The Social Life of Small Urban Spaces*. New York: Projects for Public Spaces, 1980.

Wiese, Andrew. *Places of Their Own: African American Suburbanization in the Twentieth Century*. Chicago: University of Chicago Press, 2005.

Wilgoren, Jodi. "Detroit Urban Renewal without the Renewal." *New York Times*, July 7, 2002. http://www.nytimes.com/2002/07/07/us/detroit-urban-renewal-without-the-renewal.html.

Williams, Corey. "For Some Detroit Services, Call the D.I.Y. Dept." *ABC News*,

May 9, 2013. http://abcnews.go.com/US/wireStory/detroit-services-call-diy-dept-19143262#.UZKYSjtuq3A.

Williams, Paige. "Drop Dead, Detroit!" *New Yorker,* January 27, 2014.

World Health Organization. *Meeting the MDG Drinking Water and Sanitation Target: The Urban and Rural Challenge of the Decade.* Geneva, Switzerland: World Health Organization and UNICEF, 2006. http://www.who.int/water_sanitation_health/monitoring/jmpfinal.pdf.

Yiftachel, Oren. "Critical Theory and Gray Space." *City* 13, nos. 2–3 (2009): 240–56.

Index

Kimberley Kinder is assistant professor of urban planning at the University of Michigan. She is author of *The Politics of Urban Water: Changing Waterscapes in Amsterdam.*